Europe's Union in Crisis

The European Union faces a set of inter-related crises that it struggles to contain and address. By exploring how the EU responds to crises and conflict, this volume addresses both its resilience and vulnerability. The EU faces significant challenges: European integration is increasingly politicised; democratic politics within member states are increasingly volatile; challenger parties threaten the status quo; and party systems are shifting throughout Europe. These crises test both the EU and individual states, especially those that had to exchange interdependence in the Union for dependence on the Troika. Despite the tension of hard times, this volume points to patterns of continuity and change as the single market, somewhat side-lined and forgotten in the heat of crises, retains its role as the hard core of the Union and the EU's most significant achievement.

This book was originally published as a special issue of *West European Politics.*

Brigid Laffan is Director and Professor at the Robert Schuman Centre for Advanced Studies, European University Institute (EUI), Florence. She has published widely on European Integration including *Core-periphery Relations in the European Union* (London: Routledge, 2016), *Ireland and the European Union* (2008), *Renovation or Revolution: new territorial politics in Ireland and the United Kingdom*, (2005), *Europe's Experimental Union. Re thinking Integration* (1999) and *The Finances of the Union* (1997).

West European Politics Series

Edited by
***Klaus H. Goetz**, University of Munich, Germany*
***Anand Menon**, King's College London, UK*
***Wolfgang C. Müller**, University of Vienna, Austria*

West European Politics has established itself as the foremost journal for the comparative analysis of European political institutions, politics and public policy. Its comprehensive scope, which includes the European Union, makes it essential reading for both academics and political practitioners. The books in this series have originated from special issues published by *West European Politics*.

For a complete list of titles in this series, please visit https://www.routledge.com/West-European-Politics/book-series/WEP

Recent titles in this series include:

Towards a New Executive Order in Europe
Edited by Deirdre Curtin and Morten Egeberg

The Structure of Political Competition in Western Europe
Edited by Zsolt Enyedi and Kevin Deegan-Krause

Dynamics of Change in the European Union
Edited by Daniel Naurin and Anne Rasmussen

Assessing Political Representation in Europe
Edited by Christine Arnold and Mark N. Franklin

From Europeanisation to Diffusion
Edited by Tanja A. Börzel and Thomas Risse

The Party Politics of Territorial Reforms in Europe
Edited by Emanuele Massetti and Simon Toubeau

The Role of Parties in Twenty-First Century Politics
Responsive and Responsible?
Edited by Luciano Bardi, Stefano Bartolini and Alexander H. Treschel

Decision Making in the EU before and after the Lisbon Treaty
Edited by Madeleine Hosli, Amie Kreppel, Běla Plechanovová and Amy Verdun

Party Politics and Democracy in Europe
Essays in honour of Peter Mair
Edited by Ferdinand Müller-Rommel and Fernando Casal Bértoa

Europe's Union in Crisis
Tested and Contested
Edited by Brigid Laffan

Europe's Union in Crisis

Tested and contested

Edited by

Brigid Laffan

LONDON AND NEW YORK

First published 2018
by Routledge

2 Park Square, Milton Park, Abingdon, Oxfordshire OX14 4RN
52 vanderbilt Avenue, New York, NY 10017

Routledge is an imprint of the Taylor & Francis Group, an informa business

First issued in paperback 2019

British Library Cataloguing in Publication Data
A catalogue record for this book is available from the British Library

ISBN13: 978-1-138-04003-8 (hbk)
ISBN13: 978-0-367-22976-4 (pbk)

Typeset in Minion Pro
by RefineCatch Limited, Bungay, Suffolk

Publisher's Note
The publisher accepts responsibility for any inconsistencies that may have arisen during the conversion of this book from journal articles to book chapters, namely the possible inclusion of journal terminology.

Contents

Citation Information

The chapters in this book were originally published in *West European Politics*, volume 39, issue 5 (September 2016). When citing this material, please use the original page numbering for each article, as follows:

Chapter 1
Europe's union in crisis: tested and contested
Brigid Laffan
West European Politics, volume 39, issue 5 (September 2016) pp. 915–932

Chapter 2
Politicisation and integration through law: whither integration theory?
Sabine Saurugger
West European Politics, volume 39, issue 5 (September 2016) pp. 933–952

Chapter 3
The EU's problem-solving capacity and legitimacy in a crisis context: a virtuous or vicious circle?
Gerda Falkner
West European Politics, volume 39, issue 5 (September 2016) pp. 953–970

Chapter 4
Fleeing the centre: the rise of challenger parties in the aftermath of the euro crisis
Sara B. Hobolt and James Tilley
West European Politics, volume 39, issue 5 (September 2016) pp. 971–991

Chapter 5
After the Spitzenkandidaten: fundamental change in the EU's political system?
Thomas Christiansen
West European Politics, volume 39, issue 5 (September 2016) pp. 992–1010

Chapter 6

The Commission: boxed in and constrained, but still an engine of integration
Stefan Becker, Michael W. Bauer, Sara Connolly and Hussein Kassim
West European Politics, volume 39, issue 5 (September 2016) pp. 1011–1031

Chapter 7

Reinterpreting the rules 'by stealth' in times of crisis: a discursive institutionalist analysis of the European Central Bank and the European Commission
Vivien A. Schmidt
West European Politics, volume 39, issue 5 (September 2016) pp. 1032–1052

Chapter 8

Europe's crises and the EU's 'big three'
Ulrich Krotz and Richard Maher
West European Politics, volume 39, issue 5 (September 2016) pp. 1053–1072

Chapter 9

EU experimentalist governance in times of crisis
Jonathan Zeitlin
West European Politics, volume 39, issue 5 (September 2016) pp. 1073–1094

Chapter 10

Why the single market remains the EU's core business
Jacques Pelkmans
West European Politics, volume 39, issue 5 (September 2016) pp. 1095–1113

Notes on Contributors

Michael W. Bauer is Jean Monnet Professor and holds the Chair of Comparative Public Administration and Policy Analysis at the German University of Administrative Sciences, Speyer.

Stefan Becker is a research associate at the Jean Monnet Chair of Comparative Public Administration and Policy Analysis at the German University of Administrative Sciences, Speyer.

Thomas Christiansen holds a Chair in European Institutional Politics in the Department of Political Science at Maastricht University, The Netherlands and is also part-time Professor at the European University Institute, Florence, Italy.

Sara Connolly is Professor of Personnel Economics in Norwich Business School at the University of East Anglia, UK.

Gerda Falkner is Professor of Political Science and Director of the Institute for European Integration Research at the University of Vienna, Austria.

Sara B. Hobolt is the Sutherland Chair in European Institutions at the London School of Economics and Political Science, UK, and an Associate Member of Nuffield College, University of Oxford, UK. She is also the Vice Chair of the European Election Studies.

Hussein Kassim is Professor of Politics at the University of East Anglia, Norwich, and a Visiting Professor at the College of Europe in Bruges, Belgium.

Ulrich Krotz is Professor at the European University Institute, Italy, where he holds the Chair in International Relations, and is Director of the Schuman Centre's 'Europe in the World' programme.

Brigid Laffan is Director and Professor at the Robert Schuman Centre for Advanced Studies, Italy, and Director of the Global Governance Programme, European University Institute, Florence, Italy.

Richard Maher is a Research Fellow in the 'Europe in the World' programme at the Robert Schuman Centre for Advanced Studies at the European University Institute, Italy.

Jacques Pelkmans is a Senior Research Fellow at the Centre for European Policy Studies (CEPS), Belgium, and has been a Professor at the College of Europe in Bruges, Belgium, since 1992.

Sabine Saurugger is Professor of Political Science and Research Dean at Sciences Po Grenoble, France.

Vivien A. Schmidt is Jean Monnet Professor of European Integration, Professor of International Relations in the Pardee School, USA, and Professor of Political Science at Boston University, USA, where she is also Founding Director of BU's Center for the Study of Europe.

James Tilley is a Professor of Politics at the University of Oxford and a fellow of Jesus College, Oxford, UK.

Jonathan Zeitlin is Professor of Public Policy and Governance, and Distinguished Faculty Professor in the Department of Political Science and the Faculty of Social and Behavioural Sciences (MG) at the University of Amsterdam, The Netherlands.

Europe's union in crisis: tested and contested

Brigid Laffan

ABSTRACT

This special issue explores how Europe's Union is tested though crises but also faces explicit contestation in troubled times. Crises are 'open moments' that impact on rulers and ruled, testing existing paradigms, policies, politics, institutional roles and rules. The papers in this special issue test the resilience of the Union in crisis conditions, the post-functionalist interpretation of contemporary integration, the legacy of the crisis for politics and institutions in Europe and the impact of the crisis on key bilateral relations. Four thematic issues are addressed: the resilience of the EU, multilevel politics, patterns of continuity and change and the relationship between the whole (EU) and the member states.

Europe's Union faces a set of inter-related crises that it struggles to contain and address. This special issue seeks to explore how the Union is tested through crises but also faces greater contestation. The dual emphasis on testing and contesting allows us to focus on how the EU addresses crises but also faces explicit contestation in troubled times. Since 2008 the Union and its member states have confronted two major exogenous shocks. These shocks in turn led to internal turbulence within the Union. The first exogenous shock was the global impact of the collapse of Lehman Brothers which triggered a deep financial and economic downturn, the worst economic crisis since the Great Depression of the 1930s. The Great Recession had a severe impact on the European Union as the global financial crisis morphed into a deep crisis of the eurozone in autumn 2009. The credibility and sustainability of the eurozone was tested. Market pressure, in addition to political, economic and social pressures, gave rise to deep cleavages between creditors and debtors, the strong and the vulnerable. The EU did not face a single eurozone crisis but instead a confluence of overlapping and interrelated political, institutional and governance crises for the eurozone as a whole and its member states. The EU's legal system, institutions and governance capacity were tested, perhaps like never before. At the same time, the Union's policies, instruments, the commitment of the member states to a shared endeavour and even the underlying rationale of integration became ever more contested as democratic politics in Europe bore the strain of recession and the asymmetric manner in which the crisis affected the member states.

The second exogenous shock came from Europe's neighbourhood. Having essentially been created to pacify inter-state relations in Europe and negate geopolitics, the Union was confronted with the re-emergence of an assertive Russia when Putin annexed Crimea and began a proxy war in Eastern Ukraine. This shattered the Union's neighbourhood policy, a policy that was built on market access, a diffusion of governance norms and soft conditionality. Europe's normative power came face to face with Russian hard power. As optimism concerning the Arab Spring abated, Europe was confronted to its south with a multiplicity of states that were either failing, ravaged by civil war or characterised by heightened political uncertainty. Instability to the south manifested itself in a humanitarian crisis and extensive movement of people across the Mediterranean that left the member states on its northern shores struggling to cope with the influx of people. By summer 2015, the refugee and migration crisis threatened the sustainability of the Schengen system, a core European regime. The emergence of ISIS and the number of Europeans willing to fight as jihadists for the group heightened security concerns and concerns about the integration of migrants in Europe. The return of some battle-hardened jihadists to Europe exposed deep vulnerabilities in Europe's internal security as it was confronted with terrorist attacks in Paris and Brussels. The combination of external transboundary shocks and their impact on Europe gave rise to deep instability in two of the Union's core regimes and began to threaten the EU's sense of itself. How Europe deals with the forces unleashed by these multiple crises will shape the future of the Union and the continent. The timing, combination and consequences of the two external shocks placed extraordinary pressure on the EU and its governing capacity. Given that the Union does not exist in a sealed container immune from developments on its borders, the special issue is attentive to the growing pressure on the Union from outside, although the primary focus is on the multifaceted eurozone crisis.

Crises are 'open moments' that impact on rulers and ruled, testing existing paradigms, policies, institutional roles and rules. They are 'moments of truth', critical junctures replete with risk and characterised by a high level of contingency (Panizza and Philip 2013). According to Rosenthal *et al.* (2001: 6), modern crises 'are increasingly characterized by complexity, interdependence and politicization'. They generate uncertainty, threat and discontinuity and tend to act as focal points for institutional, policy and political change that leave significant legacies (Gourevitch 1992). A crisis is rarely a distinct event but a process whereby different forces interact and intersect to create collective stress across many domains. From a constructivist perspective, 'a crisis is not a natural event, but a social event, and therefore is always socially constructed and highly political'

(Gamble 2009: 38). The stakes are very high for political leaders when faced with crises, as they are confronted with situations that demand action in an environment of heightened uncertainty and contingency. Who owns the crisis and who is responsible for addressing it is a major question in the heat of a crisis (Boin 2009: 367). Moreover as a crisis unfolds, there is inevitably a 'drama of accountability and blaming' (Boin *et al.* 2010: 706). Institutions and their leaders are attentive not just to the framing of a crisis but to how to justify and legitimise their crises responses. A crisis offers both danger and opportunity and crises have been part of the dynamic of European integration from the outset. In fact, it could be argued that all too often and too easily any blockage or setback in integration was deemed to be a crisis. Applying the term crisis or crises is, however, truly applicable to the compound challenges that the EU faces at this juncture. Europe's relatively young Union is facing the severest test in its short history.

Why this special issue?

On the eve of the financial crisis, the EU had become a viable regional economy, underpinned by law, and a system of multilevel governance, but neither a state nor a nation, and there were very few indications of a desire by mass publics to change this state of affairs. The Lisbon treaty finally came into operation in December 2009 just as the euro crisis was about to unfold. The treaty was the culmination of the Union's constitutional decade and its provisions would operate in an environment very different from the first decade of the twenty-first century. In addressing the consequences of the crisis for the Union, this special issue draws a distinction between political integration, on the one hand, and institutional and functional integration on the other. Nye, writing in 1971, argued that in order to gain analytical leverage in the study of integration, it was fruitful to 'break apart the concept of integration' into a number of component parts (Nye 1971: 26). Institutional and functional integration encapsulates the systemic features of the Union, notably its treaty framework, institutions and policy range (the formal system) and political integration relates to political processes and the political behaviour of elites and citizens. The value added of this special issue is, primarily, its range and the manner in which the papers address different facets of integration that are usually treated separately. The politics of integration, both domestic and supranational, are rarely studied in conjunction with governance and institutions. The special issue does not begin from deductively-led hypotheses shaped by a general theory given the diversity and complexity of the crises-induced political and institutional conditions. Rather, the approach is to test the following: the resilience of the Union in crisis conditions, the post-functionalist interpretation of contemporary integration, the legacy of the crisis for Europe's supranational institutions and the impact of the crisis on key bilateral relations. In addition, the special issue pays particular attention to the dynamic of politicisation in the context of enhanced contestation in hard times. The papers draw on a range of theoretical and analytical approaches, including traditional integration theory, comparative politics, experimental governance and institutionalism.

Just before the financial and economic crisis unfolded, Hooghe and Marks (2009) developed a post-functionalist theory of European integration. They began from the premise that 'Domestic and European politics have become more tightly coupled as governments have become responsive to public pressures on European integration' (Hooghe and Marks 2009: 2). They pointed to the growing politicisation of European integration and their post-functionalist theory assigned a central role to identity politics. This combination, they suggested, led to 'downward pressure on the level and scope of integration' in the presence of a 'constraining dissensus' (Hooghe and Marks 2009: 21). The politicisation of integration was widely addressed in the integration literature during the 2000s in response to greater contestation around issues of European integration (Grande and Kriesi 2015; Stratham and Trenz 2013; De Wilde 2011; De Wilde and Zurn 2012). There was in addition a normative discussion about whether or not greater politicisation was desirable (Bartolini 2006; Hix 2006). The eurozone crisis provides an important test of the post-functionalist theory of integration and the dynamic of politicisation in crisis conditions. Five papers in this special issue address different dimensions of 'post-functionalism' and 'politicisation'. Falkner's paper on the 'EU's Problem-Solving Capacity and Legitimacy in a Crisis Context: A Virtuous or Vicious Circle?' analyses across a range of policy areas how and why reforms were possible and a joint decision trap avoided notwithstanding the constraining dissensus identified by Hooghe and Marks (2009). Pelkmans' paper on 'Why the Single Market Remains the EU's Core Business' reminds us of the centrality of the single market to European integration and the enduring functional logic of market integration. Saurugger's paper, 'Politicisation and Integration through Law: Whither Integration Theory?', analyses the challenges the eurozone crisis created for theoretical explanations of European integration and does so through the lens of key characteristics of the crisis, namely increasing politicisation of the domestic level and the strong call for legal regulation of and court responses to the EU's economic governance. The Hobolt and Tilly paper, 'Fleeing the Centre: The Rise of Challenger Parties in the Aftermath of the Euro Crisis', addresses directly the political consequences of the crisis for party politics in the member states by focussing on the rise of challenger parties. The level of analysis moves to EU-level political dynamics in Christiansen's paper on 'Electoral Politics and Executive Appointment in the EU: The Impact of the *Spitzenkandidaten*'. This paper provides a bridge to a number of papers on the institutional consequences of the crisis.

Scholarly debate and contention about the role of individual EU-level institutions and the institutional balance is as old as the Union itself. One reading of the crisis and its consequences places an emphasis on intergovernmental decision-making, albeit in a new form (Bickerton *et al.* 2015; Fabbrini 2013; Puetter 2014). These scholars point to the dominance of the European Council in making the 'big' crisis management decisions and to the preference for extra-treaty measures and policy instruments during the course of the crisis (Bickerton *et al.* 2015). In other words, the Commission is the big loser. Becker *et al.* take issue with this core conclusion of the new intergovernmentalist literature in their paper 'The Commission Boxed In and Constrained: Still an Engine of Integration?' They provide an account of the Commission during the crisis that covers the interplay of factors at different levels (i.e. political and institutional environment as well as internal organisation) and argue that the crisis has acted as a catalyst for a more pronounced move towards both policy management and presidentialism. The latter was reinforced by the *Spitzenkandidaten* experiment analysed by Christiansen. Schmidt, in 'Reinterpreting the Rules by Stealth in Times of Crisis: The European Central Bank and the European Commission', addresses how two of the supranational institutions, the Commission and the ECB, governed under the pressure of the crisis. The central argument is that they did so by reinterpreting the rules without admitting to this publicly – in other words, they did so by stealth. The focus in Zeitlin's paper, 'EU Experimentalist Governance in Times of Crisis', is on the fortunes of the Union's mode of experimentalist governance in crisis conditions. Experimentalist governance was one of the main varieties of new governance modes identified by the 1990s' 'governance turn' in EU studies (Héritier and Rhodes 2011; Kohler-Koch and Rittberger 2006). The two case studies in the paper, financial regulation and the European Semester, provide a robust test of the resilience of 'experimentalist governance' given the tendency towards centralisation and hierarchy in crisis conditions.

The European Union is a compound polity in which its member states provide the indispensable foundation. Although formally equal in the Union treaties, the Union consists of an admixture of large, medium-sized and small states. Historically, two large states – France and Germany – have been central to efforts to deepen integration and have provided the essential political capital to advance European integration. Hence their bilateral relationship lies at the core of the Union. UK membership in 1973 added a third 'Big State', but one characterised by an ambivalent relationship with the Union and the process of integration. Exploring how the crisis has affected bilateral and trilateral relationships across the 'Big Three' is essential to understanding the legacy of the crisis on the Union's core power structures. This is addressed by Krotz and Maher in 'Europe's Crises and the EU's "Big Three"', in which they analyse the impact and significance of the Ukraine and eurozone conflicts on the EU's big three member states.

What we have learnt?

In this concluding section we outline the conclusions that may be drawn from the articles in this special issue. We will address a number of different facets of institutional-functional integration and political integration. We begin with a discussion of the resilience of the Union when confronted with crises. This is followed by an analysis of the changing politics of integration and the links between domestic politics, transnational politics and EU-level politics. This leads in turn to a discussion of the whole and the parts and the manner in which integration logics are coupling and de-coupling. Finally we address the patterns of continuity and change that may be observed.

Resilience, but at a price

The EU faced its most severe test during the eurozone crisis and although the acute phase of the crisis has abated, the single currency zone remains an unstable hybrid between a centralised monetary union and an economic union replete with unresolved tensions. That said, the Union's institutions and leaders proved capable of reaching agreement on far-reaching changes in the system of economic governance, the establishment of the European Stability Mechanism (ESM), the role of the European Central Bank (ECB) as defender of the currency union, the creation of a banking union and the re-establishment of the credibility of the euro vis-à-vis the financial markets. Banking union represents a step-change in integration although it remains incomplete. The rescue of the eurozone was characterised by both muddling through and muddling up. The exit of any one member state from the eurozone was avoided albeit with great difficulty. The EU institutions demonstrated a remarkable capacity to gradually put together a 'package' of policy instruments for coping with the crisis and 'governancing' the fiscal and budgetary processes of the member states. Moreover, many other areas of EU public policy adapted to the changing circumstances and pressures. Given the lack of readiness for the crisis and the deep design faults in the euro's architecture, this suggests that the EU, a relatively young social construct, has achieved a degree of maturity and robustness through being tried and tested. Three papers in this special issue support a conclusion that points to the resilience of the Union. Falkner demonstrates that across a wide range of policy fields the Union did not descend into a 'joint decision trap' or stalemate but managed to reach agreement. She outlines how the crisis itself was a trigger for change particularly in situations of urgent time pressure, harsh consequences for inaction and a tipping point towards serious outcomes such as the break-up of the eurozone or financial contagion across Europe. Zeitlin's analysis of the testing of experimental governance in two fields pointed to its durability and robustness even in relation to 'hard cases', financial regulation and the European Semester. The explanation offered lies in the diverse and polyarchic conditions of the EU; the Union continues to have to navigate the tensions between the 'logic of integration' and the 'logic of diversity' identified already in the 1960s by Hoffman (1966). Pelkmans brings the continuing significance of the single market sharply into focus. In a wide-ranging analysis,

Pelkmans argues that the single market was and remains the hard core of the EU and that it is the foundation of the Union for the future. All three papers point to resilient problem-solving dynamics in the Union and the continuing importance of functional pressures and the functional content of policy integration. The 'constraining consensus' identified by Hooghe and Marks (2009) did not prove so constraining as thought and functional pressures continue to play a major role in integration.

Resilience in the eye of the storm came at a price. While the Union's institutional and functional capacity was successful in stabilising the eurozone and regaining market credibility, it was only possible by stretching formal-legal provisions to their limits. The 'no bailout' clauses of the Treaty on European Union (TEU) were breached and there was pronounced mandate-stretching by EU institutions, notably the ECB, and numerous extra-treaty instruments were created. Schmidt traces the manner in which the ECB moved from a focus on credibility at the beginning of the crisis to a later focus on stability. A deep concern about stability - financial contagion and the survival of the euro - led the ECB to engage in non-standard measures such as buying bonds in the secondary markets and to become a de facto lender of last resort. Given the mandate-stretching involved in saving the euro, the ECB adopted a legitimising discourse of privileging the core features of its mandate - price stability and the monetary transmission mechanism - as a shield against legal challenge. Law is constitutive of the European Union and 'integration though law' one of its structural characteristics (Cappelletti *et al.* 1986; Joerges 2014). A pronounced feature of the crisis response was the use of law in legitimising action. However, the pressures of the crisis resulted in the development of numerous legal instruments outside the formal treaty framework which led to legal challenges in the German Constitutional Court and the European Court of Justice. Law was not just a route to integration but also a weapon in greater contestation about what the EU could do and how its institutions behaved in crisis conditions. The resort to courts brought contestation about policy responses out of the realm of politics into the realm of courts. Saurugger concludes in her paper that the EU when confronted with a systemic crisis situation did not introduce more soft law mechanisms aimed at making EU governance simpler, more flexible and less formal. Rather the legal frame became harder (Saurugger 2016). The crisis has left many unresolved questions about the relationship between the new instruments and the existing corpus of European law, their impact on the Union's system of competences and institutional balances and on the relationship between euro and non-euro states. It has also opened up a focus on the relationship between law and politics as the political capacity of the Union and its member states was stretched to its limits.

Although resilience was characteristic of the Union's response to the eurozone crisis, the system remains extremely vulnerable. The retrofitting of the single currency is incomplete even in relation to the major policy and institutional fix, banking union. Functional integration advances, but only up to an unsatisfactory point that leaves the whole edifice more vulnerable than it should be. The politics of the 'least necessary' at any one decision point predominates. The tensions between the 'debtor' and the 'creditor' states, which have their roots in the structural imbalances of the various economies, have not been resolved either, but strongly aggravated by the euro crisis, with the political radicalisation of the European South as a consequence. The Five Presidents Report on the Economic and Monetary Union (EMU) points to further policy and institutional development but not in the immediate future. Resilience during the eurozone crisis, largely prompted by the unknowable consequences of a dramatic rupture, is not being matched in the other crisis situations that Europe confronts. Europe continues to struggle to address the myriad external crises in its neighbourhood, although it has managed to maintain cohesion, albeit with great difficulty, when faced with a resurgent Putin. The refugee crisis is, however, even more challenging for the EU and its member states than the crisis in the eurozone. There is no supranational institution like the ECB that can intervene decisively in the refugee crisis. The functional equivalent of acute market pressures that forced the member states and ECB to take urgent decisions when faced with the prospect of contagion do not exist. And although the eurozone crisis triggered anti-EU sentiment, European electorates remained committed to euro membership even in Greece, where the crisis was at its most turbulent. Rather the refugee crisis has become bound up with acute tension within some member states around issues of migrant integration and terrorist attacks in Europe.

Multilevel politics

The EU, long characterised as a system of multilevel governance, is moving to a system of multilevel and perhaps transnational politics. Writing in 2000, Mair concluded that 'Europe fails to impact on national party systems because it is held at one remove by the competing political leaderships, such that, in terms of domestic politics at least, it is often depoliticised' (Mair 2000: 48). This was challenged during the 2000s and is no longer tenable after the crisis. The Great Recession had a profound impact on politics in the member states and on the consequences of EU-level action for domestic politics. One pressing crisis legacy was and remains the volatility of domestic politics and party systems given the weight of the crisis that has gone hand in hand with the continuation and deepening of grand coalitions in supranational politics. Saurugger argues that the political character of integration has been brought sharply into focus by the crisis and that integration theories have difficulty in explaining the intensification of politicisation in the Union. Theorising and conceptualising multilevel politics is a central challenge to scholars of integration. Hobolt and Tilley's analysis of the rise of the challenger parties underlines the need to revisit domestic politics to understand the political dynamics unleashed by the crisis. The focus on the rise of challenger parties provides an illuminating lens on the manner in which party systems and party competition are been reshaped. Mainstream parties both in government and opposition have suffered losses to parties on the left and right.

The Hobolt and Tilley paper challenges the post-functionalist theory of politicisation in the European Union. It shows that both 'identity' and 'left-right' politics are at play, but for different voting cohorts. Voters who defect to left-wing challenger parties are concerned about redistribution and those favouring greater redistribution are more likely to defect to the left. Redistribution remains a core left-right conflict. Defection to the right, however, is bound up with 'identity politics'. Voters who defect to right-wing challenger parties are much more anti-immigration and anti-EU than mainstream loyalist voters. Many possible consequences flow from this analysis. The mainstream parties, even those in opposition, are being squeezed on both the left and the right, which has implications for government formation and the content of political programmes. From an EU perspective, the limited competences of the EU in the social sphere and the size of the EU budget militates against greater European-level responsiveness to those seeking further redistribution and EU economic governance rules limit the capacity of national parties to expand welfare budgets and entitlements. Defection to right-wing challenger parties points to a growing number of Europeans who combine an anti-EU and anti-migrant profile. These are the voters who object to the undermining of national political and cultural community through immigration and the undermining of national autonomy though a deepening of integration. This confirms Grande and Kreisi's finding that EU politicisation was part of a deeper structural shift in European politics that is leading to a restructuring of domestic politics in Europe (Grande and Kriesi 2015; Kriesi 2009). Both left-right and identity dynamics and politics may recombine in relation to labour mobility and immigration. Migration is playing a prominent role in the UK referendum debate on membership. Pelkmans points to the negative impact of forms of worker mobility across intra-EU borders on the wages and jobs of specific segments of the workforce and in certain sectors. These segments of the labour force feel threatened by the availability of lower cost workers who of course benefit from intra-EU mobility. The distributive consequences of labour mobility and of migration are likely to further affect domestic politics in the member states and make it much more challenging for the EU to address the refugee and migration crisis.

The rise of challenger parties and anti-EU mobilisation is also evident at the European level, notably in the European parliament. The 2014 EP elections were noteworthy for a number of reasons. Eurosceptic parties amassed votes across the continent and polled over 25 per cent of the votes in five member states – France, the UK, Italy, Greece and Denmark. The 2014 elections were also an occasion for political experimentation. This was the first time in the history of direct elections that the European party groupings put forward their candidate for Commission president, known as *Spitzenkandidaten*. Christiansen analyses this change and its consequences for electoral politics and executive appointment in the Union. He underlines the possibilities but also the limits of this development. He points to the paradox that electoral competition between the heavyweight political groupings led in the end to the formation of an even stronger 'grand coalition' of centre-left and centre-right in the parliament. The *Spitzenkandidaten* process enhances the ties that bind the centrist parties in the EP and because of the growth of anti-EU parties, these parties are bound to engage in greater cooperation because of the need for constructive majorities in the parliament. This then leaves political space to those on the left and right of the grand coalition. A complex pattern of multilevel politics is emerging in the Union driven by the rise of challenger parties and the deepening of cooperation among the centrist parties in reaction to this.

The whole and the parts

The EU created a special type of relationship between states by transforming Europe's nation states into member states engaged in a common enterprise operating within a shared framework of laws and institutions. However, the crisis tested not just the EU and eurozone collective but also its parts, the member states. The impact was particularly acute in the programme countries that had to exchange interdependence in the Union for dependence on the Troika. This was of course envisaged as a time-bound episode of dependence rather than a permanent feature of eurozone membership. As the crisis unfolded, increasing attention was directed towards the 'E' in EMU when economic governance was emphasised as a key feature of crisis prevention. A number of papers addressed the Union's and eurozone's evolving system of economic governance. A system of 'rules-based integration' was enhanced in the fiscal and budgetary spheres through a series of new far-reaching legal provisions, the so-called 'Six-pack' and Two-pack' which were encased in a new institutional and process architecture known as the European Semester. All papers agree that the EU's role has become more intrusive and visible in scrutinising and guiding core national policies in the economic and social spheres, especially within the eurozone. Becker *et al.* conclude that under the new provisions the Commission assumed greater powers in policy management and surveillance. The objective of the new rules and monitoring processes was to emphasise the responsibility of each member state to the collective, to the common concern of the member states. The extent to which the relationship between the collective and individual member states was fundamentally altered by the strengthening of the Union's system of economic governance remains an open question. Schmidt concludes that the Commission was forced because of declining output legitimacy to interpret the rules in a much more flexible manner as the crisis unfolded. Zeitlin's fine-grained assessment of the European Semester process demonstrates how the Commission has to respond to deteriorating economic and social conditions in Europe by balancing fiscal policy with other considerations and by moving from 'a one-size-fits-all' to a more nuanced approach. The changing policy priorities are accompanied by discernible shifts in process and procedure aimed at expanding deliberation and mutual learning across the member states and allowing more leeway for member states in implementing recommendations in national conditions. Zeitlin concludes that even in the 'hard case' of the economic governance, the Union had to rely on experimentation and learning rather than on hierarchical imposition. That said, membership of the eurozone has deepened interdependence across its members and thus also deepened their mutual vulnerability. The treaty stipulation concerning the common concern of the member states has taken on new meaning.

The crisis also affected relations among the member states. 'Exit' emerged as a possibility in relation to two member states. A Greek exit from the euro surfaced many times but became a real possibility in July 2015. As Krotz and Maher emphasise in their paper, the UK was a bystander in the eurozone crisis and in relation to the Ukrainian crisis. The former was not unexpected as the UK is a non-euro state but the latter was significant as the UK was traditionally a major power in foreign policy. Underlying a growing UK detachment from the Union was the decision by the UK Conservative government to renegotiate the terms of EU membership and to put the result to the UK electorate as an 'in' or 'out' proposition in a referendum scheduled to take place in June 2016. The departure of the United Kingdom would represent a major systemic blow to the EU as it would alter power and policy balances in the Union. More importantly, it would add a degree of contingency to the membership of all states. Krotz and Maher, in their paper, analyse the evolving relationship between the Union's two other large powers, Germany and France. They conclude that this relationship has been reconfigured during the crises. Essentially Germany emerged as the Union's indispensable power and the Franco-German relationship, while retaining significance, became one in which Germany is the leading state. This was sharply underlined during the eurozone crisis, as Germany had very strong preferences concerning the policy instruments it would countenance and the risks it was prepared to take. Chancellor Merkel was the face of the Union during both the eurozone crisis and the Ukrainian negotiations. Germany's role in relation to Ukraine marks a pronounced shift in German foreign policy given its tradition of now wanting to take a leading role in geo-politics. Whether or not French weakness is merely episodic or more structural will become clearer over the next decade. Both these large states have a combined interest in ensuring that their relationship continues to play a central role in the European Union. Germany has no desire to lead alone and France does not want its influence to wane even further.

Continuity and change

The analysis in this volume points to patterns of continuity and change notwithstanding the severity of the crises challenging the Union and its member states. The single market, somewhat side-lined and forgotten in the heat of the crisis, retains its role as the hard core of the Union and the EU's most significant achievement. The single market remains the foundation for by far the larger part of the Union's substantive activities and other policies piggyback on its dynamics (Pelkmans 2016). In fact it could be argued that the single market, characterised by deep integration across a whole range of sectors, the embeddedness of economic actors in the process and the economic benefits it has brought, is the glue that held the EU-28 together. In addition, the single market is the centrepiece of the 'E' in EMU and even the UK grappling with BREXIT would not want to lose its access to this sizeable market. Dominated by regulatory and sectoral politics, the single market endeavour has remained largely outside the turmoil of EU decision-making on crisis measures. Although aspects of the single market have become deeply politicised, notably the services directive and the chemical regulation, these are exceptions to the rule of meso-level technical rule-making. More remarkable is the fact that having agreed the services directive following three years of contestation in the EP and at times on the streets, the implementation phase has not become politicised and is proceeding largely below the radar. The one aspect of the single market that may prove to be neuralgic, given the political dynamics outlined above, is the distributive impact of free movement on some cohorts of European labour markets. Intra-EU mobility, refugees and extra-EU migration are becoming entangled in the political debates on mobility.

There is continuity too in the persistence of experimentalist governance processes in the Union, notwithstanding the enhanced supervisory and monitoring powers of the centre. The creation of banking union and the concomitant establishment of a single supervisory mechanism (SSM) represents a step-change in banking supervision in Europe, a form of functional federalism. The new federal system is designed in such a way that the supervisory teams consist not just of ECB supervisors but also members from the host country supervisory authorities and from other member states. National supervisory teams have been transformed into multinational teams chaired by the ECB. Although still in its embryonic phase, Zeitlin (2016) underlines the perpetuation of a significant role for and presence in the new structures of national supervisory bodies. Pelkmans (2016) emphasises how the Commission has moved from regarding member states as 'sinners' when they failed to comply with European law to a system of modern enforcement whereby the Commission has evolved into a partner of the member states with the objective of making the single market work better. Only as a last resort will the Commission rely on its policing powers and begin expensive and time-consuming infringement proceedings. The explanation for the persistence of experimentalist governance, albeit with different institutional properties and the move to modern enforcement, lies in large measure with a structural characteristic of the Union, namely its polyarchic and polycentric nature which is the polity response to a high level of heterogeneity and the uncertainty accompanying the many complex problems and challenges facing the Union and its member states. There has been persistence but also change, and in some cases deep change. The crisis forced the Union and the eurozone into the establishment of new policy instruments, largely outside the formal treaty framework, new regulatory provisions in the sphere of economic governance and enhanced central powers, notably in the banking sector. Two dimensions of the change are of significance for the EU polity and EU governance. First, the institutional landscape in a number of sectors has become much thicker at the EU level. This is most apparent in the area of financial regulatory governance. The Lamfalussy level three committees have been transformed into European Supervisory Authorities (ESAs) with independent legal personalities and enhanced powers; they are a central part of the European System of Financial Supervision (ESFS) together with the national authorities, known as the National Competent Authorities (NCAs). The system of financial regulation and supervision was further strengthened with the creation of the SSM under the authority of the ECB. Second, at least in the eurozone, the ties that bind the member states have also thickened. New legal provisions and new processes bring the Commission, the Economic and Financial Affairs Council (EcoFin), the eurogroup and the member states into ever deeper processes of engagement, monitoring, reviewing and perhaps mutual learning. Co-responsibility, which represents the common concern of the member states as a collective, has not hollowed out domestic autonomy but has encased the domestic in more tightly coupled forms of EU governance. Domestic autonomy and policy choice have become part of a deliberative process with EU institutions and partners rather than being ring-fenced a priori. The member states have not surrendered their autonomy but have accepted that they share a mutual interest in their domestic policies and choices. The Commission, armed with the provisions of the Six-pack and Two-pack, has had to moderate its approach and accept that domestic headroom at the implementation stage is necessary and desirable. EU governance, which had traditionally been rather loosely coupled, has become more tightly coupled, particularly in the eurozone. The process of retrofitting the eurozone is not over and there is likely to be considerable contestation about just how much more centralisation will be acceptable to the member states in eurozone governance over the next decade.

Scholarship on the crisis reopened one of the perennial debates in the literature on the EU – that is, the balance between supranational and intergovernmental institutions and dynamics in the Union. One prominent reading of the crisis and its consequences places an emphasis on intergovernmental decision-making, albeit in a new form (Bickerton *et al.* 2015; Fabbrini 2013;

Puetter 2014). Three of the contributions to this special issue lead to the conclusion that the new intergovernmentalism must be explored in conjunction with a 'new supranationalism' (Dehousse 2015). Schmidt highlights the powerful role of the 'independent' ECB as it navigated the crisis. Beginning within the limits of its mandate and policy toolkit, it moved to the deployment of non-standard measures and the intervention by President Draghi in July 2012 brought the acute phase of the crisis to an end. The decision to locate the SSM in the ECB, albeit with Chinese walls between it and monetary policy, was largely to build banking union on the credibility of the ECB, the eurozone's indispensable institution. The Commission too emerged from the crisis not with less power but with a pronounced shift in its role from 'policy entrepreneur' to that of policy manager (Becker *et al.* 2016). The EP felt that it was side-lined during the crisis but it did play an important role in the legislative process on economic governance, and because of its lack of a real public finance capacity, it lacked the legitimacy to be a central player in rescue and bailout. The implementation of the provisions of the Lisbon treaty at the same time as the crisis unfolded enabled the EP to engage in political experimentation that is likely to have lasting effects, namely the system of *Spitzenkandidaten* that appears to have altered the process of executive appointment in the Union (Christiansen 2016). If scholars increasingly point to the emergence of both a 'new' intergovernmentalism and supranationalism in the Union, perhaps we need to revisit our categories and move on from the dichotomy posited by these two paradigms of European integration. If we treat the EU as a multilevel polity that has melded its member states into a system of shared governance and that has moreover created a collective polity that is more than the sum of its parts, the emphasis should be on how the levels interact and intersect and on how a system of 'competitive cooperation' operates in an environment of asymmetry and diversity.

Perhaps the most important change brought sharply into focus by the crisis was the growing salience of the EU and EU policies in the domestic politics of the member states. The Union was a major issue in most crisis elections and Eurosceptic parties have gained further traction at both the national and EU levels. The rise of challenger parties has altered party competition and electoral competition in many member states. The combination of anti-EU and anti-immigration sentiment in a cohort of Europe's electorates will have consequences for domestic politics and the search at EU level for ways of addressing the growing contestation concerning mobility and immigration in Europe. Centrist parties in both government and opposition are being squeezed and are finding it difficult to offer their electorates choice. This leaves the political space to challenger parties that are not part of the consensus on the politics of 'there is no alternative' (TINA). Parties of the centre have done the heavy lifting and borne the strain and political costs of the crisis. A decoupling of domestic politics from EU-level beltway politics carries long-term dangers for the Union. That is why it is imperative that EU level policy-making, particularly in relation to sensitive areas of domestic policy, is prudent and designed to allow the maximum space for domestic choice.

Further exploration?

This special issue touches on many aspects of integration and Europe's evolving Union. Five topics stand out as areas that should be addressed further by social science. First is the Union of multilevel politics which is little understood, notwithstanding the increasing attention to dynamics of politicisation. How we theorise, conceptualise and analyse the politics of the different levels (supranational and domestic) and, most importantly, the interaction and intersection between nested and connected politics in the EU is a major challenge facing scholars of integration. This involves a focus on just on the vertical axis - EU-domestic - but also on the horizontal axis across the member states as the effects of politics in one or more member states spill over into others. A focus on multilevel and transnational politics would bear fruit. Second is the relationship between multilevel politics and governance, which requires deepening links between comparative politics and comparative public policy. The governance turn in EU studies greatly enhanced our knowledge of the dynamics of governance in the Union but it came at a cost: the cost of largely ignoring politics other than technocratic politics and the cost of paying insufficient attention to power. It is important to understand better the relationships between the institutional-functional dimension of integration and political and social integration. There are essential questions about connections, tensions and contradictions between multilevel politics and governance that need attention. Resilience in the Union's system of governance may come at the cost of fragility in politics and a further weakening of the Union's legitimacy. Third, a pronounced feature of the two big crises facing the Union is the strong barriers to redistribution. Redistributive politics are inherently more difficult for political actors than regulation. Yet addressing the crises may require a stronger capacity for redistribution which is being framed as 'solidarity'. Fourth, we need to continue to pay attention to the relationship between the whole and the parts - the Union as a polity and its member states. The focus must be on the intensification of the links between the domestic and the EU, the intrusion of the EU in domestic policy-making and the adaptation of the system of experimental governance to more Europe. Another crucial facet of the relationship between the whole and the parts is the balance of power across the member states and the cleavage patterns that are emerging among the member states. Fifth is the need for a focus on different integration logics that may be coupling and de-coupling. Responses to the eurozone crisis deepened functional-institutional integration, on the one hand, while weakening political cohesion both across and within member states, on the other.

Acknowledgements

I would like to thank two anonymous reviewers for their insightful comments, the editors of *West European Politics* and Graeme Crouch, whose support was invaluable in bringing this special issue to fruition.

Disclosure statement

No potential conflict of interest was reported by the author.

References

Bartolini, Stefano (2006). Should the Union Be 'Politicised'? Prospects and Risks. Paris: Notre Europe, Policy Paper, No.19, available at http://www.unizar.es/euroconstitucion/library/working%20papers/Hix,%20Bartolini%202006.pdf

Becker, Stefan, Michael W. Bauer, Sara Connolly, and Hussein Kassim (2016). 'The Commission: Boxed in and Constrained, but Still an Engine of Integration', *West European Politics*, 39:5, doi:10.1080/01402382.2016.1181870.

Bickerton, Christopher, Dermot Hodson, and Uwe Puetter, eds. (2015). *States and Supranational Actors in the Post-Maastricht Era*. Oxford: Oxford University Press.

Boin, Arjen (2009). 'The New World of Crises and Crisis Management: Implications for Policymaking and Research', *Review of Policy Research*, 26:4, 367–77.

Boin, Arjen, Paul T. Hart, Allan McConnell, and Thomas Preston (2010). 'Leadership Style, Crisis Response and Blame Management: The Case of Hurricane Katrina', *Public Administration*, 88:3, 706–23.

Cappelletti, Mauro, Monica Seccombe, and Joseph H. Weiler, eds. (1986). *Integration through Law: Europe and the American Federal Experience*, Vol. 3. Boston, MA: Walter de Gruyter.

Christiansen, Thomas (2016). 'After the *Spitzenkandidaten*: Fundamental Change in the EU's Political System?', *West European Politics*, 39:5, doi:10.1080/01402382.2016.1184414.

Dehousse, Renaud (2015). *The New Supranationalism*, Paper Prepared for Presentation at the ECPR General Conference, Panel on Reflections on the Euro-Crisis and the Future of Representative Democracy, Montreal, August 26-29, available at http://ecpr.eu/Filestore/PaperProposal/281383a5-0285-4417-a613-eed8cd5d36bd.pdf (accessed 10 November 2015).

De Wilde, Pieter (2011). 'No Polity for Old Politics? A Framework for Analyzing Politicization of European Integration', *Journal of European Integration*, 33:5, 559–75.
De Wilde, Pieter, and Michael Zürn (2012). 'Can the Politicization of European Integration Be Reversed?', *Journal of Common Market Studies*, 50:1, 137–53.
Fabbrini, Sergio (2013). 'Intergovernmentalism and Its Limits Assessing the European Union's Answer to the Euro Crisis', *Comparative Political Studies.*, 46:9, 1003–029.
Falkner, Gerda (2016). 'The EU's Problem-Solving Capacity and Legitimacy in a Crisis Context: A Virtuous or Vicious Circle?', *West European Politics*, 39:5, doi:10.1080/01402382.2016.1186386.
Gamble, Andrew (2009). *The Spectre at the Feast: Capitalist Crisis and the Politics of Recession*. London: Palgrave Macmillan.
Gourevitch, Peter A. (1992). *Politics in Hard Times: Comparative Responses to Economic Crises*. New York, NY: Cornell University Press.
Grande, Edgar, and Hanspeter Kriesi (2015). 'The Restructuring of Political Conflict in Europe and the Politicization of European Integration', in Thomas Risse (ed.), *European Public Spheres: Politics is Back*. Cambridge: Cambridge University Press, 190–223.
Héritier, Adrienne, and Martin Rhodes (2011). *New Modes of Governance in Europe: Governing in the Shadow of Hierarchy*. London: Palgrave MacMillan.
Hix, Simon (2006). 'Why the EU Needs (Left-Right) Politics? Policy Reform and Accountability Are Impossible without It', Notre Europe Policy Paper, 19, available at http://www.unizar.es/euroconstitucion/library/working%20papers/Hix,%20Bartolini%202006.pdf
Hoffman, Stanley (1966). 'Obstinate or Obsolete? The Fate of the Nation-State and the Case of Western Europe', *Daedalus*, 95:3, 862–915.
Hooghe, Liesbet, and Gary Marks (2009). 'A Postfunctionalist Theory of European Integration: From Permissive Consensus to Constraining Dissensus', *British Journal of Political Science*, 39:1, 1–23.
Joerges, Christian (2014). 'Law and Politics in Europe's Crisis: On the History of the Impact of an Unfortunate Configuration', *Constellations*, 21:2, 249–61.
Kohler-Koch, Beate, and Berthold Rittberger (2006). 'The "Governance Turn" in EU Studies', *Journal of Common Market Studies*, 44:1, 27–49.
Kriesi, Hanspeter (2009). Rejoinder to Liesbet Hooghe and Gary Marks, 'A Postfunctional Theory of European Integration: From Permissive Consensus to Constraining Dissensus', *British Journal of Political Science*, 39:1, 221–24.
Krotz, Ulrich, and Richard Maher (2016). 'Europe's Crises and the Eu's "Big Three"', *West European Politics*, 39:5, doi:10.1080/01402382.2016.1181872.
Mair, Peter (2000). 'The Limited Impact of Europe on National Party Systems', *West European Politics*, 23:4, 27–51.
Nye, Joseph S. (1971). *Peace in Parts: Integration and Conflict in Regional Organization*. Boston, MA: Little, Brown.
Panizza, Francisco, and George Philip (2013). *Moments of Truth: The Politics of Financial Crises in Comparative Perspective*. London: Routledge.
Pelkmans, Jacques (2016). 'Why the Single Market Remains EU's Core Business', *West European Politics*, 39:5, doi:10.1080/01402382.2016.1186388.
Puetter, Uwe (2014). *The European Council and the Council: New Intergovernmentalism and Institutional Change*. Oxford: Oxford University Press.
Rosenthal, Uriel, Arjen Boin, and Louise K. Comfort (2001). *Managing Crises: Threats, Dilemmas and Opportunities*. Springfield, IL: Charles C. Thomas.

Saurugger, Sabine (2016). 'Politicization and Integration through Law: Whither Integration Theory?', *West European Politics*, 39:5, doi:10.1080/01402382.2016.118 4415.
Stratham, Paul, and Hans Joerg Trenz (2013). 'How European Union Politicization can Emerge through Contestation: The Constitution Case', *Journal of Common Market Studies*, 51:5, 965–80.
Zeitlin, Jonathan (2016). 'EU Experimentalist Governance in Times of Crisis', *West European Politics*, 39:5, doi:10.1080/01402382.2016.1181873.

Politicisation and integration through law: whither integration theory?

Sabine Saurugger

ABSTRACT
This article aims to analyse the challenges the eurozone crisis created for theoretical explanations of European integration. Starting from a definition of the two central characteristics of the crisis – the increasing politicisation of the domestic level and the strong call for legal regulation of, and court response to, the EU's economic governance – this article systematically analyses the capacities of mainstream theoretical frameworks to explain the way the EU has dealt with the situation since 2008. Liberal intergovernmentalism, neofunctionalism, and constructivism explain parts of the processes, but do not sufficiently link the domestic level and the EU level to answer the crucial question of why a more politicised and opposed domestic level leads to continued integration through (hard) law. It is in broadening these main theoretical frames and in combining them that tools are found that allow for an understanding of contemporary EU integration through law in politicised times.

The last 15 years have consisted of constant ups and downs for European Union politics: the resignation of the Santer Commission in 1999, the rejection of the Constitutional Treaty by French and Dutch voters in 2005, the financial and economic crises - starting in 2008 and coming to full bloom in 2010 - and the European elections in 2014, resulting in a significant increase in seats for Eurosceptic and extremist parties in the European Parliament. While crises also occurred during the first 50 years of European integration, such as the rejection of the European Defence Community (EDC) in 1954 or the Empty Chair Crisis in the 1960s, that prevented the EU from institutionalising new policies or treaties, the eurozone crisis has a different significance: it called into question an existing EU regime, and thus its political and legal system more broadly.

From a theoretical perspective, the economic and financial crisis puts great pressure on the capacity of integration theories to explain integration outcomes. This does not call for replacing one conceptual framework with another, but introduces a puzzle in all theoretical frameworks that explain the EU. More generally, the crisis put stress on the cognitive frames politicians and academics use to think about European integration processes, and hence provide an impetus to reframe the narrative of these processes (Manners and Whitman 2016).

The reason for this stress is linked to two key dimensions of European integration: a systemic and a socio-political one. The 'systemic' dimension of integration refers to integration through law, a cornerstone of our understanding of European integration; the socio-political dimension includes politics and politicisation. The former (systemic integration or functional-institutional integration as it is called in the introduction of this special issue) has always been the core of the narrative of formal integration. While it came partially under strain during the crisis - through the establishment of extra treaty policy instruments and stretching of legal mandates - we observe the continuing importance of a legal shield to legitimise action. Member states still perceive the EU as a union of law, albeit of a specific type. Political integration on the other hand has increasingly come under strain. We observe enhanced politicisation and opposition in domestic politics. This makes legal integration a tested dimension, and political integration a contested one.

This article aims to analyse the challenges to theoretical explanations of European integration created by the eurozone crisis. Starting from a definition of the two central characteristics of the crisis – the increasing politicisation of the domestic level and the call for legal regulation of and court responses to the EU's economic governance – this article analyses the capacities of two integration theories, neofunctionalism and liberal intergovernmentalism, as well as the broad conceptual framework of social constructivism to explain how the EU has responded since 2008 (see also Leuffen *et al.* 2012). While conceptual frameworks that study the EU's workings have helped us to understand the day-to-day politics of the EU, the two theories explain not only the functioning of the European political system but the forces that influence the nature of the system (Wiener and Diez 2009). Social constructivism, on the other hand, insists on understanding the cognitive frames which influence actors' preferences and positions. It therefore opens the black box of agency in the conceptual mosaic of European integration. How do these two theories and one conceptual framework help us to answer the crucial question of why a more politicised and EU-critical domestic level leads to continued integration through (hard) law.

The article will first outline the two main empirical puzzles of this crisis: the reinforced politicisation of the member states' domestic levels and the continued resort to integration through law. Part two of the article analyses how these two empirical puzzles challenge the three theoretical frames and argues that only by adding three dimensions - aspects of politicisation, the specificity of EU negotiation structures and the influence of cognitive frames - to all three theoretical frames are we able to understand the extent to which the nature of European integration has changed since the onset of the Eurozone crisis.

Political and functional-institutional integration under stress

The eurozone crisis put in question the institutional capacity of the EU to collectively address the issues raised: how to deal with the economic and financial breakdown in a period where public support for the European integration project as a whole, but also for specific issues, was decreasing. The increased vertical pressure from the public on domestic policies, and the horizontal spillover of these public opinion pressures to other member states, reinforce the existing feedback loops of EU policy-making. The institutional responses of the EU to the crisis paradoxically show, however, that functional-institutional integration, which was based on a very specific combination of hard law and soft governance mechanisms (Terpan 2015; Zeitlin in this special issue), seems to turn to a specific type of hard law in times of crisis.

Politicised integration

Since the beginning of 1990, one of the central characteristics of European integration is the increasing politicisation of European citizens with regard to European issues. Since the 1990s, European integration has become measurably more contentious – in the media as well as in public opinion (De Vreese 2003; De Wilde and Zürn 2012; De Wilde *et al.* 2016; Franklin and Van der Eijk 2004). As Hooghe (2007) pointed out, more democratic control over EU decision-making – such as stronger national parliamentary oversight, greater powers for the European Parliament, majority voting in the Council, and more EU referendums – brought political parties and the public into EU decision-making. Hence, the era in which relatively insulated elites bargained grand treaties in the shadow of an uninterested and generally approving public has come to an end. Hooghe and Marks (2009) describe this new phenomenon as a 'constraining dissensus' in their postfunctionalist theory. They convincingly argue that neither identity nor economic interests alone explain the member states' preferences over jurisdictional architecture. The problem of their argument, however, is that postfunctionalism aims to explain the brake on European integration. What we observe however is the contrary: member states and European institutions do not put a brake on European integration as they reinforce specific forms of hard law and judicial oversight in dealing with the eurozone crisis.

The crisis, starting in 2008, reinforced the situation where citizens blamed both European integration and their governments for their perceived difficulties. The crisis itself makes opposition more visible, and broader. When the salience of an issue, understood as the perception of the importance of the issue for the public, increases, even complex and highly technical issues such as economic and financial regulations become more contentious. In other words, in periods of crisis, policies influence politics even more significantly

(Wlezien 2005). A higher degree of politicisation, understood as 'an increase in polarisation of opinions, interests, or values and the extent to which they are publicly advanced towards the process of policy formulation within the EU' (de Wilde 2011: 566–7), can be observed during the current economic and financial crisis in the EU (Hobolt and Tilley 2014; Hobolt and Wratil 2015). Heightened politicisation influences the policy positions of member states which seek to renegotiate policies at the EU level. This makes it necessary not only to concentrate on the negotiation process of new policy instruments at the European level but also implementation at the domestic level, and subsequent renegotiation at the EU level. In other words, domestic opposition is taken up by national representatives and translated again at the EU level: member states reopen debates on specific policy instruments, insisting on the difficulty of implementing them at the domestic level and ask for a reinterpretation of these issues. The crisis debates about fiscal, economic or bailout regulations cannot be contained in the realm of purely technical debate. In domestic political debates, political viewpoints are increasingly taken into account, as we observe in national election campaigns. And yet, despite this high level of politicisation, we still seem to observe integration through law, albeit of a specific kind.

Integration through law and institutional engineering

The EU is considered one of the most densely regulated and judicialised supranational political systems in the world (Alter 2001; Stone Sweet and Caporaso 1998). European integration has taken place through law establishing common policies and competences shared between member states and the Commission, and less through a transfer of loyalty or the creation of a common identity. Scholars point to integration through law to be a form of the constitutionalisation of the EU (see amongst others Scicluna 2012; Tuori and Tuori 2014; Tuori 2015), of which the Economic and Montary Union (EMU) is but one specific example initially combining a series of soft and hard law mechanisms. Hard law predominated in the monetary field whereas soft law predominated in the economic policy sphere.

Hence we observe mostly delegated legislation - i.e. law neither adopted by the Community Method nor implemented through the usual institutions in the member states (Tuori 2012). Rather, it empowers supranational agencies, such as the European Central Bank in the case of the Banking Union, or the Commission with regard to the European semester. These institutions use their new powers to issue executive decisions that are not subject to parliamentary procedures at the EU or the domestic level. While in the past, these procedures have been used to depoliticise issues, this is not the case today. Politicisation remains important *despite* integration through law.

Macro-economic integration through national coordination mechanisms (Articles 2 and 3), while foreseen by the Treaty of Rome, was created explicitly by the Treaty of Maastricht, and more specifically the 1997 Stability and Growth Pact (SGP).[1] The coordination of macro-economic policies was organised through informal mechanisms like programmes, codes of conduct, recommendations, guidelines, benchmarking or best practices. Even the more constraining rules in the SGP were 'soft' because they were placed outside the reach of the Court of Justice of the EU (CJEU) (or any independent institution).

Economic governance - e.g. the economic part of EMU - was affected by two main crises in 2002–2005 and 2009–2013. Whereas the first non-systemic crisis, triggered by France and Germany, led to a softening of the SGP's hard law (Hodson and Maher 2004), the systemic crisis starting in 2009 led to a consistent deepening of integration in the field of economic governance, instead of a dismantling of shared governance institutions and market structures (Jones *et al.* 2016; Saurugger and Terpan 2016). EMU was revised in 2010/2013 (with the six-pack,[2] the two-pack and the fiscal compact/TSCG),[3] hardening the obligations and the enforcement mechanisms aimed at ensuring compliance with the obligations. In 2012, European Heads of State and Governments agreed to create a Banking Union, based on two pillars – single supervision and resolution. Hence, with regard to the wider crisis, the EU member states' coordinated response took the form of a new set of rules enhancing EU economic governance.

These institutional reforms contain several rules that come very close to hard law or at least may be considered as a hardening of soft law. The Treaty on Stability, Coordination and Governance (TSCG)/Fiscal Compact seeks to reinforce the SGP through the introduction of new control mechanisms. It requires national budgets to be balanced or show a surplus: this so-called 'golden rule' has to be incorporated into national law. With the entry into force of the TSCG, the CJEU supervises the enforcement of the new budget rules. These new hard enforcement mechanisms mean that fiscal surveillance has entered the realm of hard law, or has at least moved very far towards hard law.

The legal status of the bailouts, however, is situated in between hard law and soft law. Financial loans decided by international financial institutions inhabit a grey area 'in the interstices of soft law, technical norms, public international law, and international private law. They are not soft law - that is, legally non-binding - since the violation of certain conditions affects disbursement, and the repayment of the loan with interest is a contractual obligation. The conditions themselves, on the other hand, do not amount to contractual obligations according to the legal opinion of international financial institutions, because they are set by the government requesting legal assistance' (Anders 2008: 188; Terpan 2015). In this sense, the rigour plans indicate political and economic targets that have to be reached in the future. The fact that bailed out countries officially present the plans as their own gives an aura of 'ownership' and aids ease of implementation.

What we see here is a series of legal improvisations (Tuori 2012): a reliance on intergovernmental agreements referring coordination and monitoring tasks to the Commission, performing these both outside and inside its Treaty-based functions as well as the ECB's role in monitoring and ensuring the eurozone's financial stability. These legal innovations (although similar to those observed in the case of the Schengen agreement and the Charter of Fundamental Rights), triggered legal reactions at the domestic level, illustrating the continued relevance of integration through law embedded in both the European and domestic realms.

We observe judicial reactions on both the domestic and the European level from a number of domestic supreme courts and the CJEU as crisis measures were tested for their legality and compatibility with the treaties (Tuori 2012). Finland's Constitutional Law Committee concluded in December 2011 that if the EMS's Emergency Procedure covered not only the granting of financial assistance but also directly affected the liability of member states - such as calls for unauthorised unpaid capital - it would have to be agreed through a qualified majority in Parliament. The controversial draft provision was amended by leaving decisions affecting the liability of member states outside the emergency procedure, thereby removing the contradiction with the Finish Constitution.[4]

In addition, the German Constitutional Court (FCC) has issued a series of important rulings on crisis measures, notably the Greek rescue package, the ESF, and the ESM. In its judgment of 7 September 2011, the FCC concluded that the Monetary Union Financial Stabilisation Act, which authorised the loans granted to Greece, and the Act Concerning the Giving of Guarantees in the Framework of the ESM did not violate the plaintiffs' rights to elect the Bundestag under Article 38(1) of the Basic Law.[5] The second ruling on the TSCG, issued on 12 September 2012, stated that the liabilities of ratifying the treaty were in compliance with the Basic Law, but only under certain conditions. The FCC held that the Bundestag cannot transfer its own powers to control the budget to a permanent international mechanism which would be subject to decisions taken by other states. The government has to obtain the approval of the Bundestag prior to participating in every large-scale rescue measure, so that the legislature can effectively control budget decisions. On 18 March 2014, the FCC gave its final judgment in the ESM case,[6] confirming its 2012 interim ruling. The starting point in this ruling too is that in order to protect the people's right to vote, and thus the principle of democracy, the Bundestag may not transfer its overall budgetary responsibility to an international body. To this end, the Court asked the German legislator to ensure that no decision made in the ESM's governing bodies be agreed to without the participation of the German representatives. According to Article 4(8) in the ESM Treaty, this would be the case if Germany had no veto rights. However, as Germany's voting rights amount to a blocking minority, since decisions of the ESM bodies are taken either unanimously or with at least 80 per cent of the voting rights (e.g. emergency procedure), the veto position of the German government is ensured.

The CJEU was drawn into crisis law in a number of cases, one sent from the Irish Supreme Court and the other from Germany's highest court. The Pringle ruling (C-370/12 *Pringle*) addressed a question referred to the CJEU by the Irish Supreme Court: whether the setting up a permanent international body competent to grant financial assistance to eurozone members in financial difficulties went against the foundations of EMU, which aims at ensuring price stability through sound government budgets. In its ruling, the CJEU confirmed the competence of the EU member states to conclude the ESM Treaty and hence the compatibility of the 'no bail-out' clause (Article 125 TFEU) with the ESM Treaty.

The CJEU's second ruling with regard to the crisis mechanisms started with an opinion issued on 14 January 2015 by Advocate General (AG) Cruz-Villalón in the reference to the preliminary ruling in *Gauweiler et al. v. Deutscher Bundestag* on the ECB's Outright Monetary Transactions (OMT), or indirect bond-buying through the ECB. This case was especially important because for the first time in the history of European integration the FCC made a request for preliminary ruling to the CJEU. The FCC asked whether the ECB had transgressed the limits of its powers derived from the treaties. The OMT Programme launched in September 2012 was part of a series of measures taken by the ECB in response to the euro crisis (European Financial Stability Facility – EFSF, European Stability Mechanism – ESM). In his opinion, the AG concluded that the OMT programme was compatible with the TFEU, under two conditions: first, if the ECB 'refrains from any direct involvement in the financial assistance programs to which the OMT program is linked, and complies strictly with the obligation to state its reasons and adheres to the requirements deriving from the principle of proportionality' and, second, provided that the timing of its implementation permits the actual formation of a market price in respect of the government bonds.[7] Based on the AG's opinion, the Court delivered its final decision on 16 June 2015 (C-62/14 *Gauweiler*), where it concluded that the programme was compatible with EU law. Both the *Gauweiler* and *Pringle* decisions continued in the vein of ratifying a move towards both a rules-based and policy-based EMU in the wake of the crisis, legitimised by judicial decision-making undertaken by the Court.

Hence it seems, that, confronted with a systemic crisis situation, policy-makers in the EU did not introduce more soft law mechanisms aimed at making EU governance simpler, more flexible and less formal (see also Genschel and Jachtenfuchs 2013). This had been done in 2005, when the SGP was first revised, with a view to decreasing citizen opposition to specific EU policies (Sabel and Zeitlin 2008). There was no systemic crisis at this time, but more limited breaches of the SGP. During the most recent crisis, on the contrary, the EU's legal frame became harder. Besides, although some of the new rules adopted in

2010–2013 were not adopted under the Community method but through more intergovernmental procedures (Bickerton *et al.* 2015), both EU institutions and member states were careful to constantly refer to the EU's legal framework.

Theories and integration through law in politicised times

Part two of the article moves the focus to integration theories to test how well they address crisis responses. Without attempting to present the entire panoply of theoretical and conceptual approaches to European integration, we critically analyse two theories and one broad conceptual framework of European integration and their explanatory power in the context of the crisis.

Liberal intergovernmentalism

Liberal intergovernmentalism (LI) explains the politics to cope with the crisis as the interaction of national preferences, governmental bargaining power and institutional choices designed to commit euro area countries credibly to the currency union, in line with its general three-step model (Moravcsik 1998; Schimmelfennig 2015). More specifically, domestic preference formation leads to interstate bargaining and, finally, to supranational institution-building according to the principal–agent model.

LI convincingly explains, on the one hand, the role of interstate bargaining as the main decision-making mode in producing the reinforced legal frames of the new economic governance architecture of the EU since the beginning of the crisis in 2008, and on the other hand why member states prefer integration through law and judicial control as means to reduce transaction costs. However, changes to preference formation based on the dynamic interaction between domestic public opinion and the European level is more difficult to explain. LI, while acknowledging the influence of domestic politics, argues that the preferences of governments on European integration result from a domestic process of preference formation. These preferences are based on national economic interests. LI distinguishes between organised interests (economic interest groups) and diffuse interests (public opinion), arguing that the more institutionally represented and organised they are, the more influence they have. Diffuse interests, on the contrary, are more likely to lead to the prevalence of ideological preferences (Moravcsik and Nicolaïdis 1999: 61; Schimmelfennig 2015). Once defined, preferences remain stable throughout negotiations (Moravscik and Schimmelfennig 2009). As a consequence, LI does not take feedback loops into account - i.e. the debate triggered when the implementation of decisions in domestic realms feed back into debates at the EU level - for the simple reason that policy implementation is not part of the explanatory framework. However, we observe empirically that domestic preferences in intergovernmental bargaining processes are constantly influenced and framed by debates that take place at the domestic level, be it in their own constituency or those of other member states. There is a constant back and forth between the European and the domestic level, which on the one hand does not allow for considering preferences as fixed or stable, and on the other leads to a blurring of the distinction between economic and identity-based preferences. The findings on public opinion research illustrate this change. Recent studies by Hobolt and Wratil (2015), Hobolt and Tilley (2014), as well as Kriesi and Grande (2015) suggest that, as the issue of monetary integration became more salient and citizens more aware of it, identity concerns of citizens decreased, whereas utilitarian concerns about the EU's institutional effectiveness and benefits of integration became more important.

Negotiations on the Greek, Portuguese and Irish bailouts illustrate this problem. Member states' positions and discourse have varied significantly during the crisis, influenced by electoral cycles and issue salience. Increased politicisation was one of the results that led to the necessity of renegotiating the mechanisms at the European level. With regard to the bailout plans, after an initial refusal to support Greece, the member states agreed to rescue the country in May 2010, followed by similar rescues in November 2010 (Ireland) and May 2011 (Portugal). In October 2011 a short-term EFSF was established to shore up the markets for European sovereign debt, finally ratified in October 2011 as the ESM.

However, national use of these processes varied, indicating contestation. French President Hollande used the debate on the EU for electoral purposes in order to please the left wing of his electorate, declaring that he would argue for a renegotiation of the 'Fiscal Pact' and strong support for the Greek bailout if he won the election (Howarth 2007). For over a year he argued, based on this electoral premise, in favour of an economic government, a principle to which Angela Merkel agreed in 2013.

German Chancellor Angela Merkel's use of domestic constraints was similar in another context. The debate on whether to save Greece or not was based on internal electoral calculus in Germany. After having subsidised the eastern Länder for a decade in order to make reunification possible, many Germans worried whether the European crisis would lead the German economy to redistribute its wealth to its southern neighbours (Hall 2012). Confronted with difficulties in regional elections – in particular Germany's largest state, North Rhine-Westphalia, where the Chancellor's party lost by a landslide in 2012, as it did in the Schleswig-Holstein 2012 elections – Angela Merkel severely criticised the idea that Germany was going to pay for countries such as Greece or Portugal which were blamed for their fiscal imprudence (Hülsemeyer 2016). This position was widely shared throughout the northern European member states. Radical right- and left-wing parties exploited the nationalist reaction: politicisation increased. The Dutch and the Finnish government both had huge difficulty defending, and subsequently implementing the decision to financially support the southern periphery.

We observe similar reactions in the troubled countries themselves. Greece's President Papandreou's call for a referendum, leading to his resignation in November 2011, serves as another illustration of the influence of national debates on European policies: why would French President Sarkozy and German Chancellor Merkel force the Greek Prime Minister Papandreou to choose between the referendum, on the one hand, and staying in the eurozone and receiving further financial support on the other at the Cannes G20 meeting in October 2011, but then not do so in 2015 when the new Prime Minister Alexis Tsipras announced a referendum on precisely the same question? Neither in 2011, nor in 2015 was it possible for a national head of state or government to dismiss the public opinion of another member state. But in 2015, doing so would have meant the political opinion of the Greek citizens would contest European integration forcefully enough to push the Greek government to consider openly its exit from the eurozone. Hence, domestic debates, organised interests and the public opinion in other member states must be taken into account in order to understand how European politics function (Saurugger 2016). Domestic and European politics have never been as intertwined as during the euro crisis. It seemed as if every public statement by a European decision-maker was followed in other countries, which feel obliged to comment (Risse 2015).

Neofunctionalism

Neofunctionalism's concentration on spillover, more than its interest in transfer of loyalty, seems to make it another interesting candidate to explain the current crisis situation. In distinguishing between three forms of spillover – functional, whereby an original objective can only be assured by taking further integrative steps; political, whereby domestic elites come to the conclusion that problems of substantial interest cannot be addressed by the domestic level alone; and finally cultivated spillover, according to which supranational institutions purposefully advance the integration process – neofunctional accounts convincingly explain the deepening of the integration process described above (Niemann and Ioannou 2015). The establishment of new rules at the European level, attempting to improve the incomplete EMU architecture created at Maastricht, and the reinforcement of the positions of supranational actors – the Commission and the ECB – illustrate this argument. The functional rationalities of European integration were reinforced by integrative pressures from non-state actors such as banks, supranational institutions and markets.

While this contemporary neofunctionalist explanation allows us to understand the specific forms and instruments of this renewed legal integration, it is mainly focused at the European level, and excludes domestic public opinion and feedback loops that might emerge once policy implementation has occurred. The increasing politicisation of the European public sphere – which is not necessarily linked to a higher level of Euroscepticism, but has certainly led to more contentious politics and opposition at both domestic and European level to certain aspects of the European project – however, has already been mentioned by early neofunctionalists such as Lindberg and Scheingold (1970). Schmitter's (1969, 2004) curvilinear hypothesis argues that, up to a certain point of integration, the relationship between integration and homogeneity is linear (more commercial transactions lead to the creation of a more homogenous group). However, when change becomes too rapid, actors are once more inclined to adopt Eurosceptic attitudes. Both public contestation and the resulting politicisation of European issues exert influence on bargaining between member states and European institutions, and hence on the legal frames which resulted from these negotiations.

The negotiations of the European semester illustrate this point. The European member governments decided on the creation of the 'European semester', which refers to a mechanism according to which the member states, after having received EU-level recommendations, submit their policy plans ('national reform programmes' and 'stability or convergence programmes') to be assessed at the EU level. Member states, however, renegotiate the specifics of these rules: in presenting their budget at the EU level, they engage in a negotiation process in which domestic macro-economic policies and national political opposition are crucial negotiation factors. Domestic political time plays a crucial role:

> European economic governance is not a single 'time-rule' exercise. It reflects different functional specificities and differences in potential of issues to mobilise political opposition. As seen most clearly in the Lisbon strategy, threats of constraints on member states' capacity to act as time setters in economic reforms from domestic electoral time rules induce governments to evade commitments that 'bind their hands' and to avoid delegating power to the European Commission. (Dyson 2009: 287)

This can be observed in the way member state governments respond to incentives and pressure to synchronise fiscal, employment or macro-economic coordination first under EMU rules and now under the new economic governance framework.

The implementation of the European semester which aimed to strengthen economic coordination illustrates this point. This integrated surveillance framework governs the implementation of fiscal policies under the SGP to strengthen economic governance and ensure budgetary discipline, and the implementation of structural reforms in the context of 'Integrated Guidelines' outlined in 'National Reform Programmes' to ensure progress towards the agreed goals of the EU Strategy for Growth and Jobs ('Europe 2020').

In 2012, when negotiating its European semester, the Spanish reaction to the European semester illustrates domestic resistance and the associated adjustment process. The government declared that Spain remained a sovereign country and would not follow EU guidelines without having the final word. Spanish Prime Minister Mariano Rajoy declared that economic difficulties at the domestic level were so great that a mechanically applied austerity programme would not lead to the expected results.[8] The exercise therefore cannot be interpreted as the pure implementation of a European rule, but as an adjustment process in which general EU rules are renegotiated and adapted to national constraints of how best to solve the crisis at the domestic level: during the regional election campaign, Prime Minister Rajoy was increasingly criticised by the extreme left parties – which secured a landslide victory in the 2015 municipal and regional elections in Spain.

This process cannot be understood if domestic politics are not taken into account. Domestic-level politics and debates influence the positions and discourse of political actors and lead to processes in which member states adjust these instruments at the European level. 'Negotiated multilevel politics' (Laffan 2016) takes place: economic and financial mechanisms, albeit based on specific regulations and directives, foresee instruments that can only be defined through negotiation between member states and European institutions. The current economic and financial crisis makes the usages of the EU (Jacquot and Woll 2010) increasingly salient at the domestic level: EU norms and instruments are instrumentalised by policy actors to help them stall or advance their reform projects, be it by providing bargaining assets, legitimisation, room for manoeuvre, blame-avoidance or increases in power.

Hence, European governments act under the pressure of domestic electoral timing. These are not only national – presidential or parliamentary - elections, but also regional or local ones. Electoral vulnerability is a crucial element explaining both ex ante and ex post domestic attitudes and positions on economic governance that member states defend at the EU level, which instead of choosing less legally binding norms, opt for more law. Both member states and institutions were careful to constantly refer to the shield and cover of law. The ECB's arguments to act only 'within our mandate' and 'in the interests of the monetary transmission system' are central examples.

Constructivism

On the most general level, constructivism refers to the assumption that social norms and frameworks on which reality is based are constructed and redefined through permanent interaction. Actors' interests cannot be understood as deduced from a solely material structure, as rational choice approaches would argue. On the contrary, constructivists assume that social, political and economic contexts structure these interests; thus actors and structures are co-constituted – one of the most central terms in constructivist research. In other words, the way we think about the world makes the world as we perceive it. Thus, constructivists have a very different understanding of how interests change. For materialists, actors' interests evolve as changes in their environment alter their situation. Constructivists, on the contrary, assume that interests change as agents alter their understanding of their changing world and recalculate their priorities (Béland and Cox 2011).

One of the central concepts – the logic of appropriateness - refers to ideas (Béland 2009), or, in other words, to the 'collective understandings of social facts', as the primary source of political behaviour. These 'claims about descriptions of the world, causal relationships, or the normative legitimacy of certain actions' (Parsons 2002: 48) influence policy development in three ways (Béland 2009: 702). First, they help to construct the problems and issues that enter the policy agenda. Second, they frame the basic assumptions that influence the content of reform proposals. Finally, ideas can act as discursive tools that shape reform imperatives.

To what extent does this help us better understand the current economic and financial crisis European integration is confronted with? Not paying attention to the embeddedness of actors in cognitive frames may indeed obfuscate major aspects of policy-making. Not only is it important to understand why policy decisions have been taken and policy reforms implemented, as liberal intergovernmentalist and neofunctionalist approaches allow us to do, but it is also crucial to understand why the agents of policy processes sometimes do not react as they were expected to. Their rationality is embedded in specific cognitive frames that must be understood in order to make sense of sometimes ambiguous behaviour. When and why, for example, do European leaders evoke the neoliberal paradigm in their messages, and when and why does this idea not find its way into official documents and discourse? In crisis situations, this question is crucial, as actors are confronted with a transformed environment in which they must frame problems and decide on solutions. In other words:

> Since structures do not come with an instruction sheet, economic ideas make such an institutional resolution possible by providing the authoritative diagnosis as to what a crisis actually is and when a given situation actually constitutes a crisis. They diagnose 'what has gone wrong' and 'what is to be done'. (Blyth 2002: 10)

With regard to the recent crisis situation, actor-centred constructivism (Jabko 2006; McNamara 1998) allows us to understand how specific economic ideas framed the solutions to the crisis that were put on the table, but at the same time how these solutions were used strategically. In studying the ECB's role during the crisis, Fontan (2014a, 2014b), for instance, starts from a crucial question: why did the ECB continue to defend an orthodox model of central banking while its response to the crisis deviated from it – and how did it manage to do so? Fontan argued that while the creation of the ECB was prominently inspired by the orthodox model of the Bundesbank and the new classical economy, the ECB's decision to implement heterodox monetary measures in order to tackle the eurozone crisis triggered internal and external tensions. These tensions, illustrated by the 2011 resignations of Axel Weber, president of the German Central Bank, followed by Jürgen Stark, member of the ECB's executive board, endangered its organisational unity. The ECB dilemma consisted of implementing the necessary crisis measures while protecting its original orthodox reputation. Fontan argued that these strategies helped the ECB agents protect and enhance their reputation within crucial economic and financial arenas as well as the market.

Other studies on the reforms of the European economic policy framework show that while the idea of German ordoliberalism was as strong in 2003/2004 as it is today, German stakeholders use the paradigm strategically in negotiations (Bulmer 2014): The German government accepted Axel Weber's resignation, although he represented German ordoliberalism in a very clear form, because the German government perceived compromises to be crucial in 2011 in order to go beyond the deadlock in which the ECB found itself with regard to saving the eurozone (Jones 2013). The French government's position defending the need for an economic government that takes more variables into account than just low inflation and spending control, is another illustration of the interaction between ideas and strategies in this particular crisis. More specifically, neo-liberal ideas are perceived as particularly resilient because they adapt to actors' strategies: Mügge (2013) and Thatcher (2013), for example, underline these strategic usages of neo-liberal ideas in the regulation of European financial and economic markets.

The main issue is, however, the capacity of constructivism, or more precisely actor-centred constructivism, to take crisis-induced 'multilevel politics' into account. While the power of actor-centred constructivism to explain the influence of ideas and paradigms on the framing of policy solutions applied to the economic and financial crisis – those defended by supranational institutions, national governments and non-state actors more generally – is high, the reciprocal influence between domestic-level politics and European-level negotiations and the use of judicial politics seems so far underestimated, but not at all impossible to introduce in the framework.

Conclusion

In terms of the current state of European integration, is there one conceptual framework that provides a more valid explanation of why a more politicised and opposed domestic level leads to continued integration through a specific form of (hard) law? The crisis has led to a situation in which the EU is yet again deeply involved in the exercise of core state powers. Does the demand for integration largely grow from the desire of member states to limit policy externalities and to realise economies of scale, as the neofunctionalist-inspired understanding of Genschel and Jachtenfuchs (2013) suggests? According to this view, consensus requirements of intergovernmental decision-making are high and make the integration process also seemingly irreversible. This often forces political decision-makers to cope with follow-on problems of integration by more integration, even though these problems induce publics to prefer less. Instead of strengthening solely the power of governments in European integration, the power of bureaucrats and judges is also being strengthened at the expense of directly elected legislative representatives.

While we indeed observe these phenomena, the question remains how to conceptualise the increasing politicisation of the domestic level, politicisation that leads to unstable power relations, the emergence of new parties and, in some countries, deep social unrest. Can we say that the greater the domestic opposition to European integration, the higher the probability that legal frames harden and judicial politics may, yet again, be a central feature of European integration?

If this is the case, each of the three theoretical approaches above can only partially explain this outcome. While liberal intergovernmentalists can explain reinforced legal integration with the argument of the necessity of decreasing transaction costs through intergovernmental bargaining, the reinforced horizontal and vertical influence of public opinion and party politics from the domestic level and other member states is not yet part of their explanatory framework. Contemporary neofunctionalist accounts of the crisis, on the other hand, conceptualise the deepening of integration – i.e. reinforced legally binding rules and judicial oversight through a spillover effect – but do not take into account domestic-level politicisation or feedback loops when explaining the outcomes of EU-level bargaining. Furthermore, neither of the two refer to actors' cognitive frames used to legitimise or disqualify specific solutions in designing the legal instruments of the EU's economic governance. Finally, actor-centred constructivist frameworks convincingly explain the resilience of certain economic ideas in European-level bargaining procedures and their strategic use in the bargaining processes, allowing for the analysis of the influence of supranational actors, which liberal intergovernmentalist accounts would neglect. This approach, however, is again much less interested in the influence of horizontal and vertical politics and the politicised public opinion on the positions and preferences of member states and supranational actors.

While it would be tempting to propose another new conceptual framework at the end of this article, which might solve all the problems encountered in the three approaches above, my aim is much humbler. All three theories and frameworks offer partial explanations to what we observe in the most recent developments of European integration. One finds LI's intergovernmental bargaining (Fabbrini 2015), but without member state preferences that purely concentrate on a decrease of transaction costs; neofunctionalist 'failing forward' (Jones *et al.* 2016) adding new forms of legally binding rules and judicial control, and, finally, cognitive frames that help explain the legitimacy of specific solutions compared to others developed by member states and supranational actors. All three theoretical frameworks, however, might need to engage more systematically with the question of under what circumstances domestic politics influence European bargaining both horizontally and vertically, from the domestic level to the European level and between the different member states' domestic levels and create feedback loops. In other words, why these crisis situations lead in some cases to harder law and/or more integration, and why in other situations we observe a softening of rules and/or less integration. To answer these questions, theories and conceptual frameworks need to be conceptually open to other explanations, as already proposed by Ernst Haas and his colleagues (Haas 1968) in their revision of neofunctionalism. Even if European integration continues to combine intergovernmental and supranational elements, it becomes increasingly 'normalised'. Scholars may need to combine theoretical frameworks to understand its complexity, just as theories of state building would do.

Notes

1. Regulation (EC) 1467/1997, OJ L174, 7.7.05.
2. Regulation (EU) no. 1173/2011 of the Parliament of the Council of 16 November 2011; Regulation (EU) no. 1174/2011 of the Parliament of the Council of 16 November 2011; Regulation (EU) no. 1175/2011 of the Parliament of the Council of 16 November 2011, amending Regulation (EC) 1466/1997; Regulation (EU) no. 1176/2011 of the Parliament of the Council of 16 November 2011; Regulation (EU) no. 1177/2011 of the Council of 8 November 2011 amending Regulation (EC) no. 1467/97; Council Directive 2011/85/EU of 8 November 2011. These acts have been published in OJ L306, 23 November 2011.
3. Regulation (EU) no. 472/2013 of 21 May 2013, OJ L140, 27 May 2013; Regulation (EU) no. 473/2013 of 21 May 2013, OJ L140, 27 May 2013. Treaty on Stability, Coordination and Governance in the Economic and Monetary Union signed on 2 March 2012, entered into force on 1 January 2013, Doc/12/2, available at http://europa.eu/rapid/press-release_DOC-12-2_en.htm, accessed 10 December 2014.
4. Reports of the Constitutional Law Committee PeVL 22 and 25/2011, and PeVL 13/2012 (Tuori 2012: 41).
5. BVerfG, 2 BvR 987/10 (no. 103).
6. BVerfG, 2 BvR 2728/13 of 14 January 2014, Rn. (1–24).
7. eur-lex.europa.eu, Opinion of Mr Advocate General Cruz Villalon delivered on 14 January 2015, ECLI:EU:C:2015:7.
8. 'FT Interview: Mariano Rajoy', *Financial Times*, 13 January 2013.

Acknowledgements

I would like to thank Brigid Laffan, Gerda Falkner, the participants of the 2015 workshop at the EUI in Florence and of the 2016 Summit Conference in Brussels, and particularly Fabien Terpan and Mathias Götz for their remarks and constructive criticisms. I am very grateful to the two anonymous reviewers for their precise suggestions and comments.

Disclosure statement

No potential conflict of interest was reported by the author.

References

Alter, Karen J. (2001). *Establishing the Supremacy of European Law: The Making of an International Rule of Law in Europe*. Oxford: Oxford University Press.

Anders, Gerhard (2008). 'The Normativity of Numbers: World Bank and IMF Conditionality', *Political and Legal Anthropology Review*, 31:2, 187–202.

Béland, Daniel (2009). 'Ideas, Institutions, and Policy Change', *Journal of European Public Policy*, 16:5, 701–18.

Béland, Daniel, and Robert Henry Cox, eds. (2011). *Ideas and Politics in Social Science Research*. Oxford: Oxford University Press.

Bickerton, Christopher, Dermott Hodson, and Uwe Puetter, eds. (2015). *The New Intergovernmentalism: States and Supranational Actors in the Post-Maastricht Era*. Oxford: Oxford University Press.

Blyth, Mark (2002). *The Great Transformation: Economic Ideas and Institutional Change in the 20th century*. Cambridge: Cambridge University Press.

Bulmer, Simon (2014). 'Germany and the Eurozone Crisis: Between Hegemony and Domestic Politics', *West European Politics*, *37*:6, 1244–63.

De Vreese, Claes (2003). *Framing Europe: Television News and European Integration*. Amsterdam: Aksant Academic Publishers.

De Wilde, Pieter (2011). 'No Polity for Old Politics? A Framework for Analyzing the Politicization of European Integration', *Journal of European Integration*, *33*:5, 559–75.

De Wilde, Pieter and Michael Zürn (2012). 'Can the Politicization of European Integration be Reversed?', *Journal of Common Market Studies*, 50:s1, 137–53.

De Wilde, Pieter, Anna Leupold, and Henning Schmidtke (2016). 'Introduction: The Differentiated Politicisation of European Governance', *West European Politics*, 39:1, 3–22.

Dyson, Kenneth (2009). 'The Evolving Timescapes of European Economic Governance: Contesting and Using Time', *Journal of European Public Policy*, 16:2, 286–306.

Fabbrini, Sergio (2015). *Which European Union? Europe After the Euro Crisis*. Cambridge: Cambridge University Press.

Fontan, Clément (2014). 'Frankenstein en Europe: L'impact de la Banque centrale Européenne sur la Gestion de la Crise de la Zone Euro', *Politique Européenne*, 42, 10–33.

Fontan, Clément (2014). 'L'art du grand écart', *Gouvernement et action publique*, 2, 103–23.

Franklin, Mark, and Cees van der Eijk (2004). 'Potential for Contestation on European Matters at National Elections in Europe', in Gary Marks and Marco Steenbergen (eds.), *European Integration and Political Conflict*. Cambridge: Cambridge University Press, 32–50.

Genschel, Philipp, and Markus Jachtenfuchs, eds. (2013). *Beyond the Regulatory Polity?: The European Integration of Core State Powers*. Oxford: Oxford University Press.

Haas, Ernst B. (1968). *The Uniting of Europe. Political, Social, and Economic Forces, 1950–1957*, 2nd ed. Stanford: Stanford University Press.

Hall, Peter (2012). 'The Economics and Politics of the Euro Crisis', *German Politics*, 21:4, 355–71.

Hobolt, Sara B., and James Tilley (2014). *Blaming Europe?: Responsibility Without Accountability in the European Union*. Oxford: Oxford University Press.

Hobolt, Sara B., and Christopher Wratil (2015). 'Public Opinion and The Crisis: The Dynamics of Support for the Euro', *Journal of European Public Policy*, *22*:2, 238–56.

Hodson, Dermot, and Imelda Maher (2004). 'Soft Law and Sanctions: Economic Policy Co-ordination and Reform of the Stability and Growth Pact', *Journal of European Public Policy*, 11:5, 798–813.

Hooghe, Liesbet (2007). 'What Drives Euroskepicism? Party-Public Cuing, Ideology and Strategic Opportunity', *European Union Politics*, 8:1, 5–12.

Hooghe, Liesbet, and Gary Marks (2009). 'A Postfunctionalist Theory of European Integration: From Permissive Consensus to Constraining Dissensus', *British Journal of Political Science*, 39:1, 1–23.

Howarth, David J. (2007). 'Making and Breaking the Rules: French Policy on EU 'Gouvernement Économique' and the Stability and Growth Pact', *Journal of European Public Policy*, 14:7, 1061–78.

Hülsemeyer, Axel (2016). 'The Transformation of Germany's Position in the Eurozone Crisis. From Greek Bailouts to Eurobonds', in Sabine Sauruggerand Fabien Terpan (ed.), *Crisis and Institutional Change in Regional Integration*. Abingdon: Routledge, 60–78.

Jabko, Nicolas (2006). *Playing the Market: A Political Strategy for Uniting Europe, 1985–2005*. Ithaca: Cornell University Press.

Jacquot, Sophie, and Cornelia Woll (2010). 'Using Europe: Strategic Action in Multi-level Politics', *Comparative European Politics*, 8:1, 110–26.

Jones, Erik (2013). 'The Collapse of the Brussels-Frankfurt Consensus and the Future of the Euro', in Vivien Schmidt and Mark Thatcher (eds.), *Resilient Liberalism in Europe's Political Economy*. Cambridge: Cambridge University Press, 145–70.

Jones, Erik, Daniel Kelemen, and Sophie Meunier (2016). 'Failing Forward? The Euro Crisis and the Incomplete Nature of European Integration', *Comparative Political Studies*, available at http://scholar.princeton.edu/sites/default/files/smeunier/files/failingforwardjoneskelemenmeunierfinal.pdf.

Kriesi, Hanspeter, and Edgar Grande (2015). 'The Europeanization of the National Political Debate', in Olaf Cromme and Sara B. Hobolt (eds.), *Democratic Politics in a European Union under Stress*. Oxford: Oxford University Press, 67–86.

Laffan, B. (2016). 'Europe's Union in Crisis: Tested and Contested', *West European Politics*, doi:http://dx.doi.org/10.1080/01402382.2016.1186387.

Leuffen, Dirk, Berthold Rittberger, and Frank Schimmelfennig (2012). *Differentiated Integration. Explaining Variation in the European Union*. Basingstoke: Palgrave MacMillan.

Lindberg, Leon, and Stuart Scheingold (1970). *Europe's Would Be Polity. Patterns of Change in the European Community*. New Jersey: Prentice Hall.
Manners, Ian, and Richard Whitman (2016). 'Dissident Voices in Theorizing Europe: Another Theory is Possible', *Journal of Common Market Studies*, 54:1, 1–18.
McNamara, Kathleen (1998). *The Currency of Ideas: Monetary Politics in the European Union*. Ithaca & London: Cornell University Press.
Moravcsik, Andrew (1998). *The Choice for Europe: Social Purpose and State Power from Messina to Maastricht*. Ithaca, NY: Cornell University Press.
Moravcsik, Andrew, and Kalypso Nicolaïdis (1999). 'Explaining the Treaty of Amsterdam: Interests, Influence, Institutions', *Journal of Common Market Studies*, 37:1, 59–85.
Moravscik, Andrew, and Frank Schimmelfennig (2009). 'Liberal Intergovernmentalism', in Antje Wiener and Thomas Diez (eds.), *European Integration Theory*. Oxford: Oxford University Press, 67–87.
Mügge, Daniel (2013). 'Resilient Neo – Liberalism in European Financial Regulation', in Vivien Schmidt and Mark Thatcher (eds.), *Resilient Liberalism in Europe's Political Economy*. Cambridge: Cambridge University Press, 201–25.
Niemann, Arne, and Demosthenes Ioannou (2015). 'European Economic Integration in Times of Crisis: A Case of Neofunctionalism?', *Journal of European Public Policy*, *22*:2, 196–218.
Parsons, Craig (2002). 'Showing Ideas as Causes: The Origins of the European Union', *International Organization*, 56:1, 47–84.
Risse, Thomas (2015). 'European Public Spheres, the Politicization of EU Affairs and its Consequences', in Thomas Risse (ed.), *European Public Spheres. Politics is Back.*, Cambridge: Cambridge University Press, 141–64.
Sabel, Charles F., and Jonathan Zeitlin (2008). 'Learning from Difference: The New Architecture of Experimentalist Governance in the EU', *European Law Journal*, 14:3, 271–327.
Saurugger, Sabine (2016). 'Sociological Approaches in Times of Turmoil', *Journal of Common Market Studies*, 54, 1, 70–86.
Saurugger, Sabine, and Fabien Terpan (2016). 'Do Crises Lead to Policy Change? The Multiple Streams Framework and the European Union's Economic Governance Instruments', *Policy Sciences*, 49:1, 35–53.
Schimmelfennig, Frank (2015). 'Liberal Intergovernmentalism and The Euro Area Crisis', *Journal of European Public Policy*, 22:2, 177–95.
Schmitter, Philippe C. (1969). 'Three Neofunctionalist Hypothesis about International Integration', *International Organization*, 23:1, 161–6.
Schmitter, Philippe C. (2004). 'Neo-Neofunctionalism', in Antje Wiener and Thomas Diez (eds.), *European Integration Theory*. Oxford: Oxford University Press, 45–74.
Scicluna, Nicole (2012). 'EU Constitutionalism in Flux: Is the Eurozone Crisis Precipitating Centralisation or Diffusion?', *European Law Journal*, 18:4, 489–503.
Sweet, Alec S., and James A. Caporaso (1998). 'La Cour de Justice et l'intégration Européenne', *Revue Française de Science Politique*, 48:2, 195–244.
Terpan, Fabien (2015). 'Soft Law in the European Union – The Changing Nature of EU Law', *European Law Journal*, 21:1, 68–96.
Thatcher, Mark (2013). 'Supranational Neo-Liberalization: The EUs Regulatory Model of Economic Market', in Vivien Schmidt and Mark Thatcher (eds.), *Resilient Liberalism in Europe's Political Economy*. Cambridge: Cambridge University Press, 171–200.
Tuori, Kaarlo (2012). The European Financial Crisis: Constitutional Aspects and Implications. *EUI Working Papers LAW No. 2012/28*, available at SSRN:http://ssrn.com/abstract=2171824.

Tuori, Kaarlo (2015). *European Constitutionalism*. Cambridge: Cambridge University Press.
Tuori, Kaarlo, and Klaus Tuori (2014). *The Eurozone Crisis: A Constitutional Analysis*. Cambridge: Cambridge University Press.
Wiener, Antje, and Thomas Diez (2009). *European Integration Theory*, 2nd ed. Oxford: Oxford University Press.
Wlezien, Christopher (2005). 'On the Salience of Political Issues: The Problem with the 'Most Important Problem', *Electoral Studies*, 24:4, 555–79.

The EU's problem-solving capacity and legitimacy in a crisis context: a virtuous or vicious circle?

Gerda Falkner

ABSTRACT
This article focuses on which mechanisms enabled the eurozone to escape from gridlock. At present, the EU is in a state of profound and multiple crises. Nonetheless, it managed to bring about a medium-term stabilisation of its banking system and economic governance, and a systemic implosion has so far been prevented. Considering that crucial regulations in the financial markets and economic governance are not a new idea but had been politically blocked for many years preceding the crisis, it is a major political science puzzle how and why the reforms were actually possible in an acute crisis. Drawing on Fritz W. Scharpf's theory of the joint-decision trap, the article evaluates if, how and under what conditions crisis situations actually make a difference. Can crises possibly introduce dynamics that – at times – help overcome stalemate? Nine EU policies are being considered. The conclusions discuss insights for the EU's overall system development.

Even Commission President Jean-Claude Juncker admits today that 'our European Union is not in a good state' (Juncker 2015). Indeed, the EU finds itself in the midst of a series of profound and multiple crises, triggered by the Lehman Brothers bank's collapse in the US, which evolved into an international banking and then sovereign debt crisis, and soon led to an economic crisis. Not even the financial aspects of the crisis may yet be resolved for good but, without any doubt, the broader problems are still in full swing since the economic turmoil also triggered political and social mayhem and now Euroscepticism is destabilising the EU at a time when the worst refugee crisis since World War II requires solidarity between member states.

Where do we stand? Where could this crisis lead us? The first part of this article will focus on the development of a range of EU policies in the heat of the crisis.[1] What were the effects of increased functional and time pressures on the policy-specific decision-making processes? Are there mechanisms that enable the EU to escape deadlock when action is most needed? The second part of the article then adopts a meta-level perspective across policies and considers the overall EU system to discuss what can be done to meet the challenges ahead and where we might end up.

Background: the EU and intergovernmental stalemate

Much has been written about the EU being in crisis, about the sources of the conglomerate of crises and the manifold problems still persisting. With the refugee crisis reaching new heights in autumn 2015, the challenges facing European cooperation and EU integration appear to get worse by the day. At the same time, it is worthwhile considering that despite all that, there have actually been a number of accomplishments in the recent past. At least the EU managed to bring about a medium-term stabilisation of its banking system and its economy. Despite severe downturns in a couple of countries, a sweeping breakdown has been prevented. Notwithstanding democratic shortcomings in, and wide-ranging criticism of, the details on how the EU proceeded, top politicians succeeded in finding ways to jointly steer through the stormy waters and keep the integration process going, at least until today.[2] Considering that crucial regulations in the financial markets and economic governance are not a recent project but had been politically blocked for many years preceding the crisis, it is a major political science puzzle how and why the reforms have actually been possible now.

After all, the mainstream academic view has been that the EU, just like Germany's federalist system, represents an example of interlocking politics with detrimental effects on the efficiency of decision-making. The EU has frequently been characterised as a 'joint-decision trap' following Scharpf's (1988) diagnosis, which originally stems from the early 1980s (the first, German version was published in 1985).[3] Looking through this lens, member state governments are the predominant decision-takers on the higher EU level and they import the immediate self-interests of the lower-level units into the EU without any systematic precaution to ensure that they take the common European good as seriously (Scharpf 1988: 255). With a requirement for unanimous or nearly unanimous decisions, be it formally or at least de facto, this structure amounts to a 'trap' where even single or a few dissenting governments can easily block much-needed political reforms (Scharpf 1988: 239, 254). Under these decision rules, and in a purely 'intergovernmental' perspective of rational-choice institutionalism, European policy choices would appear to be completely determined by the initial constellations of interests or political preferences among member state governments. European action would serve common interests only if these are harmonious. If they are in conflict, one could expect compromises at the level of the 'lowest common denominator', or even complete blockage.[4] In terms of problem-solving, joint-decision systems generally lead to suboptimal policy outputs (Scharpf 1988: 258), not only because of the initial difficulties of agreement on a European policy, but also because European policies, once in place, would be equally resistant to reform and would displace the capacities for independent action of the constituent units. In other words, the European Union might not be able to act while the member states no longer have the capacity to do so.[5]

This analysis is part of the 'intergovernmental' family of integration theories (see, most importantly, Moravcsik 1993, 1998) with a particularly sceptical view of policy development. In any case, the notion of the EU being stuck in a 'decision trap' has always had and still has immediate appeal for many policy analysts who follow the daily business in Brussels. For sure, the parsimonious original argument is a useful ideal type of European integration, but we know from a wealth of both theoretical and empirical literature that this is not the whole story. There is also an autonomous influence of supranational institutions, though it varies as a function of at least four factors: 'the distribution of preferences among member state principals and their supranational agents, the institutional rules governing EC policy-making, the information available to member governments and supranational agents, and the ability of supranational institutions to build transnational constituencies within the member states' (Pollack 1997; see also Pollack 2003). Many authors have pointed at, for example, the EP's growing role over time (Tsebelis 1994), the Commission's various routes for strategic action to press for policy innovation against the preferred choices of the governments (Schmidt 2000), the EU's business actually being conducted in '*day-to-day politics*' (rather than 'grand bargains', Peterson 1995) and by EU-socialised bureaucrats rather than the governments themselves (Lewis 1998, 2000) and/or even in a realm of 'subterfuge' (Héritier 1997, 1999).

Nonetheless, seemingly insuperable consensus requirements and entrenched antagonistic interests still frequently characterise EU decision-making processes, despite the fact that the formal consensus requirements have been relaxed over time. However, this has – at minimum – been countervailed by successive enlargements which have made the EU not only larger but much more diverse, and by the still existing tendency to act by common consensus rather than by outvoting dissenting members. Last, but not least, the European Council as the major political pace-setter still acts on a consensual basis and governments cannot be outvoted there.

Be that as it may, even the most parsimonious, original formulation of the 'decision trap' model had mentioned that external shocks or crises can propel the EU out of a joint-decision trap. The EU's recent conglomerate of grave pressures can certainly be considered as such and therefore it makes sense to consider the effects of the crisis on the development of the various EU policies. An international, collaborative research project has recently done this across a range of nine crucial EU policy areas (Falkner 2016).

The basic approach was to acknowledge the structure of the EU as a system crucially based on government compromise with the ensuing danger of stalemate (as highlighted by intergovernmental approaches). At the same time, the potential influence of supranational actors and processes as well as functional pressures was acknowledged (as stressed by supranational perspectives and neo-functionalism). So both ideal-typical characterisations of the integration process were taken on board as possible scenarios and the authors of the policy studies were invited to discuss how far any one of the two, or what kind of mix, occurred in their area. The present article cannot go into the findings in depth, but it is of interest to mention that authors found a variety of modes. High-level summitry was responsible for the basic decisions in immediate crisis management and where new competences were shifted to the EU level (e.g. the banking union), governments often kept the most contested parts in the intergovernmental realm. However, the classic community method was used to follow up on the guiding decisions in important cases (e.g. in economic governance with the two-pack and six-pack regulations) and supranational actors such as the Commission, ECB and EP had significant roles to play in almost all decisions studied. Overall, the team saw no rush towards a 'new intergovernmentalism' (Bickerton *et al.* 2014; Puetter 2011) that would clearly set apart the recent period of European integration from earlier times.

Most important in our context here is that the above-mentioned study actually brought to light a number of examples of how the EU may actually end stalemate in times of crisis and adopt crisis-related reforms which are outlined in the following section in addition to the factors driving these developments – and their limits.

EU policies in times of crisis

Part of the study addressed EU financial market regulation, economic governance, competition policy, trade policy, energy and climate policies, health, research and innovation, migration and foreign policy. None of them escaped significant crisis-induced pressures. At the very least, the crisis was continuously being discussed as a relevant new condition affecting the economy and the budgets. However, the various fields were affected by different elements of the crisis and the pressures were quite different in kind.

All fields suffered financial pressures and austerity became a key concern. Economic considerations overshadowed, in particular, climate protection and health policy issues. Financial aspects also triumphed in the blocking of reforms crucial to counter new challenges in the EU's external policies and regarding the migration issue (although the real crisis in that area only occurred more recently, but this could have been prevented had the EU invested more in its near neighbourhood). Compared to some other EU policies, however, these were still minor pressures: between the outbreak of the crisis in 2008 and early 2015, three areas experienced threats that were so grave that a systemic breakdown that would have affected all (or almost all) member states could not be excluded. Evidently, this is true for the financial markets. Similarly, economic governance reforms were introduced based on the consideration that in the absence of these far-reaching changes, the markets would not regain trust. Finally, the Commission's competition policy covers state aid for the banking sector, and this also became a core area of crisis-related action (see below).

In several of the studied fields, but by no means all, the crisis-induced pressures have triggered a sizeable amount of policy change. On closer examination, the specific crisis-related factors that enabled the eurozone to escape from pre-existing decision traps – i.e. the factors in addition to those that allow exits from decision traps in more normal times (for a summary see Falkner 2011) – were a combination of extreme time pressures and high functional pressures on the EU. This tends to make a large number of actors reconsider their preferences and has a high potential to end blockages. Where pressures are lower (e.g. because there is no deadline or because only a small number of member states have to bear the burden of non-action), stalemate may continue as too few actors are willing to reconsider their positions. These factors are discussed below alongside the most interesting developments in each EU policy. I will start with policies that have so far not been in the focus of public attention when it comes to crisis effects.

In the area of energy policy and climate protection, the broad policy objectives and the basic preferences of EU member states have remained stable. However, the crisis has strengthened those actors that had always been reluctant to accept an ambitious climate policy and it has shifted attention away from environmental concerns (Slominski 2016). Conflicts became harsher and even environmental pace-setters such as Germany are now more worried about costs. The main impact of the crisis so far has been on the level of discourse, but there are examples of de facto policy effects such as the 2009 energy and climate package where political compromise could only be reached after the EU alleviated the economic burden of the policy.

The increased economic pressures also affected the field of health policy. In some member states, the financial crisis, with its consequences of economic crisis and bailout programmes even came as a 'system shock' (Földes 2016). Increases in mental illness and drug and alcohol abuse are just the tip of the iceberg of heightened costs to be borne by national budgets that, at the same time, became smaller due to the economic downturn and rising unemployment. With instability and between-country imbalances growing in the Economic and Monetary Union (EMU), the EU's focus seems to have increasingly shifted towards an economic perspective on health policy reform. Most interesting from the political science perspective is the informal creeping of competences to the EU even in areas that are explicitly still the prerogative of the member states, such as the organisation of health care and, more broadly, social systems. During recent years, the EU has actually acquired supervisory powers that clearly impinge on national autonomy. There are degrees of leverage over different groups of member states: the EU Commission has the most impact when it acts as a part of the 'Troika' in countries where external funds are indispensable; second come countries under the Excessive Macroeconomic Imbalance Procedure or the Excessive Deficit Procedure (European Commission 2014), where the European Semester process gives the Commission the possibility of using sanctions if its recommendations are not respected; finally, for all other countries the Commission may issue policy warnings – still a significant innovation considering that the Treaty basis which protects member state responsibility for health policy has not been changed.[6] While earlier EU activities in the area related to policies additional to national ones or trans-border in nature (such as free access to health care elsewhere, as established by the ECJ in a famous line of judgments), recent developments under the Stability and Growth Pact actually touch on issues of sovereignty (see Földes 2016, with further references). Even basic aspects of national politics are impinged on since, usually, for the amount spent on social and health policy is one major political line of division between ideological camps and may be decisive in national elections. Now such decisions may be removed from the national political process to a large extent and 'sucked' into EU-level politics.

It needs to be mentioned that there are similar consequences of the crisis in areas such as social assistance and pensions. In fact, no spending-based policy will nowadays escape supranational monitoring and potential inclusion in country-specific EU recommendations. It stands to reason that higher levels of conflict are to be expected in the future if the Commission exercises the new powers more fully.

In research policy, the EU has a complementary competence and – similar to the situation in health and social policies – the member states are expected to remain the main level of political steering. Over time, the EU has started promoting cooperation in research between its member states and (co-)funding of research activities. This has neither changed nor declined in times of crisis; to the contrary, the EU's spending in the field has been significantly increased (unlike the other spending lines under the 2014–2020 multiannual financial framework). Moreover, the EU strongly encourages its member states via the European Semester Monitoring Process to retain and reinforce their spending on research and innovation, notwithstanding the EU's overall orientation towards austerity. Research policy is a rare area where the crisis years have actually brought about expansion. However, as much as the Commission stresses investment in research and innovation as a 'way out of the crisis', Ulnicane (2016) also shows that the 'research advocates' within the European Commission were nonetheless outweighed by the 'austerity advocates' when it came to the decision whether the so-called 'investment clause' should be activated to allow deviations from the fiscal targets of the Stability and Growth Pact when the money is spent on research and innovation.

Let us now turn to those policies where the crisis led to truly dramatic developments. As outlined above, it seems to have been a mix of strong functional pressures and extreme time pressures that provoked change. Confronted with the knowledge that only decisive action within a specific and rather narrow time frame would prevent sectoral breakdowns (of the banks, of the states' finances), the EU has proven fit for decisive action in at least three policy areas: financial market regulation, economic governance and state aid policy. By contrast, strong functional pressure to reform a policy without a specific deadline impending seems not to suffice, as the examples of EU foreign policy and migration policy show.

The peak of urgency occurred when in 2012 the financial markets started speculating against larger EU member states such as Italy and Spain with relatively high debt and poor economic performance. The EU needed to show resolve, and it did: the banking union was set up (if begrudgingly) and the ECB president promised to 'do whatever it takes' (see Kudrna 2016, with further references). Indeed, the looming end of the euro and possible Europe-wide contagion of the banking sector made the EU exit from a joint-decision trap that had for the previous two decades blocked the supranationalisation of banking supervision. The banking union is a case in point, where the member states held on to their prerogatives until the only viable alternative to Europeanisation of banking supervision and risk sharing was the breakdown of the euro. A banking union had seemed the only functionally adequate follow-up to the existing – partial – EMU ever since the debates preceding the 1992 Maastricht Treaty. However, it took the severe crisis of recent years until the governments finally gave in and acted rather speedily in 2012. The Council and the European Council were key actors during the acute crisis period since issues of utmost importance in terms of national interest and even stability were at stake. However, Kudrna (2016) highlights that, at the same time, the Commission, the EP and the ECB were also deeply involved. Overall, about 30 packages of reform regulations were adopted in the field of financial market regulation. Although it remains to be seen if the still partial solutions suffice to keep further dangers at bay, the EU demonstrated a response capacity that was at the least surprising given past experiences.

Stabilisation and stricter control of banks and insurances were not enough to calm the financial markets' distrust in EU member states' economies and finances at large. As a consequence, another very clear effect of the crisis was in the field of economic and fiscal governance reform. Several substantial initiatives strengthened the credibility and enforceability of the EMU's economic coordination regime through further formal transfer of competences. That had previously been a no-go area, but confronted with a breakdown of the euro and a contagion of instability into the other EU economies, the governments and later also many parliaments gave in. Laffan and Schlosser (2016) argue that doing nothing was simply not an option given the extreme degree of market pressure and the evidence of contagion. However, the EU was an ill-prepared system that lacked the instruments to deal with the challenges it faced when the eurozone crisis came as an exogenous shock. The first policy to counteract the volatility of the bond markets was the reform of the Stability and Growth Pact with the Fiscal Pact as well as the six- and two-pack reform packages. Although public attention focused on the former two, the strongest effect on the competence distribution between member states and the EU occurred under the two-pack reforms.

In the recent economic governance reforms, EU institutions actually gained competences at the expense of the national level. The European Commission's supervisory and enforcement powers were significantly strengthened as control and even sanctioning of spending that is considered excessive is now speedier and more effective. The EP has made the most of its new powers under the Lisbon Treaty and, for example, created a package deal of all six-pack measures although formally it only had co-decision powers over two of them. It also needs to be mentioned that the influence of the individual governments on the Council has been reduced with the introduction of Reverse Qualified Majority Voting - e.g. on sanctions if member states do not comply with fiscal or macroeconomic targets. All in all, it seems that the much stronger role of the EU and its 'higher and more intrusive scrutiny' (Laffan and Schlosser 2016) over all domestic macroeconomic and fiscally relevant policies are a hitherto much under-estimated crisis-induced development of recent years. Most probably, the broader public will only realise this during years to come, for example if the procedures become visible to outside expert circles due to either newly heightened instabilities and necessary counter-steering and/or due to new actors rising in governments and possibly making these procedures a matter of debate.

The third policy where EU politicians were actually threatened by immediate breakdown scenarios is state aid to ailing banks and weakening in the broader realm of competition policy. As Botta (2016) discusses, the immediate reflex of some governments (above all, the French) was to exempt state aid to banks from the application of the EU's supranational state aid control regime. That would not only have been a 'spillback' of Europeanised competences but could also have triggered a subsidies war between the member states. Hence, the Commission put up a fierce battle for its powers. Since it was clear that its usual state aid procedures could not have matched the urgency imposed by the crisis (bank rescue deals usually had to be forged overnight or over a weekend respecting the pulse of the globalised stock exchange), the Commission quickly proposed an ad hoc framework of soft law to speed up its decision-making routines. In the end, the Commission managed to preserve its exclusive powers – but it also needs to be mentioned that the banks were saved by national subsidies, not by a common EU fund, and that, in the longer run, this strategy endangered the sustainability of national budgets and fed back into the loop of crises.

Trade policy has from the outset been one of the most supranational areas with exclusive competences for the EU. Nonetheless, it has been further supranationalised in recent times. Both the Lisbon Treaty and an ensuing Comitology reform gave the Commission's proposals in the field even more weight: now a qualified majority suffices when international trade agreements are adopted, and the same majority is needed to overturn a Commission proposal for protective measures. In actual practice, however, Bollen *et al.* (2016) reveal that the Commission seems to have been more successful recently in liberalisation moves (or at least their initiation, as with the Transatlantic Trade and Investment Partnership [TTIP]) than with protective measures. As opposed to the 1930s, a profound financial, economic and banking crisis has this time not made European countries more protectionist. While liberalisation now seems even more of a consensual goal, protection against unfair competition from abroad (most importantly from China) has recently run into a stalemate between two coalitions of almost the same size after members of the formerly more protectionist southern camp changed their view.

That severe crisis by no means ends all controversies is also outlined by the cases of foreign policy and migration policy. Considering that a large part of the recent conglomerate of crises stems from radical changes in the EU's close neighbourhood, such as the Arab Spring, the war in the Ukraine and the decline of transatlantic relations, it may be considered a remarkable development that the EU's foreign policy has so far remained without any truly significant reform (see Müller 2016, with further references). There is certainly no lack of pressure towards reforms and the transfer of functions to the EU level has often been framed as an economic necessity and as essential to make the EU's voice heard. However, much of the pressure was deflected since some member states relied on cooperation in selective groups and in NATO. Additionally, the pressures often immediately concerned only some of the EU member states (e.g. those geographically close to the Arab Spring or Ukrainian events) but not enough in terms of numbers to cause a breakthrough. And compared to the financial market problems, the foreign policy ones had no immediate deadline attached to them. Since the urgent crowds out the important, the EU focussed on other issues.

How wrong that turned out to be is already visible in the area of migration. Similarly to the external policy field, the EU had seen these challenges grow for a long time but had not responded. By September 2015, however, the EU's lack of action on foreign policy and asylum policy had resulted in a dramatic development. Refugees, mostly from the war in Syria, no longer stay in Lebanese camps (where lack of aid had even led to starvation) or in Turkey (which was overwhelmed by millions of refugees from Syria). They started to march towards the EU, and in particular Germany. Until recently, the functional pressures had been considerable but the burden fell only on the countries with external borders, such as Italy and Greece. There was no generalised threat - i.e. for all EU member states - and, moreover, no specific deadline that would make the problem really urgent and possibly more threatening for the less affected states. It seems a consequence of these factors that additional competences in asylum issues have not been shifted to the EU level and burdens have not so far been shared equitably amongst EU partner states. However, even before summer 2015, the EU turned out to be indispensable in securing at least some respect for human rights in migration management in the European south. As Trauner (2016) recently outlined, a minimal degree of solidarity has been shown on the EU level with financial and practical assistance programmes supporting those member states that de facto could not manage their migration inflows on their own. They were developed as a new layer to the EU's policy in the migration and asylum area.

Overall, this suggests that, yes, crises can indeed make the EU exit from decision traps. However, this is not true of just any crisis that creates any kind of pressure. Tight deadlines and harsh alternatives in the sense of a tipping point towards the worst scenario (such as the breakdown of the eurozone or a domino effect of state bankruptcies) seem necessary and, most importantly, crises should produce pressures affecting all or almost all governments alike. This arises from the consensus-oriented decision mode that is still dominant, particularly in the European Council. Any deal will depend on the relevant decision rule and its practice, and on the new interest constellation. In the absence of a sufficiently high number of decision-takers changing their mind to end a blockage, beggar-thy-neighbour policies instead of common policies may be the outcome of crises – as the crisis in asylum policy is proving at this moment.

The crisis beyond the policy level: could it turn into a vicious circle?

On the basis of the policy-specific developments outlined above, it seems worthwhile to reverse the causal arrow and think about spillover processes not from one sector to another, but from the policy level to the overall system of multi-level governance in the EU.[7] Re-thinking European integration in the shadow of the crisis, as suggested by Brigid Laffan in this issue, needs to combine perspectives. This article unites two. One is the policy-specific analysis concentrating on the prime output of the EU - i.e. policies - and hence 'output legitimacy' (Scharpf 1999: 267) created (or not). However, more is needed than just adding up the already known developments in order to speculate about the future of European integration in general. General aspects need to be taken into account on a policy-transgressing level that highlights overall democracy and 'input legitimacy' (Scharpf 1999: 267) as well as aspects of multi-level politics after the end of the permissive consensus, as highlighted by post-functionalism

(Hooghe and Marks 2009). Factors like Euroscepticism and mutual distrust could turn out to be crucial in not allowing functional pressures to be translated into joint EU-level action, as recent revisions of neo-functionalism have also discussed (e.g. Lefkofridi and Schmitter 2015; on the European Commission, see Bauer and Becker in this issue). Euroscepticism and mutual distrust also do not bode well for the intergovernmentalist view on European integration dominated by governments with their interest being to delegate to EU institutions.

Euroscepticism has manifold roots but it needs to be mentioned that the recent crisis has contributed, in bringing about political demand for EU-level solutions that, first, had distributional consequences disliked by many and, second, went beyond the powers that had been conferred in the Treaties. Ad hoc and partly out-of-Treaty solutions were chosen at times (e.g. the European Stabilisation Mechanism, the Fiscal Pact) and new instruments have been invented (e.g. rescue credits tied to conditionality fixed in successive memoranda of understanding, the excessive deficit and macro-economic imbalance procedures with country-specific recommendations and potential penalties) that stand outside the well-known toolkit from past times. If the former EU governance model rested on specific, conferred powers and rule-based governance, many present tasks involve a significant marge of appreciation[8] that is now de facto located on the EU level. It now serves as fuel for anti-EU agitation that the member states' autonomy seems no longer to be protected and that the Treaty allocation of competences seems at times disabled (consider the case of health policy outlined above).

On the level of policy preferences, the empirical analyses of the study presented above confirm that economic and, mostly, austerity considerations are being infused into other policies. Indeed, many signs of the ideal-typical 'European consolidation state' (Streeck 2015) have become visible (and made significant parts of the electorate Eurosceptic). EU-level preferences are imported into national decision processes via the European Semester process (Laffan 2014) and via 'memoranda of understanding' in exchange for credit.[9] As highlighted by Scharpf (2015), national governments in many areas now have accountability without choice while the EU has control without accountability.

This leads to the conclusion that the EU is not only in a financial, economic and neighbourhood crisis, but possibly also in a kind of legitimacy and political crisis: the stretching of mandates has triggered a debate (and court cases, for example at the German *Bundesverfassungsgericht*) whether the problem-solving needs and the success in terms of output legitimacy justify the deviations from previously agreed rules of the game. Moreover, that and the distributional consequences of the economic crisis and some EU policies have favoured hostility towards the EU by populist politicians that fuels disintegration tendencies – which in these 'postfunctionalist' times cannot be taken lightly (Hooghe and Marks 2009; see also Hobolt and Tilly, and Saurugger, in this issue). Where will this lead us?

Most fundamentally, for the long run, the crucial question is whether the crisis may this time not only keep the EU following a muddling-through model of combined successes and failures, as happened in previous crises, but if it might actually lead to a disruptive scenario. Just adding up the policy-specific developments outlined above will not suffice to formulate an educated expectation. First, we can only discuss the snapshot perspective of one point in time (here, up to October 2015), not knowing what tomorrow will bring and how this will tip the balance. Second, it could turn out that one development in a specific policy is of disproportionate significance in terms of the larger picture. One can, for example, imagine a version of the future that is based on the present short-term failure to jointly manage the sudden steep increase of asylum requests in the EU, which since late 2015 has produced a vicious

Table 1. Alternative scenarios of crisis development (highly stylised).

	Mounting challenges lead to a dangerous tipping point (financial, economic, political, social etc.) and press towards policy reforms (at this moment, particularly in migration policy and external affairs) ↓	↓
State of crisis	*Vicious circle*	*Virtuous circle*
Political discourse + interaction orientation	Antagonistic 'national' interests + advantages of autonomy are stressed, competition instead of cooperation ↓	EU is perceived + marketed as community of fate, necessary means to perform well in a globalised world, best available institution for effective problem-solving ↓
EU policy development	EU cannot forge a consensus and gets stuck in joint-decision traps ↓	EU manages an extension of relevant policies with innovative and integrative solutions to fight the crisis and its distributional consequences ↓
Political legitimacy: output side	Failure to agree on effective measures causes shortcomings in output legitimacy ↓	Output legitimacy is enhanced by successful problem-solving ↓
Political legitimacy: input side	Extra-Treaty forms of crisis management, e.g. side-lining EP, causes shortcomings in input legitimacy ↓	EU improves the democratic quality of its crisis management to improve input legitimacy ↓
Electoral outcomes	Next electoral cycle brings more anti-EU politicians in national and EU institutions ↓	Next electoral cycle brings more pro-integration politicians in national and EU institutions ↓
	THIS CLOSES THE FEEDBACK LOOP since with more (less) nationalist politicians in the decisive institutions, less (more) joint problem-solving will be possible in the EU. Hence, the problems figuring in the first line of this table will be reinforced (or alleviated). ↓ (Go back to line 1)	↓

Note: For easier representation, the circles are represented in two rows; in actual fact there could be several feedback loops over time. Certainly, impact from the outside of the circles cannot be excluded.

domino effect of one EU member state after the other closing its borders. The Schengen system of integration might be fading. In the worst case, mounting mutual distrust might spread to other areas of cooperation and disintegration might prove contagious. Connecting belts are, first, elections, which – usually periodically – bring into office more or less 'Europhile' politicians in parliaments and governments, the EP and the EU Commission. However, the orientations of the politicians in office can change fast, corresponding to their trust in each other and the viability of EU-level joint policies. Moreover, discursive action is crucial and so are responsive policies, as Table 1 highlights.

Ultimately, the left-hand column could bring about disintegration of the EU system. It needs to be mentioned that mistrust and hostile acts can easily kick-start a downward spiral since any example of that can be taken up elsewhere to justify new non-cooperation. We see some of that now, as one core EU country after the other builds fences to seal its borders, leaving the 'refugee problem' to countries at the periphery, like Greece and Italy, instead of contributing to a joint solution to the humanitarian crisis. In short, it is not to be ruled out that the EU may break down under the pressure of crisis-induced problems, mutual distrust and nationalist responses. We cannot know at this point. In addition to factors listed in Table 1, stabilising factors such as the stickiness of institutions, the malleable character of much EU law, and the widely held appreciation of the internal market, may possibly bring about a halt or even a reversal of the vicious circle.

Table 2. Two frames interpreting the crisis.

	'Integrative' framing	*'Disintegrative' framing*
Perceived causes of the crisis	Shared responsibility: • Uncontrolled liberalisation of globally interdependent financial markets executed at national, EU, and global levels • In the EU, *all* governments and experts from all member states agreed to decisions that are, with the benefit of hindsight, suboptimal (e.g. allowing countries without sound finances to join EMU; not giving Eurostat rights to check national data; contributing to banking bubbles, e.g. in Ireland; not giving sufficient funding to the UN to take good care of Syrian refugees in Lebanon and Turkey, etc.)	Blaming of a few: • Mismanagement and bad decisions taken in the 'crisis countries' only (despite severe deficits and blocked reforms also in the other member states) • E.g. Irish banking crisis caused only by Irish banks (despite tight interactions with EU, ECB and other member states' experts); • E.g. Greek fiscal crisis only caused by internal malfunctioning (despite close involvement of German and French banks and enterprises, and centripetal forces of incomplete EMU) • E.g. Italy and Greece to blame if refugees now come to Germany, Sweden, Austria
Promoted answers to the crisis	EU action: • To jointly reach functionally better solutions to frontier-transgressing problems • To join forces and reap benefits in a globalised world • to work towards the common good	Unilateral action with: • Perception that 'my country is better off on its own' • Neglect of globalisation and frontier-transgressing character of problems • 'National interest' pitched against others' interests

In any case, the current non-cooperative developments in migration issues highlight the existing danger of a disintegrative outcome – which could only under fortunate circumstances be expected to be restricted to the policy at immediate stake – i.e. the free movement of people.

Conclusions and outlook

Table 1 has highlighted that there is a danger that stalemate and nationalist responses to challenges from particular EU policies may 'spill over' to the level of system integration. What can citizens or other stakeholders outside the EU's immediate decision-making circles do to influence the direction the circle will actually take?

It seems that, although many factors matter and all levels listed in Table 1 play a major role, the dynamics will, at least in the short run, essentially hinge on three main aspects that interact strongly with all others and can be influenced by a rather wide range of actors:

- First, if the crisis is interpreted as a common challenge that has been caused by joint decisions in the past (such as the incomplete design of EMU; exaggerated financial market liberalisation without a safety net; and a failure to secure Europe's near neighbourhood or provide refugees at least with acceptable conditions in places nearer to their homes).
- Second, if the potentials of joint problem-solving are put centre stage, as opposed to uncoordinated national responses.
- Third, if a spiral of mutual distrust can be prevented.

In a nutshell, whether there is a vicious circle effect will be influenced by how the crisis and the crisis-induced problem-solving needs are now interpreted and communicated: in terms of an integration-friendly or a disintegrative frame (Table 2; on the role of discourse, see also Vivien Schmidt in this issue).

Therefore, how real sources and possible solutions to the crisis are communicated is a key issue at stake in our times, particularly since regaining credibility with the citizens as well as the financial markets is now a core task. Both on the European and national level, politicians, administrators, media, parties and civil society with their communicative actions are all of crucial importance. This is a promising field of activity for the European institutions in particular.[10] While nationalist politicians often pitch the interests of debtors versus creditor states, or central versus more peripheral EU countries, etc., against each other, anti-populist actors should argue in favour of upgrading the common interest, answering to the shared responsibilities in productive ways, and stressing the functional perspective: in an ever more globalised world that has only limited time and interest for mini-states, the well-being of EU citizens is no longer guaranteed (see Falkner and Müller 2014), and could after 50+

years of international integration hardly again be guaranteed, on the national level alone – at least not without major disruptions.

Notes

1. I draw on the findings from a collaborative project at the Institute for European Integration Research (http://eif.univie.ac.at/projekte/EUpoliciescrisis.php).
2. We should always keep in mind that we do not know as yet if the EU's actual performance is good enough to prevent revivals of the crisis and more systematic breakdown.
3. This section is based on chapter 1 in Falkner (2011).
4. Note that this is a simplified characterisation of Scharpf's model. Even in the original version of Scharpf's article, it was not considered impossible for a joint-decision system to avoid these problematic consequences. Within the perspective of rational-choice institutionalism, more productive solutions can be found with the help of log-rolling, most importantly in the form of side payments or package deals (Scharpf 1988: 264). And switching from a rational-choice to a 'constructivist' perspective, the article also considers the possibility that the 'joint-decision trap' could be overcome by governments interacting in a 'problem-solving' as opposed to a 'bargaining' style of decision-making. Perceptions of common identity, common fate, or common vulnerabilities (which is a significant element regarding the present crisis) may help to bring about an orientation towards common interests, values, or norms (Scharpf 1988: 261). Outside such extraordinary circumstances, however, the problem-solving mode was regarded as be highly vulnerable and rather unrealistic for the EU context. (For a full account, see Scharpf 2011).
5. A third aspect, of less importance here due to our focus on different policy areas, is that joint-decision systems were seen to block their own further institutional evolution (Scharpf 1988: 267), although institutional change was *not* perceived to be impossible (Scharpf 1988: 271). In this respect, the Single Act and later Treaty reforms produced a rich literature outlining that Intergovernmental Conferences are more than just 'intergovernmental' in a theoretical sense - i.e. not only driven by the intentional choices of governments (Christiansen and Jørgensen 1998, 1999; Christiansen *et al.* 1999, 2002).
6. Art. 168 Para. 7 TFEU: 'Union action shall respect the responsibilities of the Member States for the definition of their health policy and for the organisation and delivery of health services and medical care. The responsibilities of the Member States shall include the management of health services and medical care and the allocation of the resources assigned to them.'
7. I owe this idea and a number of following specifics to Fritz W. Scharpf who kindly commented on the project results at the Council for European Studies' Paris Conference, 9 July 2015.
8. This has also been stressed by Renaud Dehousse in his argument around a 'new supranationalism' (Council for European Studies' Paris Conference, 9 July 2015).
9. Note that Erne (2015: abstract) characterises the new EU governance regime as a 'silent revolution from above', with the effect of governing more like a multinational corporation than a federal state and of nationalising social conflict.
10. Klaus Götz rightly stressed this at the European University Institute in a Horizon 2020 preparatory workshop in spring 2014.

Acknowledgements

Many thanks for helpful ideas to Fritz W. Scharpf, the EIF team, the anonymous referees, and the participants of the EUI's Robert Schuman Centre's Horizon 2020 consortium workshop in March 2014 and special issue workshop in September 2015.

Disclosure statement

No potential conflict of interest was reported by the author.

References

Bickerton, Christopher J., Dermot Hodson, and Puetter Uwe (2014). 'The New Intergovernmentalism: European Integration in the Post-Maastricht Era', *Journal of Common Market Studies*, 53:4, 703–22.

Bollen, Yelter, Ferdi De Ville, and Jan Orbie (2016). 'EU Trade Policy: Persistent Liberalization, Contentious Protectionism', *Journal of European Integration*, 38:3.

Botta, Marco (2016). 'Competition Policy: Safeguarding the Commission's Competences in State Aid Control', *Journal of European Integration*, 38:3.

Christiansen, Thomas, and Knud Erik Jørgensen (1998). 'Negotiating Treaty Reform in the European Union: The Role of the European Commission', *International Negotiation*, 3, 435–52.

Christiansen, Thomas, and Knud Erik Jørgensen (1999). 'The Amsterdam Process: A Structurationist Perspective on EU Treaty Reform', *European Integration Online Papers*, 3:1, 1–23.

Christiansen, Thomas, Knud Erik Jørgensen, and Wiener Antje (1999). 'The Social Construction of Europe', *Journal of European Public Policy*, 6:4, 528–44.

Christiansen, Thomas, Gerda Falkner, and Knud Erik Jørgensen (2002). 'Theorising EU Treaty Reform: Beyond Diplomacy and Bargaining', *Journal of European Public Policy*, 9:1, 12–32.

Erne, Roland (2015). 'A Supranational Regime That Nationalizes Social Conflict: Explaining European Trade Unions' Difficulties in Politicizing European Economic Governance', *Labor History*, 56:3, 1–24.

European Commission (2014). 'The EU's Economic Governance Explained, Fact Sheet; Memo/14/2180, 28 November 2014, available at http://europa.eu/rapid/press-release_MEMO-14-2180_en.htm (accessed 16 January 2015).

Falkner, Gerda. (ed.) (2011). *The EU's Decision Traps: Comparing Policies*. Oxford: Oxford University Press.

Falkner, Gerda (ed.) (2016). 'EU Policies in Times of Crisis', *Journal of European Integration*, 38:3.
Falkner, Gerda, and Patrick Müller, (eds.) (2014). *EU Policies in a Global Perspective: Shaping or Taking International Regimes?*. London and New York: Routledge.
Földes, Eva (2016). 'Health Policy and Health Systems: A Growing Relevance for the EU in the Context of the Economic Crisis', *Journal of European Integration*, 38:3.
Heritier, Adrienne (1997). 'Policy-Making by Subterfuge: Interest Accommodation, Innovation and Substitute Democratic Legitimation in Europe - Perspectives from Distinctive Policy Areas', *Journal of European Public Policy*, 4:2, 171–89.
Héritier, Adrienne (1999). *Policy-Making and Diversity in Europe*. Escape From Deadlock. Cambridge: Cambridge University Press.
Hooghe, Liesbet, and Gary Marks (2009). 'A Postfunctionalist Theory of European Integration: From Permissive Consensus to Constraining Dissensus', *British Journal of Political Science*, 39:01, 1–23.
Juncker, Jean-Claude (2015). 'State of the Union: Time for Honesty, Unity and Solidarity', Speech/15/5614. 9 September 2015.
Kudrna, Zdenek (2016). 'Financial Market Regulation: Crisis-Induced Supranationalization', *Journal of European Integration*, 38:3.
Laffan, Brigid (2014). 'Testing Times: The Growing Primacy of Responsibility in the Euro Area', *West European Politics*, 37:2, 270–87.
Laffan, Brigid and Dirk Schlosser (2016). 'Public Finances in Europe: Fortifying EU Economic Governance in the Shadow of Crisis', *Journal of European Integration*, 38:3.
Lefkofridi, Zoe, and Philippe Schmitter (2015). '"Transcending or Descending?", European Integration in Times of Crisis', *European Political Science Review*, 7:1, 3–22.
Lewis, Jeffrey (1998). 'Is the "Hard Bargaining" Image of the Council Misleading?', *The Committee of Permanent Representatives and the Local Elections Directive*', *Journal of Common Market Studies*, 36:4, 479–504.
Lewis, Jeffrey (2000). 'The Methods of Community in EU Decision-Making and Administrative Rivalry in the Council's Infrastructure', *Journal of European Public Policy*, 7:2, 261–89.
Moravcsik, Andrew (1993). 'Preferences and Power in the European Community: A Liberal Intergovernmentalist Approach', *Journal of Common Market Studies*, 31:4, 473–524.
Moravcsik, Andrew (1998). *The Choice for Europe. Social Purpose and State Power from Messina to Maastricht*. Ithaca/New York: Cornell University Press.
Müller, Patrick (2016). 'EU Foreign Policy: No Major Breakthrough despite Multiple Crises', *Journal of European Integration*, 38:3.
Peterson, John (1995). 'Decision-Making in the European Union: Towards a Framework for Analysis', *Journal of European Public Policy*, 2:1, 69–93.
Pollack, Mark A. (1997). "Delegation', *Agency and Agenda Setting in the European Community*', *International Organization*, 51:1, 99–134.
Pollack, Mark A. (2003). *The Engines of European Integration: Delegation, Agency and Agenda Setting in the EU*. New York: Oxford University Press.
Puetter, Uwe (2011). 'Europe's Deliberative Intergovernmentalism: The Role of the Council and European Council in EU Economic Governance', *Journal of European Public Policy*, 19:2, 161–78.
Scharpf, Fritz W. (1988). 'The Joint-Decision Trap: Lessons from German Federalism and European Integration', *Public Administration*, 66:3, 239–78.
Scharpf, Fritz W. (1999). 'Legitimacy in the Multi-Actor European Polity', in Morten Egeberg and Per Lægreid (eds.), *Organizing Political Institutions. Essays for Johan P. Olsen*. Oslo: Scandinavian University Press, 261–88.

Scharpf, Fritz (2011). 'The Joint-Decision Trap Model: Context and Extensions', in Gerda Falkner (ed.), *The EU's Decision Traps: Comparing Policies*. Oxford: Oxford University Press, 217–36.
Scharpf, Fritz W. (2015). 'Comments on the Project 'EU Policies in Time of Crisis'. Conference of the Council for European Studies, Paris, 9 July 2015.
Schmidt, Susanne K. (2000). 'Only an Agenda Setter?', *The European Commission's Power over the Council of Ministers', European Union Politics*, 1, 37–61.
Slominski, Peter (2016). 'Energy and Climate Policy: Does the Competitiveness Narrative Prevail in times of Crisis?', *Journal of European Integration*, 38:3.
Streeck, Wolfgang (2015). 'The Rise of the European Consolidation State', *Max-Planck-Institute für Gesellschaftsforschung Discussion Paper*, 15:1, 1–28.
Trauner, Florian (2016). 'Migration Policy: Does Less Money Lead to Fewer Rights?', *Journal of European Integration*, 38:3.
Tsebelis, George (1994). 'The Power of the European Parliament as a Conditional Agenda Setter', *American Political Science Review*, 88:1, 128–42.
Ulnicane, Inga (2016). 'Research and Innovation as Sources of Renewed Growth? EU Policy Responses to the Crisis', *Journal of European Integration*, 38:3.

Fleeing the centre: the rise of challenger parties in the aftermath of the euro crisis

Sara B. Hobolt and James Tilley

ABSTRACT
The eurozone crisis has altered the party political landscape across Europe. The most visible effect is the rise of challenger parties. The crisis not only caused economic hardship, but also placed considerable fiscal constraints upon a number of national governments. Many voters have reacted to this by turning their back on the traditional parties and opting instead for new, or reinvigorated, challenger parties that reject the mainstream consensus of austerity and European integration. This article argues that both sanctioning and selection mechanisms can help to explain this flight from the centre to challenger parties. First, voters who were economically adversely affected by the crisis punish mainstream parties both in government and in opposition by voting for challenger parties. Second, the choice of specific challenger party is shaped by preferences on three issues that directly flow from the euro crisis: EU integration, austerity and immigration. Analysing both aggregate-level and individual-level survey data from all 17 Western EU member states, this article finds strong support for both propositions and shows how the crisis has reshaped the nature of party competition in Europe.

'There is no alternative' was the recurring refrain from many national governments during the euro crisis, referring to the necessity for austerity and structural reforms. The consequences of the sovereign debt crisis that followed the global financial crisis of 2008 have been felt acutely in many European countries. Yet in most of Europe the policy response by the mainstream, on both the left and right, focused on tackling debt rather than reducing unemployment. The external constraints on national governments' room to manoeuvre also became more obvious, especially in the countries facing a sovereign debt crisis. Governments of debtor states were asked to impose severe spending cuts and structural reforms in return for bail-outs from the European Union and the International Monetary Fund (IMF). The emergency politics of the crisis dramatically limited the political choices available to citizens (Cramme and Hobolt 2014; Hobolt and Tilley 2014; Laffan 2014; Scharpf 2011).

Voters have reacted to this by rejecting the traditional parties and turning instead to challenger parties. Challenger parties seek to challenge the mainstream political consensus and do not ordinarily enter government. These parties are unconstrained by the responsibilities of government and tend to compete on extreme or 'niche' issue positions (Adams *et al.* 2006; van de Wardt *et al.* 2014). There are multiple examples of the success of challengers in the aftermath of the euro crisis. These include the emergence of successful new parties, such as the Alternative for Germany, the Five Star Movement (Italy) and Podemos (Spain), the surge in support for the established radical right parties across Northern Europe, and notably the election of a radical left-wing Syriza-led government in Greece in 2015.

Why did certain voters defect from mainstream political parties and opt for challenger parties in the aftermath of the crisis? We offer two explanations. The first is rooted in the classic theory of retrospective voting, where voters punish incumbents for poor economic performance. The expectation is that voters will 'throw out the rascals' in government when the economy performs poorly. However, given the perception that mainstream parties, whether currently in government or not, were responsible for the economic woes, we expect the sanctioning to extend beyond government parties to all mainstream parties, including those currently in opposition. We thus hypothesise that voters negatively affected by the crisis—e.g. through job loss or reduced earnings—will punish mainstream parties and turn to challenger parties instead.

This retrospective model of economic voting helps to explain the electoral punishment of governing parties during the crisis, but it cannot be the full story. Our second explanation thus focuses on the specific appeal of different challenger parties. Our argument is that defectors choose challenger parties because they offer a rejection of, and an alternative to, the mainstream response to the crisis. Whereas the mainstream left and right have converged on a policy of austerity and an adherence to the fiscal policy-making guidelines of the EU, successful challenger parties have sought to offer clear alternatives. On the left, challenger parties reject the austerity agenda and are critical of the EU's insistence on reduced government welfare spending. On the right, the focus is on the desire to reclaim national sovereignty, specifically to control immigration and repatriate powers from the EU. In both cases, challenger parties reject the 'there is no alternative' argument and instead claim that national governments can control their own destiny and offer distinct policies.

To test these propositions we examine who defected from mainstream parties after the onset of the crisis. First, we track the changes in the success of challenger parties since the beginning of the crisis and show that there has been a sharp increase in support across Western Europe since 2010. Then we use the 2014 European Election Study to show that retrospective economic voting matters to people's decision to defect from the mainstream to challenger parties: people who were personally adversely affected by the crisis are more likely to defect. Crucially, we demonstrate that voters not only punish parties in government, but also mainstream opposition parties. Defection is also likely when individuals are disconnected from mainstream party policy, not least regarding three issues that are closely tied to the EU and the euro crisis: EU integration, austerity measures and immigration. We conclude by discussing whether the rise of challenger parties is likely to be a temporary blip due to the crisis or a more permanent feature of West European politics.

Fleeing the centre

The financial crisis that erupted in late 2008 vividly demonstrated both the interconnectedness of financial markets and the increasingly limited power of national governments. As the financial turmoil travelled from the US to Europe, it evolved into a sovereign debt crisis. By 2012, eight out of 28 EU member states had received some form of financial bailout (Cyprus, Greece, Hungary, Ireland, Latvia, Portugal, Romania and Spain). In return for these credit arrangements by the EU, jointly with the IMF, the debtor countries had to engage in significant fiscal retrenchment and structural reforms, mainly to social welfare programmes. The economic and social consequences of the crisis within the EU have been far-reaching, with high levels of unemployment and low levels of growth. This situation was worst in debtor countries in Southern Europe, notably in Greece, Spain and Portugal, where a quarter of the workforce were unable to find a job in 2014,[1] whereas other countries such as Germany enjoyed a considerable current account surplus and relatively low levels of unemployment. The contrast with the reluctantly provided rescue credit to debtor states under rigid 'conditionalities' formulated by the EU/IMF/ECB 'Troika' is stark (Scharpf 2014). Looming over these unpopular decisions by certain national governments were the constraints that European integration imposed. Even in areas at the very heart of state power, namely fiscal policy-making, national governments looked impotent (Laffan 2014). Unsurprisingly, there has been a political backlash. The most notable sign of this reaction has been the rise of challenger parties that reject the mainstream consensus. Challenger parties highlight issues such as European integration and immigration that have often been downplayed by the mainstream, and foster new linkages with voters who feel left behind by established parties (Meguid 2008; van de Wardt *et al.* 2014; Wagner 2012).

A variety of terms have been used to describe such parties that challenge the mainstream, including 'niche parties' (Adams *et al.* 2006; Jensen and Spoon 2010; Meguid 2008), 'challenger parties' (Hino 2012; van de Wardt *et al.* 2014), 'populist parties' (Kriesi 2014; Mudde 2007; Pauwels 2014) and 'new politics parties' (Poguntke 1987). Regardless of nomenclature, all these authors focus on parties that defy existing patterns of party competition by rejecting the traditional economic dimension of politics and mobilising on new issues or adopting more extreme positions on existing issues. In the case of populist parties, this also involves a more wholesale rejection of the existing 'corrupt' elite and the claim that they alone are the true voice of the people (Canovan 1999; Kriesi 2014; Mudde 2007).

Not surprisingly, there is no consensus on how to define or measure such parties in the literature. As an example, niche parties have become one of the most used labels in the literature (see e.g. Adams *et al.* 2006; Jensen and Spoon 2010; Meguid 2005, 2008; Wagner 2012), yet there is no agreement on the actual distinction between niche and mainstream. Some studies define niche parties as those that reject the traditional class-based orientation of politics, raise novel issues (Meguid 2005, 2008), and 'compete primarily on a smaller number of non-economic issues' (Wagner 2012). Others propose a more inclusive definition where niche parties represent 'either an extreme ideology (such as Communist and extreme nationalist parties) or a noncentrist "niche" ideology (i.e. the Greens)' (Adams *et al.* 2006: 513).

This paper also seeks to identify parties that challenge the mainstream party political consensus, but we adopt a novel approach to the measurement that focuses on participation in government. We argue that measuring whether or not parties ordinarily participate in government has the advantage that it indirectly captures many of the features of niche and populist parties (the mobilisation of new issues and/or extreme positions on existing issues as well as the rejection of the political establishment), yet with greater parsimony and simplicity than measuring what qualifies as 'niche', 'populist' or 'extreme'. Moreover, it highlights an important aspect of challenger parties that is not captured by existing classifications, namely the degree to which a party has government responsibility for political outcomes for which they can be held to account.

Hence, in our classification, mainstream parties are those parties that frequently alternate between government and opposition. Their policy platforms are likely to be affected by both their past experience in office and their desire to enter office again. In the eyes of voters, such parties find it difficult to escape responsibility for prolonged crises, such as the eurozone crisis. By their very nature, mainstream parties, in opposition and in office, are also more cautious in mobilising around new issues or adopting positions far from other parties, since both would make it more difficult to enter into coalition government (de Vries and Hobolt 2015; Tavits 2008; van de Wardt *et al.* 2014). By contrast, challenger parties are untarnished by office. While these parties are not necessarily new, they have not formed part of any government. Rather they have sought to reshape the political landscape by putting new issues on the agenda (de Vries and Hobolt 2012).[2] Successful challenger parties include Front National in France, Podemos in Spain and the Five Star Movement in Italy. Such parties have changed the nature of party competition and restructured the political

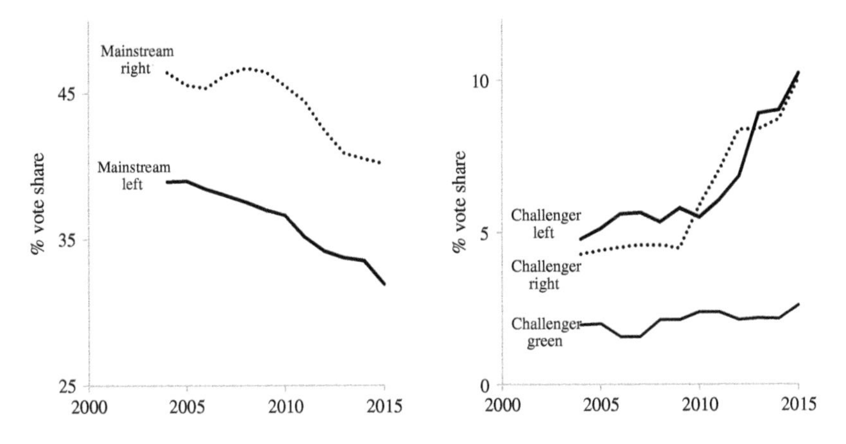

Figure 1. Vote shares of different types of parties in Western Europe, 2004–2015.
Note: These graphs show the mean vote share in national general elections holding vote share constant between elections.

agenda, in most cases without ever setting foot in government. Indeed, their appeal is partially based on the fact that they are not tainted by holding office when the seeds of the crisis were sown. Just as importantly, their lack of government experience and limited incentive, and opportunity, to join future government coalitions enables them to adopt more risky political platforms. This allows challenger parties to offer a clear alternative narrative to the mainstream consensus. Challenger parties on the left reject the notion that austerity politics is a necessary evil. On the right, challenger parties argue that powers should be repatriated from the EU to national government and parliaments, and that they can stem the threat of globalisation (especially foreign immigrant labour).

In this article we examine the causes of the rise of these challenger parties, focusing on the individual-level motivations of voters. Since the very notion of challenger parties assumes that there is an established party system to defy, our empirical focus is on Western European members of the EU that have established party systems.[3] To illustrate the change that has occurred since the onset of the crisis, Figure 1 plots the vote shares of mainstream and challenger parties across the 17 West European members of the EU between 2004 and 2015. We define three types of challenger party. All three types are parties that were not part of any national-level government in the 30 years preceding the euro crisis (1970–2010).[4] We also use the Chapel Hill Expert Survey (CHES) to distinguish between right-wing and left-wing challenger parties (Bakker *et al.* 2015), using the general left—right question in CHES: 'Please tick the box that best describes each party's overall ideology on a scale ranging from 0 (extreme left) to 10 (extreme right)'. Parties scoring more than 5 are classified as right-wing and parties scoring less than 5 are classified as left-wing.[5] While challenger parties often mobilise on issues that do not clearly coincide with the classic economic left—right dimension (Meguid 2008; Wagner 2012), such as issues relating to immigration, the environment and European integration (Kriesi *et al.* 2006; van de Wardt *et al.* 2014), most parties are nonetheless perceived by experts and citizens alike as belonging to either the general 'left' or the 'right' of politics.[6]

The left-hand graph in Figure 1 clearly demonstrates the decline in the vote shares of mainstream parties. In 2004 mainstream parties on the left and right dominated West European party systems with 86 per cent of the total vote share. This declined by 14 percentage points to 72 per cent in 2015. Mainstream parties on the centre-left and on the centre-right saw similar falls in their vote share, around 7 percentage points, over the 11 year period. In the right-hand figure, we observe a corresponding increase in support for challenger parties on both the left and the right, while green challenger parties have experienced less change. Overall challenger parties have increased their vote share from around 10 to 23 per cent during the period.[7] On the right, these include the Finns Party in Finland, the Swedish Democrats in Sweden and the Danish People's Party in Denmark, whereas on the left these include the Red—Green Alliance in Denmark, Syriza in Greece (although in government after the crisis) and Die Linke in Germany.

Of course, different shades of challenger party politics had unsettled Europe long before the onset of the sovereign debt crisis, as parties like the Front National in France, the Northern League in Italy or Geert Wilders' Freedom Party in the Netherlands successfully exploited popular anxieties about migration, globalisation, Islam and European integration. Could the success of challenger parties simply be a product of the secular decline of the mainstream left and right parties, or what some have called the end of the 'age of party democracy' (Mair 2013; Dalton and Wattenberg 2002)? Our aggregate data suggest not, in that most of the change is more recent. After all, in 2004 only 10 per cent of voters supported challengers. Nonetheless, aggregate data cannot tell us whether the rise of challenger parties is linked to people's experiences during the crisis. To answer this question, we need to examine the motivations of voters who defected from the mainstream to challenger parties over the last few years.

We argue that this type of defection is determined by the economic crisis, and the governmental response to the crisis. The choice to defect to a challenger party is about *sanctioning* and *selection* (Banks and Sundaram 1993; Fearon 1999). If we understand elections as mechanisms for political accountability, then they must function as a sanctioning device in which voters reward or punish incumbents on the basis of past performance (Fiorina 1981; Key 1966; Manin 1997; Powell 2000). This is the core intuition of the economic voting model, which suggests that voters punish governments for poor economic performance and reward them for good performance (Lewis-Beck and Stegmaier 2000; Nannestad and Paldam 1994). In times of crisis, we would thus expect governments to be more likely to be thrown out of office. Bartels' (2013) aggregate-level analysis of the 'Great Recession' has shown that this pattern holds. Citizens punished incumbent governments for slow economic growth during the crisis, although it does appear that heightened perceptions of the EU's economic responsibility reduced domestic economic voting in Southern Europe (Lobo and Lewis-Beck 2012).

Most empirical studies of economic voting use either macro-level indicators of the economy (e.g. unemployment and inflation) or survey data on people's view of economic change as an indicator of macro-economic performance (see Lewis-Beck and Stegmaier 2000, 2007 for overviews). These studies have shown a strong relationship between the economy and incumbent performance. There are, however, reasons why we may want to focus on people's direct experience with the crisis, rather than indicators of macro-economic change. First, country-level studies using aggregate data make it difficult to disentangle the individual-level motivations for defection. Second, although perceptions of the economy are normally highly correlated with party choice, there is increasing concern that the direction of causality is actually from party support to economic evaluations (Evans and Andersen 2006; Evans and Pickup 2010). By focusing on personal experiences, or what is known as the pocketbook model of economic voting, we circumvent many of these problems. There is also increasing evidence that personal economic circumstances, such as declining wages, benefit cuts or unemployment, are important determinants of voting behaviour (Bechtel and Hainmueller 2011; Margalit 2011; Richter 2006). In the context of the crisis, we expect that people who experienced a deterioration in their personal financial situation, such as through job loss or reduced income, will be more likely to defect from mainstream parties. This leads to our first hypothesis:

> H1: People who were adversely economically affected by the economic crisis are more likely to defect from mainstream parties to challenger parties.

However, the pocketbook voting model does not in itself fully explain why voters turn to challenger parties rather than to other mainstream parties in opposition. Voters do not see elections as simply sanctioning devices, but also as opportunities to choose a political representative with the right set of preferences and qualities (Besley 2005; Fearon 1999). This is about the prospective *selection* of specific parties, rather than retrospective *sanctioning* of the government. Our argument is that the convergence among mainstream parties during the crisis has led to defection to challenger parties from people who are dissatisfied with that consensus. During the crisis, the mainstream consensus was based on a shared acceptance of fiscal austerity and deference to the discretionary authority of the EU (Scharpf 2014; White 2014). While challenger parties are united in the fact that they offer an alternative to established mainstream policies and often mobilise new issues, they differ significantly in their focus.

Radical right challenger parties tend to mobilise support along the cultural or 'new politics' dimension, emphasising the repatriation of powers from the EU and the introduction of more restrictive immigration policies, often with a distinct ethno-centric message (Kitschelt and McGann 1995; Rydgren 2008; van der Brug *et al.* 2005). While left-wing challenger parties share the opposition to the political establishment and elite, they propose more extreme left-wing positions on the economic left—right spectrum. These typically reject the neoliberal character of the responses to the crisis and are often accompanied by mobilisation of more novel political issues such as anti-globalisation, freedom of information and direct democracy (March and Mudde 2005). Some left-wing challenger parties are also Eurosceptic, arguing that the EU is a vehicle of global capitalism and a threat to the national welfare state (Hooghe and Marks 2009; Halikiopoulou *et al.* 2012). Building on this literature, we thus expect that individuals who reject a pro-European mainstream consensus and who favour more restrictive immigration policies are more likely to defect to challenger parties on the right, while those opposed to neo-liberal economics and austerity are more likely to turn to challenger parties on the left. This leads to the following two hypotheses:

> H2a: People who are Eurosceptic and more opposed to immigration are more likely to defect from mainstream parties to a right-wing challenger party.
>
> H2b: People who strongly favour more economic redistribution are more likely to defect from mainstream parties to a left-wing challenger party.

Explaining defection from the mainstream

As Figure 1 shows, challenger parties have become increasingly important components of party systems across Western Europe, especially in the aftermath of the crisis. Our analysis here focuses on the question of why some people have defected from mainstream parties, of left and right, and lent their support to these various challenger parties. To do this we analyse the 2014 European Election Study (EES), which is ideally suited to examine individual-level motivations for defection as it asks identical questions about vote intention, vote recall, financial situation and policy preferences of representative samples of voters from all EU member states (Schmitt *et al.* 2015).[8] We focus on why certain individuals have switched support between parties over the electoral cycle in different countries in Western Europe. Specifically, we look at people who previously cast a vote for a mainstream party in the last national election, but by 2014 supported a challenger party. Before looking at the reasons behind defection, it is important to note how defection from the mainstream has been crucial to challenger party success on both the left and right.

Table 1 shows how people in the 17 Western European member states said they voted in the previous national election and how they would choose to vote in June 2014 when they were interviewed. It is noteworthy that the pattern of change that we see here matches the aggregate data shown in Figure 1. Both mainstream right and left parties have fewer people supporting them in

Table 1. Percentage vote for different types of parties (2014).

Party type	Previous vote	Vote intention	Change
Mainstream right	42%	36%	−6%
Mainstream left	37%	33%	−3%
Challenger right	8%	12%	+4%
Challenger left	10%	14%	+3%
Challenger green	4%	5%	+1%
All	100%	100%	
(*N*)	11,424	11,614	

Note: Non-voters and people who said don't know or refused to give their vote choice are not shown here.
Source: EES (2014).

Table 2. Percentage vote for different types of parties as a percentage of previous party type vote share (2014).

	Party type intending to vote for					
	Mainstream right	Mainstream left	Challenger right	Challenger left	Challenger green	None
Mainstream right	83%	6%	18%	8%	9%	12%
Mainstream left	3%	78%	9%	14%	17%	9%
Challenger right	1%	–	50%	2%	2%	2%
Challenger left	–	1%	3%	56%	2%	2%
Challenger green	–	–	1%	3%	54%	–
None	12%	13%	20%	18%	17%	74%
All	100%	100%	100%	100%	100%	100%
N	4110	3858	1385	1566	569	5515

Note: Percentages less than 1% are not shown here. The 'None' category includes people who said they did not vote, or were not intending to vote, people who didn't know how they voted, or how they were intending to vote, and people who refused to give a response to the question.
Source: EES (2014).

2014 than they did in the previous national election. Who benefits from these defections? Challenger left and challenger right parties benefit roughly equally. Both increase their support by about half.

Table 2 shows more clearly the flow of voters. The figures show the percentage vote for different types of parties as a percentage of previous party type. Loyal supporters, those who previously supported a particular party type and continue to do so, are shown on the diagonal. Roughly 8 out of 10 supporters of both mainstream right and left parties are loyalists. While there is some switching between left and right, overall to the benefit of the left, and some mobilisation from previous non-voters, the overwhelming picture is of stability. The makeup of challenger party support is very different to mainstream party support. All three types of challenger party have barely half of supporters that are loyalists. Challenger parties pick up support from both mainstream parties and from previous non-voters. Almost half of the support for challenger parties is due to defection from the mainstream or mobilisation from non-voting. But that does not mean that defection is that common. In total about 9 per cent of people who voted previously and now express a vote intention switch from the mainstream to the challengers (only 1 per cent switch the other way). While that is not a huge proportion of the electorate, it is a proportion that has transformed challenger parties from insignificant to significant players. That raises the question of what makes those people switch. Why has a tenth of the electorate turned away from mainstream parties?

As discussed above, there are two major drivers of electoral behaviour: sanctioning and selection. Our argument is that both sanctioning on the basis of economic experiences and selection on the basis of policy preferences determine whether people defect. Our dependent variable is thus defection. We restrict our analysis to those individuals who supported mainstream parties in the previous national election and we see what factors made people more or less likely to defect, in terms of supporting a different party today, to challenger parties.[9]

To capture sanctioning and selection, we use two sets of independent variables. Economic sanctioning is modelled by including a measure that captures how the crisis affected individuals financially. This consists of two questions. The first asks whether the respondent, or someone in their household, lost their job over the last two years. The second asks whether the respondent's household saw a decrease in income over the last two years. We add up the number of adverse impacts, so people who said their income decreased and someone lost their job score 2, people who just mention one adverse impact score 1 and people mentioning neither score zero; 48 per cent of people in the 17 Western European states score zero, 32 per cent score 1 and 20 per cent score 2.

To capture selection based on policy preferences, we use a series of 11-point policy scales. These concern the redistribution of wealth, raising taxes to spend more on public services, restricting immigration, furthering European integration and the trade-off between environmental protection and economic growth.[10] We have recoded these so that the more 'right-wing' responses are higher numbers. This means that high scores indicate that a person is against redistribution, against increasing taxes, against further European integration, favours economic growth over environmental protection, and favours restricting immigration further.[11]

We include a number of demographic control variables in the models: age, occupational social class, religiosity, sex, education, citizenship and trade union membership.[12] We also include political interest as an important control when looking at switches to non-voting, and this is measured on a 1–4 scale from not interested to very interested. Finally, we include a series of dummy variables for each country (fixed-effects) to control for country effects.

Table 3 shows the first two models that test hypothesis 1: does sanctioning happen and does it affect all mainstream parties? Because the sanctioning model is focused on the punishment of governments, we separate out those who previously voted for a mainstream party in government from those who previously voted for a mainstream party outside government. According to the

Table 3. Multinomial logit model predicting defection from mainstream parties.

	Model 1			Model 2		
	Defection from government mainstream			Defection from opposition mainstream		
	Opposition	Challenger	Non-voter	Government	Challenger	Non-voter
	B	*B*	*B*	*B*	*B*	*B*
Affected by crisis	0.30**	0.24**	0.15*	−0.19	0.30**	0.10
Political interest	−0.08	−0.07	−0.40**	0.13	0.00	−0.34**
Constant	−2.62**	−0.93*	−0.60	−18.4	−2.59**	−2.03**
Pseudo R-square	0.13				0.15	
N	5814				2989	

Note: Reference category for model 1 is vote intention for mainstream governing party, reference category for model 2 is vote intention for mainstream opposition party. Only people who previously voted for a mainstream government party are included in model 1, and only people who voted for a mainstream opposition party are included in model 2. Other control variables included in both models, but not shown above, are fixed effects for country, and individual-level control variables of age, occupational social class, religiosity, sex, education, citizenship and trade union membership.
Source: EES (2014).
*$p < 0.05$; **$p < 0.01$.

classic model of economic voting, we would only expect it to affect governing parties. However, if voters are sanctioning the mainstream consensus then we should expect it to affect all mainstream parties. The two models presented here are thus multinomial logit models which compare either (1) defection from mainstream governing parties to challengers or non-voting or (2) defection from mainstream opposition parties to challengers or non-voting. We group all challenger parties together.

Included in this model are the measures of the economic impact of the crisis on individuals, political interest and demographic controls mentioned earlier, although we just show the coefficients for economic impacts and political interest in the table. In the main, the effect of any of the social characteristics is small, with the exception of age. Older people are generally less likely to switch away from mainstream parties, no doubt because they have built up stronger partisan loyalties over many years (Converse 1969; Tilley 2003).

A clear story emerges from these results. People who defected from mainstream parties to challengers are those disproportionately affected by negative economic factors in their own lives. Crucially this is true whether the mainstream party they previously voted for is currently in government or not. People are not simply punishing governing parties, they are voting against mainstream parties as a whole. In fact, people in poor economic circumstances are actually more likely to defect to challengers from mainstream parties outside government than from mainstream parties within government. Hence, in line with our first hypothesis, we find that those who experience economic hardship during the crisis are more likely to turn their backs on all mainstream parties. Figure 2 shows the rates of defection from mainstream parties in government

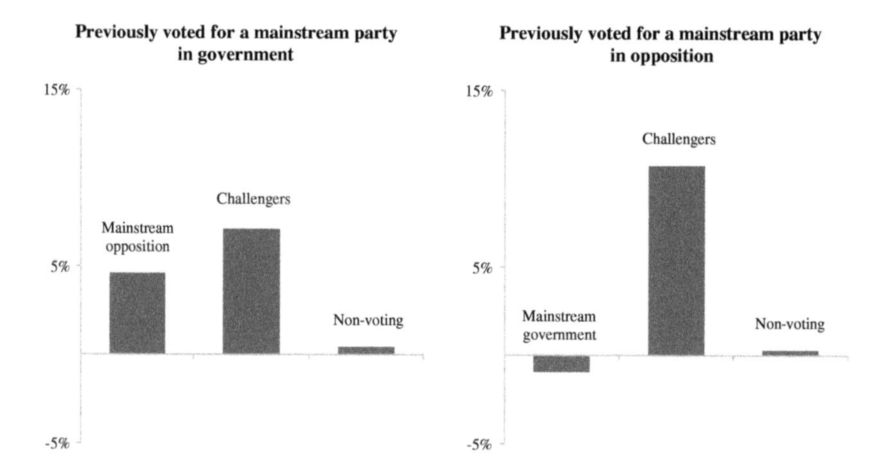

Figure 2. Changes in the predicted probability of defection for those who experience two economic impacts compared to those who experience none.

Note: These probabilities come from models 1 and 2 in Table 3. They represent the difference between people who score 2 on the economic impact scale and those who score 0 on the scale in the probability of defection/loyalty. The predicted probabilities are for a Dutch man with a white-collar job, low level of education, who is not in a trade union and has the mean age and mean political interest of someone who voted for a mainstream party in the last national election. Source: EES (2014).

and in opposition for people who experienced no negative economic effects compared to those in households who experienced both unemployment and declining income. Positive numbers indicate that parties attract more voters negatively affected by the crisis.

The left-hand chart in Figure 2 shows how defection rates differ by economic circumstance for people who previously supported a governing party. There is clearly an effect of poor economic circumstances on defection to mainstream opposition parties—they get more defectors from those severely affected by the crisis. But so do challenger parties. In fact the effect on defection to challengers is greater. More importantly though, the right-hand figure shows defection from mainstream *opposition* parties given different economic experiences. In contrast to classic economic voting models, we find that adverse experiences generate more defection to challengers from people who previously voted for mainstream opposition parties even though those mainstream parties are not in government. These are fairly sizeable effects as well. The average defection rate from both mainstream governing and opposition parties to challengers is about 25 per cent (given the specific type of person described in the figures). Moving from good to bad economic experiences thus makes a substantial difference to the possibility of defection.

Hence, there is evidence of economic sanctioning and support for our first hypothesis, but on what basis do voters decide which party to select? Table 4 shows the coefficients from a multinomial logit model that predicts defection from mainstream parties (both in government and in opposition) to the three

Table 4. Multinomial logit model predicting defection from mainstream parties to challenger parties and non-voting.

		Challenger right	Challenger left	Challenger green	Non-voter
		B	*B*	*B*	*B*
Policy position (high scores = against)	Immigration	0.16**	−0.02	−0.08*	0.00
	EU	0.14**	0.04	−0.07*	0.03*
	Environment	0.01	−0.03	−0.24**	−0.02
	Redistribution	0.02	−0.18**	−0.09*	−0.01
	Govt spending	0.07**	−0.00	−0.06	0.02
Affected by crisis		0.18*	0.19*	0.21	0.11*
Political interest		−0.11	0.04	−0.13	−0.36**
Constant		−5.02**	−2.74*	−0.53	−1.47**

Note: Reference category is vote intention for mainstream party. Only people who previously voted for a mainstream party are included in the model. Policy position is measured on a 0–10 scale for each of the five policy areas. Other control variables included in the model, but not shown above, are fixed effects for country, and individual-level control variables of age, occupational social class, religiosity, sex, education, citizenship and trade union membership.
Source: EES (2014).
$N = 8680$. Pseudo R-square = 0.15. $^{*}p < 0.05$; $^{**}p < 0.01$.

different types of challenger party and also to non-voting. It is first worth noting that all four types of defector are more likely to have directly experienced economic problems. Interestingly, the question of which specific party they defected to is not affected by the impact of the economic crisis; the size of the economic effect is rather similar across all four types of defector. How do we explain which specific party these defectors turn to?

In line with our second set of hypotheses (H2a and H2b), Table 4 shows that there is significant variation in the ideological profile of defectors to different parties. People who left the mainstream to join the challenger right-wing parties are much more anti-immigration and anti-EU than mainstream loyalists, but they differ very little in terms of their views on the environment and redistribution, and are only very slightly more in favour of restricting government spending. Defectors to the challenger left are a little more anti-EU and a little more pro-environment and immigration than mainstream party loyalists, but these are not big differences. The big difference between loyalists and defectors to the challenger left is attitudes towards redistribution. Those in favour of greater redistribution are much more likely to defect to challenger left-wing parties. This is also the case for challenger green parties, although unsurprisingly the best policy predictor is support for environmental protection. Finally the best predictor of people who become non-voters is not ideology, but political interest. While political interest appears to have little effect on defection from mainstream to challenger parties, it is the politically uninterested that leave mainstream parties and exit the system altogether.[13]

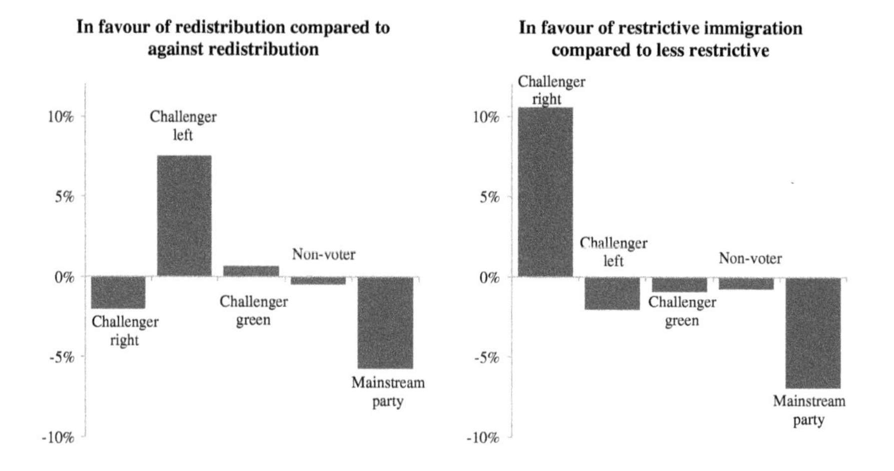

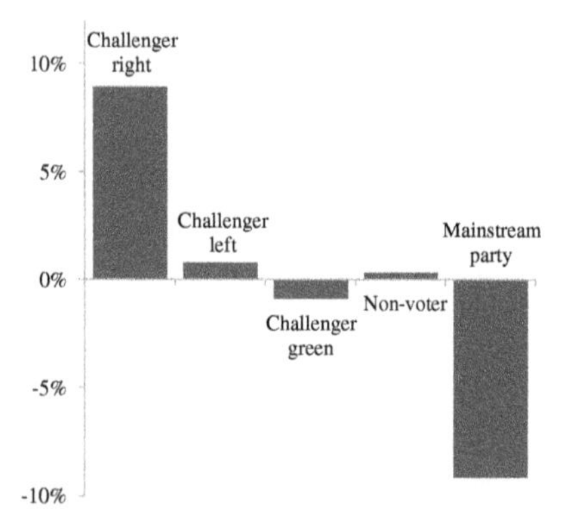

Figure 3. Changes in the predicted probability of defection/loyalty when changing policy position on the three policy scales.

Note: These probabilities come from the model in Table 4. They represent the difference between people who score one standard deviation below the mean on the policy scale compared to those who score one standard deviation above the mean on the policy scale. The predicted probabilities are for a Dutch man with a skilled manual job, low level of education, who is not in a trade union, and has the mean age, mean political interest and mean policy positions on the other four scales of someone who voted for a mainstream party in the last national election. Source: EES (2014).

These effects are not trivial. Figure 3 shows how a two standard deviation move (from a position of one standard deviation below the mean to one standard deviation above the mean) on the three most important policy scales affects rates of defection. These are clearly substantial effects given the relative rarity of defection. Challenger right-wing parties get substantially more defectors from those who are opposed to EU integration and immigration, in line with findings in the existing literature on the far right (van der Brug *et al.* 2005; Rydgren 2008), whereas challenger left-wing parties get substantially more defectors from those in favour of redistribution. Mainstream parties hang on to supporters who are more in tune with the mainstream party consensus on EU integration, immigration and redistribution. It is rejection of this mainstream consensus, in any of its forms, that motivates people to leave the embrace of mainstream parties, but the policy area that is being rejected is a crucial predictor of which challenger party will benefit from that defection.

Conclusion

Challenger parties are the political success story of the aftermath of the euro crisis. Both on the left and the right it is parties that have not recently been in government that have benefited from the exodus of voters from mainstream parties. The decline in the vote shares of mainstream parties since the onset of the financial crisis in 2008 is around 12 percentage points. With the exception of Greece, mainstream parties have remained the dominant actors in government in Western Europe, yet those defections have nonetheless transformed challenger parties from often very marginal political players to repositories of a substantial proportion of people's votes.

Why has this happened? We have argued that the classic model of elections as mechanisms for sanctioning and selection offers a helpful framework to understand defection from mainstream to challenger parties. Starting with sanctioning, defection is clearly linked to the economic crisis. People who were subject to declining economic fortunes are more likely to desert mainstream parties, whether in government or opposition. Voters are not simply reacting to the perceived failures of mainstream parties however. They are also choosing challenger parties on the basis of policy. Challengers on the right gain voters from the mainstream who disagree with the mainstream consensus on immigration and EU integration. Challengers on the left gain voters from the mainstream who disagree with the consensus on fiscal policy. Thus, both sanctioning and ideological selection matter in how challenger parties convert mainstream party voters.

While the majority of people remain loyal to the mainstream, the increasing proportion of voters that opt for challenger parties is likely to have a significant impact on party systems and European democracy. First, voters are often attracted to challenger parties because of their stances on issues such as European integration and immigration. The more Eurosceptic position adopted by most challenger parties has put pressure on national governments and made it more difficult to reach agreement on political issues, as demonstrated not least during the recent Mediterranean immigration crisis. Second, the success of challenger parties has influenced the stability of governments. Since challenger parties tend to stay in opposition, the formation, and maintenance, of stable coalitions has become more and more difficult. It has also meant the rise of 'grand coalition' governments spanning left and right mainstream parties, which has, ironically, strengthened the claims of challenger parties that all mainstream parties offer the same policies.

This raises the question of whether the success of challenger parties is a fleeting phenomenon that will dissipate as the economy improves, or whether it is the beginning of a new type of party politics in Western Europe. The crisis, and the mainstream party response to it, has facilitated the success of challenger parties, but it is not clear that the demand for such parties will simply disappear as economic conditions improve. Voters are less partisan than they were and more disillusioned with the established political class and this will continue to add to the appeal of challenger parties. Nonetheless, much will depend on how parties, both mainstream and challenger, respond to the changing political landscape. Some successful challenger parties choose to eventually enter government. If such stints in office are more than passing, these parties are likely to be held to account for the decisions and compromises taken in office, and this is likely to diminish their appeal to many of their current supporters. Such challenger parties may cease to be 'challengers' and become part of the mainstream. The example of the Syriza-led government in Greece shows how government responsibility can force challenger parties closer to the mainstream consensus. Equally, much of the appeal of challenger parties during the crisis was that mainstream parties were perceived to offer very similar positions on important issues relating to the economy, Europe and immigration. Hence, the continued success of challenger parties will also depend on the policy choices offered by the mainstream.

Notes

1. Source: Eurostat (seasonally adjusted figures from May 2014).
2. Most of these challenger parties are also 'niche parties' (Adams *et al.* 2006; Meguid 2008) and/or 'populist parties' (Mudde 2007). However, in this article we focus specifically on government experience as the distinguishing factor, since it affects whether such parties can be held to account by voters and also their ability to challenge the mainstream policy consensus (van de Wardt *et al.* 2014). To check the robustness of our party classification in comparison to other measures, we have replicated all of our analyses using the standard Adams *et al.* (2006) operationalisation of niche parties based on the Comparative Manifesto Project classification of parties into party families. Parties belonging to the Green/Ecological (10), Communist/Socialist (20) and Nationalist (70) party families as well as Special Issue parties (95) with non-centrist niche ideologies are classified as niche parties. All our main findings hold using this alternative operationalisation (see Tables A2 and A3 in the Appendix). Table A4 in the Appendix lists all parties (in 2014) included in both the challenger and niche party categories.
3. Although party systems and party competition are beginning to stabilise in Central and Eastern Europe, these political systems are still characterised by high volatility which makes it difficult to clearly identify mainstream parties (Bakke and Sitter 2005).
4. Any cut-off point in terms of government experience to determine when a party is, or is not, a challenger party is somewhat arbitrary. However, this

operationalisation both offers parsimony and captures parties without any recent government experience. Using a slightly different operationalisation that looks at post-war participation in government yields very similar results.

5. For parties scoring 5, we classify them on the basis of coalition partners or their membership of European Parliament political groups. Green parties are those parties whose ideology centres on the principles of green politics and environmentalism. The full list of challenger and mainstream parties can be found in the Appendix Table A4.
6. One exception is the Five Star Movement in Italy, which is very difficult to classify. Our results are robust to the classification of this party in either of the three challenger party categories.
7. Less than 100 per cent of vote shares were allocated, since only parties with over 1 per cent of the vote (or at least one MP) were classified. This estimate of challenger parties is therefore conservative, since most of these very small parties and candidates are likely to belong to the challenger party category.
8. Approximately 1100 respondents were interviewed in each EU member country, totalling 30,064 respondents. Our analysis only focuses on the 17 West European member states. The EES 2014 was carried out by TNS Opinion between 30 May and 27 June 2014. All the interviews were carried out face to face. More information can be found at: http://eeshomepage.net/voter-study-2014, where the EES questionnaire can also be found.
9. One issue is the coding of non-voters. We have excluded all people who refused to answer the previous vote question (9 per cent of respondents) but included 'don't knows' (2 per cent of respondents) as non-voters along with the 23 per cent of people who stated that they did not vote previously. In terms of current party support, we include anyone who did not give a party name as a non-voter, including people who answered 'don't know', did not give an answer, and people who specifically said that they would not vote. In total this includes 32 per cent of respondents. The only difference we make in terms of coding challenger party support is to categorise support for very minor parties that fail to make the 1 per cent threshold that we applied to the aggregate data.
10. Respondents were asked about the extent to which they agreed/disagreed with the following statements on an 11-point scale: 'You are fully in favour of the redistribution of wealth from the rich to the poor'; 'You are fully in favour of raising taxes to increase public services'; 'You are fully in favour of a restrictive policy on immigration', 'The EU should have more authority over the EU Member States' economic and budgetary policies'; 'Environmental protection should always take priority even at the cost of economic growth'.
11. We have also recoded 'don't know' responses to the mid points of the scale (6) in order to maximise the number of cases included in the models. Don't knows make up 4–5 per cent of the responses, and including them in this way makes no material difference to the results.
12. The occupational social class categories are self-employed, managerial, professional, white-collar worker, skilled manual worker, unskilled manual worker, student, unemployed and out of the labour force. Education is based on terminal age of education and consists of three categories: education finished before 16, education finished before 19, education finished at 20 or over. Religiosity is measured using church attendance divided into four categories: weekly, monthly, yearly and never. Age is measured in years, trade union members are distinguished from non-members and citizens are distinguished from non-citizens.

13. Table A1 in the Appendix shows similar models that look at mobilisation from non-voting to voting for the different party types. The results here echo, albeit more weakly, the same processes that we see for defection from mainstream parties. Moreover, as we might expect, mobilised voters are more politically interested than those that remain non-voters, but there are no real differences in how political interest affects mobilisation to different types of party.

Acknowledgements

We would like to thank Julian Hoerner for excellent research assistance and the European Research Council for generous funding. We are also grateful for the insightful comments from the anonymous reviewers as well as the participants in the workshop on 'Re-Thinking European Integration in the Shadow of Crisis: Politics, Institutions and Governance', organised by Brigid Laffan at the European University Institute, 2015.

Disclosure statement

No potential conflict of interest was reported by the authors.

Funding

This work was supported by the European Research Council [grant number EUDEMOS 647835].

References

Adams, J., M. Clark, L. Ezrow, and G. Glasgow (2006). 'Are Niche Parties Fundamentally Different from Mainstream Parties? The Causes and the Electoral Consequences of Western European Parties' Policy Shifts, 1976–1998', *American Journal of Political Science*, 50:3, 513–29.

Bakke, Elisabeth, and Nick Sitter (2005). 'Patterns of Stability: Party Competition and Strategy in Central Europe since 1989', *Party Politics*, 11, 243–63.

Bakker, Ryan, Erica Edwards, Liesbet Hooghe, Seth Jolly, Gary Marks, Jonathan Polk, Jan Rovny, Marco Steenbergen, and Milada Vachudova (2015). '2014 Chapel Hill

Expert Survey.' Version 2015.1. Available on chesdata.eu. Chapel Hill, NC: University of North Carolina, Chapel Hill.

Banks, Jeffrey S., and Rangarajan K. Sundaram (1993). 'Adverse Selectionand Moral Hazard in a Repeated Elections Model', in William A. Barnett, Melvin J. Hinich, and Norman J. Schofield (eds.), *Political Economy: Institutions, Competition, and Representation*. Cambridge: Cambridge University Press, 295–311.

Bartels, Larry (2013). 'Ideology and Retrospection in Electoral Responses to the Great Recession', in Larry Bartels and Nancy Bermeo (eds.), *Mass Politics in Tough times Opinions, Votes and Protest in the Great Recession*. New York, NY: Oxford University Press, 185–223.

Bechtel, Michael, and Jens Hainmueller (2011). 'How Lasting is Voter Gratitude? An Analysis of the Short- and Long-Term Electoral Returns to Beneficial Policy', *American Journal of Political Science*, 55:4, 851–67.

Besley, Timothy (2005). 'Political Selection', *Journal of Economic Perspectives*, 19:3, 43–60.

van der Brug, Wouter, Meindert Fennema, and Jean Tillie (2005). 'Why Some Anti-Immigrant Parties Fail and Others Succeed: A Two-Step Model of Aggregate Electoral Support', *Comparative Political Studies*, 38:5, 537–73.

Canovan, Margaret (1999). "Trust the People!', *Populism and the Two Faces of Democracy*', *Political Studies*, 47, 2–16.

Converse, P. (1969). 'Of Time and Partisan Stability', *Comparative Political Studies*, 2, 139–72.

Cramme, Olaf, and Sara B. Hobolt, eds. (2014). *Democratic Politics in a European Union under Stress*. Oxford: Oxford University Press.

Dalton, Russell J., and Martin P. Wattenberg, eds. (2002). *Parties without Partisans*. Oxford: Oxford University Press.

Evans, Geoffrey, and Robert Andersen (2006). 'The Political Conditioning of Economic Perceptions: Evidence from the 1992–97 British Electoral Cycle', *Journal of Politics*, 68:1, 194–207.

Evans, Geoffrey, and Mark Pickup (2010). 'Reversing the Causal Arrow: The Political Conditioning of Economic Perceptions in the 2000–2004 U.S. Presidential Election Cycle', *Journal of Politics*, 72, 1236–51.

Fearon, James D. (1999). 'Electoral Accountability and the Control of Politicians: Selecting Good Types versus Sanctioning Poor Performance', in Adam Przeworski, Susan C. Stokes and Bernard Manin (eds.), *Democracy, Accountability, and Representation*. Cambridge: Cambridge University Press, 55–97.

Fiorina, Morris P. (1981). *Retrospective Voting in American National Elections*. New Haven, CT: Yale University Press.

Halikiopoulou, D., K. Nanou, and S. Vasilopoulou (2012). 'The Paradox of Nationalism: The Common Denominator of Radical Right and Radical Left Euroscepticism', *European Journal of Political Research*, 51:4, 504–39.

Hino, Airo (2012). *New Challenger Parties in Western Europe: A Comparative Analysis*. Abingdon: Routledge.

Hobolt, Sara B., and Catherine de Vries (2015). 'Issue Entrepreneurship and Multiparty Competition', *Comparative Political Studies*, 48:9, 1159–85.

Hobolt, Sara B., and James Tilley (2014). *Blaming Europe: Attribution of Responsibility in the European Union*. Oxford: Oxford University Press.

Hooghe, Liesbet, and Gary Marks (2009). 'A Postfunctionalist Theory of European Integration: From Permissive Consensus to Constraining Dissensus', *British Journal of Political Science*, 39:01, 1–23.

Jensen, Christian B., and Jae-Jae Spoon (2010). 'Thinking Locally, Acting Supranationally: Niche Party Behaviour in the European Parliament', *European Journal of Political Research*, 49:2, 174–201.
Key, V. O. (1966). *The Responsible Electorate*. New York, NY: Vintage.
Kitschelt, Herbert, and Anthony McGann (1995). *The Radical Right in Western Europe. A Comparative Analysis*. Michigan: University of Michigan Press.
Kriesi, Hanspeter (2014). 'The Populist Challenge', *West European Politics*, 37:2, 361–78.
Kriesi, Hanspeter, Edgar Grande, Romain Lachat, Martin Dolezal, Simon Bornschier, and Timotheos Frey (2006). 'Globalization and the Transformation of the National Political Space: Six European Countries Compared', *European Journal of Political Research*, 45:6, 921–56.
Laffan, B. (2014). 'Testing Times: The Growing Primacy of Responsibility in the Euro Area', *West European Politics*, 37:2, 270–87.
Lewis-Beck, Michael S., and Mary Stegmaier (2000). 'Economic Determinants of Electoral Outcomes', *Annual Review of Political Science*, 3, 183–219.
Lewis-Beck, Michael S. and Mary Stegmaier (2007). 'Economic Models of Voting', in Russell J. Dalton and Hans-Dieter Klingemann*The Oxford Handbook of Political Behavior* (eds), *The Oxford Handbook of Political Behavior*. Oxford: Oxford University Press, 518–37.
Lobo, Marina Costa, and Michael S. Lewis-Beck (2012). 'The Integration Hypothesis: How the European Union Shapes Economic Voting', *Electoral Studies*, 31:3, 522–28.
Mair, Peter (2013). *Ruling the Void. The Hollowing out of Western Democracies*. London: Verso.
Manin, Bernard (1997). *The Principles of Representative Government*. Cambridge: Cambridge University Press.
March, Luke, and Cas Mudde (2005). 'What's left of the Radical Left: The European Radical Left after 1989: Decline and Mutation', *Comparative European Politics*, 3:1, 22–49.
Margalit, Yotam (2011). 'Costly Jobs: Trade-Related Layoffs, Government Compensation, and Voting in U.S. Elections', *American Political Science Review*, 106:1, 166–88.
Meguid, Bonnie (2005). 'Competition between Unequals: The Role of Mainstream Party Strategy in Niche Party Success', *American Political Science Review*, 99:3, 347–59.
Meguid, Bonnie (2008). *Party Competition between Unequals: Strategies and Electoral Fortunes in Western Europe*. Cambridge: Cambridge University Press.
Mudde, Cas (2007). *Populist Radical Right Parties in Europe*. Cambridge: Cambridge University Press.
Nannestad, Peter, and Martin Paldam (1994). 'The VP Function: A Survey of the Literature on Vote and Popularity Functions after 25 Years', *Public Choice*, 79:3-4, 213–45.
Pauwels, Teun (2014). *Populism in Western Europe. Comparing Belgium, Germany and the Netherlands*. London: Routledge.
Poguntke, T. (1987). 'New Politics and Party Systems: The Emergence of a New Type of Party?', *West European Politics*, 10:1, 76–88.
Powell, G. Bingham (2000). *Elections as Instruments of Democracy: Majoritarian and Proportional Visions*. New Haven: Yale University Press.
Richter, Kaspar (2006). 'Wage Arrears and Economic Voting in Russia', *American Political Science Review*, 100:1, 133–45.
Rydgren, Jens (2008). 'Immigration Sceptics, Xenophobes, or Racists? Radical Right-wing Voting in Six West European Countries', *European Journal of Political Research*, 47, 737–65.

Scharpf, Fritz (2011). 'Monetary Union, Fiscal Crisis and the Preemption of Democracy', MPIfG Discussion Papers, 11/11.
Scharpf, Fritz (2014). 'Political Legitimacy and in a Non-Optimal Currency Area', in Olaf Cramme and Sara Hobolt (eds.), *Democratic Politics in a European Union under Stress*. Oxford: Oxford University Press, 19–47.
Schmitt, Hermann, Sara B. Hobolt, and Sebastian Popa (2015). 'European Parliament Election Study 2014, Voter Study', GESIS Data Archive, Cologne. ZA5160 Data file Version 1.0.0, doi:http://dx.doi.org/10.4232/1.5160
Tavits, Margit (2008). 'The Role of Parties' past Behavior in Coalition Formation', *American Political Science Review*, 102:4, 495–507.
Tilley, James (2003). 'Party Identification in Britain: Does Length of Time in the Electorate Affect Strength of Partisanship?', *British Journal of Political Science*, 33:2, 332–44.
de Vries, Catherine E., and Sara B. Hobolt (2012). 'When Dimensions Collide: The Electoral Success of Issue Entrepreneurs', *European Union Politics*, 13:2, 246–26.
Wagner, Markus (2012). 'Defining and Measuring Niche Parties', *Party Politics*, 18:6, 845–64.
van de Wardt, Marc, Catherine E. de Vries, and Sara B. Hobolt (2014). 'Exploiting the Cracks: Wedge Issues in Multiparty Competition', *The Journal of Politics*, 76:4, 986–99.
White, Jonathan (2014). 'Politicising Europe: The Challenge of Executive Discretion', in Olaf Cramme and Sara Hobolt (eds.), *Democratic Politics in a European Union under Stress*. Oxford: Oxford University Press, 87–102.

After the *Spitzenkandidaten*: fundamental change in the EU's political system?

Thomas Christiansen

ABSTRACT
The appointment of the President of the European Commission in 2014 occurred in the context of a novel environment: in constitutional terms, the Lisbon Treaty had introduced a small but significant change, namely the requirement for the candidate proposed by the European Council to be elected by the European Parliament. Politically, the 2014 European elections took place against the background of the eurozone crisis which had polarised opinions about the direction of European integration across the member states. This article develops a framework to assess the impact of this changed environment along two crucial dimensions of EU politics – interinstitutional relations and party politics. Based on this analysis, the article argues that while there has been gradual change in certain respects, the impact of the *Spitzenkandidaten* system did not lead to a transformation of the EU's political system. Indeed, rather than creating new opportunities for party political competition, the cooperation between centre-right and centre-left in the election of the Commission President and subsequent decision-making further strengthened the long-standing 'grand coalition' in the European Parliament.

The 2014 election to the European Parliament was branded by the Parliament's own PR department as an event that would be 'different this time' (European Parliament 2014). One reason why these elections could be considered 'different' was the expectation that due to the popular upheaval about the eurozone crisis they would result in a higher turnout, reversing the decades-long trend of declining turnout.

However, the 'official' reason why the 2014 election was expected to be different was the fact that with the coming into force of the Lisbon Treaty there had been a change to the appointment procedure of the President of the European Commission. Specifically, Art. 17, paragraph 7, stipulated that the European Council needed to 'take into account the elections to the European Parliament' in proposing a candidate for the Commission Presidency, and that the successful candidate would need to be 'elected' by the majority of MEPs.

Even though these were, on the face of it, only minor changes to the existing procedure – the Parliament's approval had already been required for the European Council's preferred candidate – they had a significant impact on the nature of campaigning for the elections: the treaty change opened the door for the European party families to put forward leading candidates for the position of Commission President, giving the European electorate for the first time the opportunity to determine not only the composition of the European legislature, but also the leadership of the EU's executive. These dynamics did not occur in a vacuum but coincided, and interacted, with other developments, in particular the crisis in the eurozone, the tensions that it created among and within member states, and the political consequences this has had domestically.

Against this background, the 2014 EP election marked a unique opportunity for the EU's electorate to vote on a genuinely pan-European issue directly affecting the majority of the citizens. Together with the enhanced role of the EP in the election of the Commission President, the 2014 election could therefore be expected to usher in a new era of European Union politics in which leadership changes result from popular choice rather than bargaining behind closed doors. In other words, there was an expectation that an election being held under such circumstances could be 'really different this time', indeed that it had the potential to become a transformative event in EU politics.

Analysing developments before, during and after the appointment of Jean-Claude Juncker as Commission President, this article addresses the question as to whether such transformative change has actually occurred. More specifically, it goes beyond the analysis of the electoral campaign and the election result, and asks whether the confluence of treaty change and eurozone crisis has helped to transform EU politics in a lasting way. EU politics is conceptualised along two dimensions – interinstitutional relations and party politics – and an analytical frame identifies a number of parameters in order to assess the impact of the changing circumstances on the EU's political system.

Treaty reform, eurozone crisis and the 2014 European elections

A key factor explaining potential change in the EU's politics had been the revision of the treaty agreed at Lisbon in 2007, coming into force on 1 December 2009. In particular, the new wording of Art. 17, introducing the idea of an 'elected' Commission President, provided a powerful symbolic change to the previous practice of the holder of this post being 'appointed' by the heads of state and government and merely 'approved' by Parliament. Furthermore, in the context of latent interinstitutional battles between the EP and the European Council, it also constituted a new opportunity structure for the Parliament to enhance its powers.

However, it is worth pointing out that the Lisbon changes to Art. 17 did not *automatically* lead to the *Spitzenkandidaten* system, but instead were contingent on a number of factors. First of all, the legal change was not that far-reaching, given that the Parliament already had de facto power to elect the Commission President, and a skilful, coherent and persistent strategy on behalf of the Parliament vis-à-vis the European Council arguably could have achieved the same outcome even without this change in the wording of the article.

In this context it should also be noted that the experience of 2014 was not only based on the new treaty provisions, but also on some long-standing commitments from supporters of a more parliamentary, if not federal, Europe (Westlake 2016). These preceded the treaty change in Lisbon, influencing as they did the debates leading up to and including the Convention on the Future of Europe. One such influence on the drafting of the treaty came from the European People's Party (EPP) at its Congress in Estoril in October 2002, calling for Parliament to 'give or withhold its approval by majority vote' (European People's Party 2002: Art. 47). There is no space in this paper for a complete process-tracing of the relevant passages in the treaty, but it will be evident from even this brief look that the new system arising in 2014 was not the outcome of a sudden and abrupt change, but rather the result of a gradual process of adaptation going back through several instances of treaty revision – one that arguably began in the 1996 IGC when the synchronisation of the terms of office of the EP and of the Commission was introduced (Dinan 1997: 199). The changes arising from the Lisbon Treaty, however significant, need to be seen in the context of a long-term process of continuous treaty reform (Christiansen and Reh 2009) – a process that gradually brought the Union to the point at which it became possible for minor changes to the appointment procedure to have a major impact on the functioning of the wider political system.

Historically, the EP has been an effective player in identifying opportunities for enhancing its position in the course of this treaty reform process. The EP is widely seen as the 'winner' in recent rounds of treaty reform (Beach 2007; Craig 2008), and the additional powers the EP received through the Lisbon Treaty have been widely discussed elsewhere. However, following the logic of treaty change as a continuous process, it becomes important to also consider developments in between rounds of formal treaty revision. Farrell and Heritier, in developing their concept of interstitial change, have advanced our understanding of the way in which 'incomplete contracts' contained in the treaties have allowed the EP to influence institutional change in its own interest (Farrell and Heritier 2007).

This is relevant in the present context, given the ambiguity of the phrase 'taking into account the outcome of the elections' in Art. 17, and the manner in which this was interpreted by parliamentary actors to the EP's advantage before and after the 2014 election. On this occasion, exploiting the openness of the treaty extended beyond the political realm, involving also the efforts of the EP's secretariat in launching the concerted campaign mentioned above, all on the basis of the claim that in 2014, 'for the first time, the composition of the new European Parliament will determine who will lead the next European Commission' (European Parliament 2014) – a claim that, while it turned out to be an accurate prediction of future developments, was not necessarily in line with the formal-legal position at the time of writing.

Beyond the parliament as a whole playing an institutional role, a key part of the process was the way in which the various party groups took up and utilised the opportunity offered to them on the occasion of the 2014 elections. Here the European People's Party (EPP), in recent years the largest group, played a pivotal but also contradictory role. The early initiatives of the EPP, dating back to the time before the Constitutional Convention, were already mentioned above. The EPP, on the back of a traditionally strongly parliamentary, if not pro-federalist, attitude towards the reform of the Union's institutions, had initially been in the vanguard of pushing for the election of the Commission President by the EP, and arguably had been among the strongest proponents of the *Spitzenkandidaten* system when this was initially discussed in the abstract (Westlake 2016). However, in the run-up to the 2014 election, faced with a European Council in which the EPP held the overwhelming majority, and with the party-political outcome of the elections far from certain, the EPP was rather reticent in its engagement with the system and late with the selection of a candidate for Commission President. In the end, the EPP was the last of the five parties fielding candidates to enter the race.

The background to this prevarication from the EPP was the initiative having been 'stolen' by the other political groups, most obviously by Martin Schulz who from his position as EP President launched an early and successful bid to become the candidate for the Party of European Socialists (PES). Against the background of a strong EPP majority in the European Council and after two terms of the 'EPP candidate' Commission President Juan-Manuel Barroso, chosen by the European Council, there was little to lose and everything to gain by the PES pushing for a greater parliamentary say in the choice. However, the outcome of such an initiative was far from certain; leading centre-left politicians holding office at the national level had little incentive to risk defeat in the uncharted waters of a new European electoral process. In this context, Martin Schulz had much to gain, and little to lose, by throwing his hat into the ring for the EU's top executive post.

The PES had already produced a timeline for its own *Spitzenkandidaten* in 2011, and on that basis Schulz then formally launched his campaign in the autumn of 2013, endorsed as a common candidate by most of the PES member parties. In November 2013 he was selected as 'candidate-designate' and from then on had a free and initially unopposed run as the *Spitzenkandidat* of the centre-left. He and his party clearly took this campaign seriously, something which then created dynamic effects for other party families and for the process as a whole. Schulz was eventually joined by rival candidates from the smaller party groups in the EP: Guy Verhofstadt, selected as candidate by the Alliance of Liberals and Democrats for Europe (ALDE) in February 2014, Ska Keller and José Bové who emerged victorious from a 'virtual primary' election conducted by the Greens in January 2014, and Alexis Tsipras, who had been nominated by the European left in December 2013.

Towards the end of 2013, the dynamics of this process began to become apparent: competitive pressures leading all of the main parties to seriously consider the implications of participating – or not participating – in this campaign with a leading candidate; the rising attention from media – initially EU-specific, but gradually also mainstream – to the internal decision-making processes and the inter-party rivalry; the emerging public expectation, based on the EP's own PR campaign and generally repeated in the reporting about the events, that this process would indeed determine the Commission Presidency. These dynamics ultimately forced the hand of the EPP in also putting forward its own candidate, with Jean-Claude Juncker winning the vote against then Commissioner Barnier at the EPP Congress in Dublin in March 2014.

While Juncker had all the credentials to be a leading candidate for the Commission Presidency – indeed he is said to have been serious contender already in 2009 when he lost out during bargaining in the European Council – it was also fortuitous from the perspective of the EPP that he had become available for the European position following his party's defeat in recent national elections in Luxembourg. Having been a constant in the European Council and as Chair of the Eurogroup during 18 years as Prime Minister and 10 years as Finance Minister of Luxembourg, Juncker was out of executive office from December 2013, and hence easier to convince to enter a race for the election as Commission President at a time when it was not certain that the EPP would indeed win this race. At the EPP Congress in Dublin in March 2014, Juncker received the nomination of his party, winning a vote against former Commissioner Michel Barnier with 382 to 245 votes.

Campaigning for the 2014 EP election did not occur in a vacuum, but happened against the background of the greatest crisis the EU had to face up to this point. Since 2010, when the economic and financial crisis required a response from the members of the eurozone, there had been long-lasting and acrimonious debates about the best way to manage the danger of sovereign debt default in some member states, the need for bail-outs and the corresponding demands for structural reforms in the debtor countries. In the process, it also constituted the first time that EU policy-making invoked popular and elite responses from across the European Union, dominating the campaigns and debates by the candidates for the Commission Presidency.

The eurozone crisis brought to light severe fissures within the European polity, and the allegation that much of the crisis management had been handled in a technocratic and/or intergovernmentalist manner, without sufficient democratic legitimacy, became a point of debate in most eurozone member states. Growing support for political parties and movements in several member states that were critical of the handling of the crisis, both in the creditor states and the programme countries, provided ample evidence for this rising sceptical trend – creating an electoral landscape in which it has become increasingly difficult for incumbent governments or even mainstream parties to maintain their position in the polls. The success of Syriza in Greece, in particular, heralded electoral success for anti-austerity policies that were at loggerheads with the pre-existing consensus among governments, with further backlash from disenchanted voters in other member states.

Such contestation has politicised existing tensions, with the technocratic approach relying on the work of the 'troika' of the European Central Bank (ECB), International Monetary Fund (IMF) and European Commission officials becoming the subject of much political debate and criticism. Consequently, the Eurogroup of Finance Ministers, and indeed the European Council, became essential fora for crisis management. In the context of responding to the eurozone crisis, the EU accumulated additional competences, without recourse to formal treaty change that would improve the legitimation of the greater role played by the European institutions. Instead, key decisions have increasingly been made by non-majoritarian institutions, within intergovernmental fora or through new arrangements outside the treaty structure.

These dynamics created a new context for election campaigning: the very fact of having *Spitzenkandidaten* at the European level (in addition to the domestically leading candidates that many of the component parties nominated to head national lists) did insert a new transnational dimension in the process. As Schulz, Juncker and the other candidates were competing for a European elected office, as leading candidates of the transnational party families, they could not limit themselves to campaigning only in their own constituencies or home countries. Indeed, as neither Juncker nor Tsipras were standing for election as MEPs, they might otherwise not have been campaigning at all.

Instead, the candidates had to appeal to a broader, pan-European audience, an expectation that was reflected in the many visits that each of them made across the member states of the European Union (Hobolt 2014). While such transnational campaigning was inevitably selective and conditioned by the limited time and financial resources available to the candidates, it nevertheless marked a small, yet significant departure from past experience when European election campaigns were largely a compartmentalised affair taking place within the boundaries of the respective member states.

Beyond meeting local candidates and supporting the component parties of their respective party families, a major concern in such campaigning was the garnering of media attention and increasing the name recognition of the *Spitzenkandidaten*. While initial research has shown that such media attention has had a certain, albeit limited effect on the recognition of, and the votes for, the respective candidates, this also constituted a two-sided process: candidates were more prone to campaign in countries where they were already known, and where there could be an expectation that their appearance would have a positive effect on the electorate (Schmitt *et al.* 2015).

However, size – of member states' populations and hence their share of seats in the EP – also mattered, and consequently Germany attracted by far the largest number of campaign visits, ahead of France and Belgium. The fact that there were noticeably fewer visits by the candidates of the top three parties (Juncker, Schulz, Verhofstadt) to Spain and Italy also indicates that language matters – that there are fundamental limitations to the capacity of candidates, however polyglot they may be, in a multilingual space such as European election campaigning.

Another aspect worth mentioning is that in certain member states the *Spitzenkandidaten* were not welcome: all three of the main British parties declared their opposition to the emerging system and consequently did not invite them to join their respective national campaigns. Consequently, the UK was the only member state, apart from Hungary, that was not visited by any of the top three candidates. The fact that the leaders of these two states ended up voting against the appointment of Jean-Claude Juncker in the European Council is perhaps not entirely unrelated.

Yet more significant than campaign visits was arguably the arrival of US-style presidential debates involving all or some of the candidates. Starting with the 'First European Presidential Debate' held in Maastricht on 28 April 2014, four televised debates open to all the candidates were being organised. In addition, Juncker and Schulz sparred in a number of head-to-head debates aired by French, German and Austrian broadcasters. Even if these debates were clearly not the prime-time TV events familiar from US presidential races, they did nevertheless constitute an entirely new experience of European electioneering, raising interesting questions about the way in which a genuinely European democracy might work.

Analysing the impact of the *Spitzenkandidaten* on the EU's political system

There is no doubt that the arrival *Spitzenkandidaten* and the new style of election campaigning constituted a novel departure in the history of the EU. Yet the impact that this had on the outcome of the election was more limited, and disappointing in terms of the high expectations that advocates had of the new system. The downward trend of voter turnout was not reversed, and in comparison to national elections voting for the EP remained decidedly second-order (van der Brug *et al.* 2016). Even though there had been, as discussed, significant changes to the structural context in which the 2014 election was fought, its immediate outcome was more in line with the secular trends of previous elections.

But what about the longer-term impact of this election on the EU's political system? Implicit in the above discussion, and indeed in the wider debate about the introduction of the *Spitzenkandidaten*, was the claim that there was considerable potential for a fundamental transformation of EU politics. In analysing the degree of political change that has actually taken place, this article follows a historical institutionalist approach, a choice that is warranted given that the question about the implications of the change in appointment procedure constitutes precisely the kind of puzzle that has attracted historical institutionalist research in the past:

> Historical institutionalists address big, substantive questions that are inherently of interest to broad publics as well as to fellow scholars. To develop explanatory arguments about important outcomes or puzzles, historical institutionalists take time seriously, specifying sequences and tracing transformations and processes of varying scale and temporality. Historical institutionalists likewise analyze macro contexts and hypothesize about the combined effects of institutions and processes rather than examining just one institution or process at a time. Taken together, these three features – substantive agendas; temporal arguments; and attention to contexts and configurations – add up to a recognizable historical institutional approach. (Skocpol and Pierson 2002: 696)

Essential in such an approach is the need to consider the historical trajectory of political developments, and to identify the process that has established the institutional context in which current decisions are being made – something that is highly pertinent in the case of the *Spitzenkandidaten* as an instance of parliamentary influence in the EU's political system. In fact, ever since the first direct election to the EP in 1979, key aspects of the EU's political system – the nature of European elections, the internal politics of the EP and the position of the parliament in the EU's institutional structure – have followed a particular pattern: parliamentary business has been dominated by the two largest groups, the EPP and the Socialists and Democrats (S&D), European elections have remained second-order elections, and the influence of the EP in the EU's political system has gradually expanded.

In this regard, the historical institutionalist perspective will help to identify whether developments after the 8th parliamentary elections have continued along this path, or whether the discourse about fundamentally different elections in 2014 has translated into significant change in political practice. In theoretical terms, the question then is whether the introduction of the *Spitzenkandidaten*, in conjunction with the impact of the eurozone crisis, constituted a critical juncture in that it rearranged the EU's institutional architecture and opened up an entirely new chapter of EU politics.

In order to answer that question, we need to identify the parameters of institutional change (or continuity) along the two dimensions on which political change may occur, namely the EU's interinstitutional relations and its party politics. The subsequent analysis will be grounded in an understanding of the way EU politics operates along these two dimensions, and proceeds by identifying those aspects of the system that are considered analytically relevant for the purposes of this article.

Interinstitutional relations can be studied by assessing change with respect to the following three aspects:

- relations between the European Parliament and the European Council;
- relations between the European Parliament and the European Commission;
- the balance between supranational and intergovernmental elements of the EU's institutional structure.

In addition, investigating the potential transformation of EU party politics involves the study of:

- the nature of coalition formation among groups in the European Parliament.

While recognising the complexity of EU politics, and the challenge of measuring change in such a complex system, these four criteria constitute a logical way of determining whether interinstitutional relations and party politics have been transformed as a result of the new arrangements. They can serve as a useful heuristic device in order to facilitate a systematic analysis of the degree of change that has occurred. In the following section, these criteria structure the empirical analysis of post-election developments and allow us to come to a first assessment of the impact of the *Spitzenkandidaten* on the EU's political system.

Interinstitutional relations

A review of the institutional impact should start with the relations between the European Council and the European Parliament. These two institutions with their very different sources of legitimacy were clearly at loggerheads over their respective claims concerning the pick of the Commission President. With the legal framework not providing a clear-cut answer, as discussed earlier, this question turned into a test of political will – a test that to a large extent depended on the internal cohesion within each institution, and one that the EP ultimately decided for itself.

The European Council as an institution, and the majority of its members, had from the beginning been reserved about, if not opposed to, the assumptions behind the *Spitzenkandidaten* process. As an institution at the summit of the Union's decision-making process that had hitherto been the natural forum for the selection of the Commission President, it stood to lose significant power if the EP managed to wrest control over the process from it. Defensive measures had already started early: discourse about the European Council having the right to propose its candidate – and not one 'imposed' on it by Parliament – grew stronger as election week came closer, and became dominant in the days afterwards. European Council President van Rompuy had also scheduled an early European Council meeting right after the election – strategically, as many observers assumed, so as to pre-empt any momentum gathering behind the winning *Spitzenkandidat* (*Euractiv* 2014). The expectation was that the EP would need weeks if not months to constitute itself and to achieve sustained support for the majority candidate, giving the Heads of State and Government time to come up with a common position behind an alternative candidate.

However, in the event, the European Council never managed to coalesce around a credible alternative. Instead, the EP managed to pre-empt even the swift gathering of Heads of State and Government, with the main parties throwing their weight behind Juncker and supporting his election, albeit under certain conditions. What followed were a couple of weeks of prevarication during which the European Council as a whole, and key members such as Chancellor Merkel, seemed undecided on how to respond to the EP's challenge. There was vocal opposition to Juncker from some quarters – David Cameron in particular launched a campaign against the candidature of Jean-Claude Juncker, culminating in a mini-summit of conservative leaders in Harpsund, Sweden, on 10 June. If the objective of David Cameron here was to convince Angela Merkel to oppose Juncker's election with the help of fellow sceptics Mark Rutte (NL) and Frederik Reinfeldt (S), then it backfired, as both Rutte and Reinfeldt ultimately also voted for Juncker.

Merkel was key in this process that eventually swayed the European Council to agree on the EP's candidate. She had been less than supportive of Juncker's candidature in the run-up to the election, emphasising for example that for her there was no automatic link between selecting a leading candidate and the appointment to executive office (*Tagesschau* 2014). After the election, her apparent dithering about whether or not to accept the parliamentary majority in favour of Juncker created something of a storm in the German media, with accusations of backsliding and broken electoral promises mounting quickly (see *Frankfurter Rundschau* 2014; *NDR online* 2014). In the end, under such domestic pressure, and lacking any obvious alternative, Merkel came around to support for Juncker, which then cleared the way for a majority in the European Council and his election by the EP.

This brief period after the election demonstrated that the EP, with a high degree of internal cohesion on this issue, was able to expose the divisions and uncertainties present in the European Council. The parliament's insistence that it would oppose any other candidate than its own choice made it prohibitively risky for anyone else to let their name go forward. This was a very public inter-institutional dispute, and one that the EP managed to sway decisively in its own favour.

However, the victory of the EP vis-à-vis the European Council occurred against the backdrop of a growing intergovernmentalisation of EU decision-making which negatively affected the role of the EP, despite its gains in successive rounds of treaty reform. This development, and the empowerment of the European Council in particular, is largely due to the impact of the eurozone crisis and the manner in which governments have responded to it. The argument that scholars have advanced regarding the 'integration paradox' in the post-Maastricht era juxtaposes the expansion of EU competences with the stagnation of the powers of the supranational institutions (Bickerton *et al.* 2014). And while a critique of this view has pointed out that the impact of the eurozone crisis has been rather mixed and also involved the strengthening of supranational actors such as the Commission and the ECB (Dehousse 2015; Schimmelfennig 2015), the EP has been marginalised in the process.

In other words, the EP has gained power vis-à-vis the European Council in the context of appointment of the Commission President – an event happening only every five years – but its influence remains limited in key areas of non-legislative decision-making such as the eurozone or the refugee crisis. This means that an argument about the transformation of EU politics depends to a large extent on the relationship between the EP and the European Commission, namely the question whether the EP, through its success in choosing the Commission President, has transformed its relationship with this part of the EU's executive.

In this regard, there has been a strong sense that this link has indeed been strengthened, with a Commission President emerging from the EP's electoral process, and the winning candidate therefore being the *EP's* Commission President. Developments after the election provide evidence both for and against this particular view. First among the objections is the argument that the Parliament does not 'own' the entire Commission, however strong its ties are with the President. Commissioners continue to be appointed by the member states (via the European Council), and the President is merely a *primus inter pares* within a college that continues to decide by simple majority.

The EP had for some time managed to impose itself on the appointment procedure of designated Commission members by subjecting these to hearings before the relevant committee prior to their appointment, and has on occasion succeeded in objecting to individual appointments or specific allocations of portfolios. This long-standing pattern continued also with the members of the Juncker Commission, and indeed the EP also flexed its muscles on this occasion when it successfully objected to Alenka Bratušek, the former Slovenian Prime Minister who was nominee for the post of Energy Commissioner. After a poor performance in her hearing the MEPs voted against her appointment, and Slovenia then nominated Violeta Bulc, who in due course was appointed as Transport Commissioner.

However, none of this constituted a major shift from previous practices. On the whole, the composition of the college was dominated by member state preferences, and the allocation of portfolios negotiated between President-designate Juncker and national governments. With regard to the latter, Juncker demonstrated a degree of independence in handing Vice-Presidential positions exclusively to candidates nominated by small and medium-sized member states (with the exception of Federiga Mogherini), while at the same time recognising national preferences in assigning key portfolios such as economic and financial affairs to Pierre Moscovici (France) and financial services (Jonathan Hill). In any case, any claims that the EP would 'own' the Commission due to the new election procedure ignores the intergovernmental dimension of the European Commission which is deeply entrenched and goes beyond the point of appointment. The tensions between intergovernmental and supranational dynamics is present not only between EU institutions, but also within them, and the strong links between Commissioners and member states is a case in point (Christiansen 1997). As Fabbrini has argued, this in itself constitutes a considerable obstacle to the kind of 'parliamentary government' that advocates of the *Spitzenkandidaten* process had expected (Fabbrini 2015b).

The real test of a transformation in the relations between Parliament and Commission then lies not in the appointment of the members of the college, but rather in their interaction during subsequent legislative and other decision-making processes. Did the EP's ownership of the appointment of the Commission President result in a closer alliance between the two institutions? Did the Commission in fact evolve into a European government able to rely on a stable majority in Parliament?

Developments over the first year after Juncker's appointment paint a mixed picture. For a start, a closer personal relationship appears to have developed between the presidents of the two institutions, Juncker and Schulz. Having been the protagonists of the *Spitzenkandidaten* experience, and owing their positions to the outcome of the subsequent interinstitutional bargaining, demonstrated a capacity for close cooperation on several occasions. Under Schulz's leadership, the EP did deliver parliamentary support to Juncker on key dossiers such as the European Investment Plan, the measures proposed by the Commission in response to the 2015 refugee crisis, or the negotiations about a Transatlantic Trade and Investment Partnership (Shackleton 2015).

Beyond this, the close cooperation between EP and Commission has been institutionalised in the form of the so-called G5: regular meetings between Juncker, Schulz, Commission First Vice-President Frans Timmermans, and the leaders of the EPP and S&D groups in the EP, Manfred Weber and Gianni Pitella, respectively (Politico 2015). Forging a close alliance between the key players in the Commission and the EP, the introduction of the G5 also constituted an institutionalisation of the new coalition politics following the 2014 election, to be discussed further below. Yet beyond formalising a coalition of EPP and S&D, it also facilitated strategic cooperation between the two institutions, advancing their common position vis-à-vis the Union's intergovernmental institutions.

This arrangement does not mean that the Commission would always be assured of a majority in Parliament – the search for majority support for Commission initiatives remains a challenge on a case-by-case basis. Most strikingly, the Commission, in the context of its Better Regulation initiative, drastically reduced the number of new legislative initiatives it intends to launch, and furthermore withdrew a host of legacy proposals that had already been introduced by the Barroso Commission. In doing so, the Commission limited the role of the EP: legislation had long been the essence of parliamentary power in the EU, and the absence of a regular flow of new proposals has been likened to a room without oxygen for the Parliament.

However, the reduction in legislative proposals is to some extent balanced by a more comprehensive and predictable political agenda of the European Commission. Juncker stood for election in the Parliament not only on the basis of his party's manifesto, but a more detailed set of priorities that he announced on 15 July 2014. This 'Juncker Plan' contained 10 priority objectives for the period 2014–2019, and even though these were fairly broad, it established greater predictability of the Commission's work. Crucially, it facilitated an improvement in the EP's capacity for holding the Commission to account: annual work programmes and legislative initiatives could now be assessed in relation to the priorities Juncker had committed the Commission to at the point of his election – something he recognised when stating in his speech that 'we feel bound by a contract with this House, drawn up to run for five years. The first port of call for the new Commission will be this House' (Juncker 2014).

Furthermore, while the paucity of legislative proposals has limited the EP's involvement in decision-making in 2015, it also provided space for other kinds of parliamentary activity. Chief among these has been the EP's function as a forum for public debate on key issues. The growing number of state leaders speaking in the Parliament is evidence of this trend. In 2015, this included the French President, the German Chancellor and the Greek Prime Minister all debating with MEPs their policies in the eurozone crisis. Both the Hungarian and the Polish Prime Minister confronted MEPs in the context of criticisms from the EU institutions about domestic reforms in their respective countries. In the context of this trend, Martin Schulz's 'invitation' to David Cameron, to come to the EP and debate with them the plans for a British referendum and the negotiation of a deal to prepare for that, turned into something of an obligation – a call that Cameron only answered late and partially when agreeing to meet with group leaders in February 2016.

In this manner, the EP has arguably created a European forum in which state leaders account for their domestic policies insofar as these have relevance for the European Union as a whole, and comes in addition to the EP's scrutiny of the European institutions, with the Presidents of the Commission, the European Council and the European Central Bank facing MEPs on a regular basis to report on their work. This interaction with state leaders has helped to raise the Parliament's profile and contributed to a wider European debate about controversial policies within specific member states, albeit at irregular intervals and without formal obligation.

The politicisation of the European Commission, the closer relationship between Parliament and Commission and the emergence of the EP as an accountability forum for the member states can all be seen as evidence of the greater parliamentarisation of the European Union that has followed the introduction of the *Spitzenkandidaten* system. However, these trends come up against the structural limitations of the EU as a hybrid polity in which key areas of decision-making remain in the hands of national governments (Fabbrini 2015a).

Party politics

The 2014 election result, with its growing share of seats going to anti-European, Eurosceptic and populist parties, was remarkable, yet they did not fundamentally alter the situation within the European chamber which has traditionally relied on collaboration of pro-integrationist groups from centre-left and centre-right. Indeed, rather than an electoral 'earthquake' upsetting the traditional way of doing things, the immediate and somewhat counter-intuitive effect of the 2014 election result was to create an even stronger, more cohesive centre-ground in the parliament.

The initial bond here was the commitment from the parties participating in the *Spitzenkandidaten* process that one of their candidates, and *only* one of their candidates, would be considered a legitimate proposal from the European Council. It was a position that was quickly reaffirmed right after the election results came in, when Martin Schulz conceded defeat on behalf of the Socialists, and immediately demanded that Jean-Claude Juncker as the candidate of the EPP, holding most seats in the new parliament, should become Commission President – a position that was soon afterwards endorsed by the leaders of the majority of groups in the EP (*Spiegel Online* 2014a).

In effect, within 24 hours of the last polls closing, this marked the confirmation that the centre parties would work together, in defence of the broader parliamentary interest, vis-à-vis the European Council. And while that inter-institutional confrontation took some weeks to play out, the close cooperation between centre-right and centre-left in the election of the Commission President as well as the other appointments to senior posts demonstrated that the grand coalition was not only very much intact, but actually strengthened by this particular election outcome. On 24 June the representatives of EPP and S&D came to an agreement in order to 'shape a stable and sustainable majority in the European Parliament', an agreement to which the ALDE group then adhered only two days later (*European Voice* 2014).

While in the past such EPP-S&D agreements had been common, for example by facilitating the sharing of the post of EP President over the EP's five-year term, in the light of the *Spitzenkandidaten* this dimension of coalition politics had much wider significance, involving also the election of the Commission

President and the party-political *couleur* of other senior appointments. The cornerstones of this 'deal' were the support of the Socialists for Jean-Claude Juncker as Commission President and the support of the EPP for Martin Schulz to continue as EP President (*Spiegel Online* 2014b). This meant that the traditional 'grand coalition' at the political centre of the EP not only continued to function effectively, but that it became somewhat institutionalised in the form of the above-mentioned G5 meetings. It also meant that the Martin Schulz, as serving EP President, could remain in post – indeed, there is even the possibility that Schulz might serve out the full term of five years – an unprecedented development – as a result of the EPP-S&D power-sharing deal.

The recognition that there has been less, rather than more, left/right competition in the post-2014 EP is not only based on the formation of the grand coalition that was established in order to elect Jean-Claude Juncker and agree on the other key appointments in 2014. Cooperation among the centrist and pro-integrationist parties was also required, more than before, due to the greater size of the anti-establishment parties in the post-2014 parliament. Once it had become virtually impossible to form a constructive majority in Parliament without either the centre-right or the centre-left, these parties are bound to greater cooperation.

This strengthening of the 'grand coalition' at the centre of the EP has occurred in stark contrast to the expectations expressed prior to the election, but also clashes with the predictions made by scholars only some 10 years earlier. Before the 2004 enlargement there was an anticipation that the arrival of the 10 new member states 'should further stabilize the party system in the EP ... by increasing the size of the two main party groups against the smaller groups, and by strengthening the bi-polar nature of competition in the EP' (Hix *et al.* 2003). In the wake of the 2014 election, the exact opposite appears to have happened: the size of the two main groups has shrunk, and that in turn has strengthened the bi-partisan rather than the bi-polar nature of the chamber. If anything, the pro-/anti-European cleavage in the Parliament has become more important, not least in the wake of the eurozone crisis and subsequent years of austerity policies (Höpner 2014).

Conclusions

The European election in 2014 was indeed different, but did this new kind of electioneering transform EU politics? Looking across the two key dimensions of EU politics identified, the *Spitzenkandidaten* system produced something of a supranational moment in the evolution of the EU's institutional architecture: the EP taking the reins from the European Council in the choice over the Commission President initially strengthened the EP, but above all empowered the Commission by enhancing its legitimacy and affording it greater independence from the member states. In particular, the President of the Commission, less encumbered than his predecessor by the need for support and approval from the majority of the member states, has been able to assume a leadership role unseen since the days of Jacques Delors.

In terms of the relations between the EP and European Council, this was indeed a *moment* rather than a wider transformation, with the effects of the eurozone crisis more than counteracting the impact of the new electoral procedure. There has, however, been closer and more systematic cooperation between the EP and Commission, with the election of the Commission President by the Parliament on the basis of a set of political priorities and the formal agreements between the EPP and S&D groups. A 'governing coalition' of sorts has been established, and regular meetings between the leadership of both institutions helps to maintain this cooperative relationship. However, this does not guarantee certain support for Commission proposals in the way national governments can rely on their parliamentary majorities – the Commission's search for majority support for its proposals on a case-by-case basis continues, as does its close cooperation with member states and the European Council in a range of important non-legislative domains. In other words, there have been changes in the EU's interinstitutional relations, but these hardly amount to the kind of critical juncture that would throw the Union off its established path.

With respect to the dimension of party politics, the kind of changes that could be observed have also been limited. Indeed, neither pre-election campaigning nor post-election decision-making delivered greater party-political competition or a genuine choice between rival political programmes. Instead, with greater popular engagement and the development of a pan-European public sphere, the result has been a further strengthening of the pro-integrationist establishment in the face of rising populist opposition to further integration. In party-political terms, then, the introduction of the *Spitzenkandidaten* process has been characterised by a mismatch between, on the one hand, the promise of a clearer choice between rival candidates and a more competitive party system in the EP, and, on the other hand, the continuation of long-term trends in EU politics: the close cooperation between the pro-integrationist parties at the centre of the EP's political spectrum.

The overall conclusion of this analysis points to gradual adjustments in the EU's interinstitutional relations, combined with the continuation of pro-integrationist coalition politics among the largest parties in the EP. It does not amount to a fundamental shift in the politics of the European Union, and in fact it is remarkable how the very different kind of election campaigning under the *Spitzenkandidaten* system has been followed by the reaffirmation of bipartisan party politics. Far from having constituted a critical juncture, the impact of the 2014 election has been to confirm the continuity of key aspects of the EU's political system. Path dependency rather than fundamental transformation has characterised the EU's interinstitutional relations and party politics, even though from mid-2015 the refugee crisis and the instability on the EU's borders raises new questions about the direction of future developments.

It has to be recognised that this is a very preliminary finding, based on less than two years of political activity since the European elections in May 2014. A more thorough assessment will only be possible in 2019, when the institutions, parties and winning candidate can be judged against their performance at the end of the current parliamentary term. In fact, the real litmus test may be whether the European elections in 2019 will see greater competition between rival candidates for the Commission Presidency – involving candidates not only from the mainstream parties, but also from critical and Eurosceptic camps. Such a development would create the prospect for more relevant debates about the future of Europe, and greater potential to realise the kind of political change that the *Spitzenkandidaten* system was supposed to deliver.

Acknowledgements

Initial ideas for the article were presented at the first EUI-EP Policy Dialogue in Brussels in December 2014, and a first draft was presented at a workshop at the Robert Schuman Centre for Advanced Studies at the EUI in Florence in September 2015. I am grateful for the insightful feedback received on both occasions, and also for the valuable comments provided by the journal's two anonymous referees. The article also benefitted greatly from the author's conversations with Michael Shackleton and Martin Westlake. Any remaining errors are solely my responsibility.

Disclosure statement

No potential conflict of interest was reported by the author.

References

Beach, Derek (2007). 'The European Parliament in the 2000 IGC and the Constitutional Treaty negotiations: from loser to winner', *Journal of European Public Policy*, 14:February, 1271–92.

Bickerton, Christopher J., Dermot Hodson, and Uwe Puetter (2014). 'The New Intergovernmentalism: European Integration in the Post-Maastricht Era', *Journal of Common Market Studies*, 53:4, 703–22.

Van der Brug, Wouter, Katjana Gattermann, and Claes H. De Vreese (2016). 'Introduction: How Different Were the European Elections of 2014?', *Politics and Governance*, 4:1, 1–8.

Christiansen, Thomas (1997). 'Tensions of European Governance: Politicized Bureaucracy and Multiple Accountability in the European Commission', *Journal of European Public Policy*, 4:1, 73–90.

Christiansen, Thomas, and Christine Reh (2009). *Constitutionalizing the European Union*. Basingstoke: Palgrave Macmillan.

Craig, Paul (2008). 'The Role of the European Parliament under the Lisbon Treaty', in Stefan Griller and Jacques Ziller (eds.), *The Lisbon Treaty*. Vienna: Springer, 109–34.

Dehousse, R. (2015) 'The New Supranationalism', Paper prepared for presentation at the ECPR General Conference, Montreal.

Dinan, Desmond (1997). 'The Commission and the Reform Process', in Geoffrey Edwards and Alfred Pijpers (eds.), *The Politics of European Treaty Reform*. London: Pinter, 188–11.

Euractiv (2014). 'EU Leaders to Meet for 'Informal' Talks, Two Days After Elections', 3 February 2014, available at http://www.euractiv.com/eu-elections-2014/van-rompuy-gathers-eu-leaders-in-news-533196 (accessed 1 February 2015).

European Parliament (2014). 'Press Release: The 2014 European elections: this time it's different', (2 November 2014, available at http://www.europarl.europa.eu/news/en/news-room/content/20140210ipr35560/html (accessed 2 February 2014).

European People's Party (2002). A Constitution for a Strong Europe, Estoril, (accessed 18 October 2002).

European Voice (2014). 'Main Parties Bid to Firm up Grand Coalition', 3 July 2014, available at http://www.europeanvoice.com/article/main-parties-in-bid-to-firm-up-grand-coalition (accessed 1 February 2015).

Fabbrini, Sergio (2015a). *Which European Union? Europe After the Euro Crisis*. Cambridge: Cambridge University Press.

Fabbrini, Sergio (2015b). '*The European Union and the Puzzle of Parliamentary Government*', *Journal of European Integration*, 37:5, 571–86.

Farrell, Henry, and Adrienne Héritier (2007). 'Codecision and Institutional Change', *West European Politics*, 30:2, 285–300.

Frankfurter Rundschau (2014). 'EU-Kommissionspräsident: Das Zögern der Kanzlerin', 1 June 2014, available at http://www.fr-online.de/europawahl/eu-kommissionspraesident-das-zoegern-der-kanzlerin,27125132,27315524.html (accessed 1 February 2015).

Hix, Simon, Amie Kreppel, and Abdul Noury (2003). 'The Party System in the European Parliament: Collusive or Competitive?', *Journal of Common Market Studies*, 41:2, 309–31.

Hobolt, Sara (2014). 'A Vote for the President? The Role of Spitzenkandidaten in the 2014 European Parliament Elections', *Journal of European Public Policy*, 21:10, 1528–40.

Höpner, Martin (2014). 'Spitzenkandidaten für die EU-Kommissionspräsidentschaft: Quantensprung der Demokratie?', *Gesellschaftsforschung*, 14:1, 2–5.

Juncker, J.-C. (2014). *A New Start for Europe: My Agenda for Jobs, Growth Fairness and Democratic Change*. Brussels: European Commission.

Marks, Gary, and Liesbet Hooghe (2009). 'A Postfunctionalist Theory of European Integration: From Permissive Consensus to Constraining Dissensus', *British Journal of Political Science*, 39:1, 1–23.

NDR online (2014). 'Christdemokraten behandeln Juncker wie Aussätzigen', 28 May 2014, available at http://www.ndr.de/info/sendungen/interviews/Christdemokraten-behandeln-Juncker-wie-Aussaetzigen,lambsdorff132.html (accessed 1 February 2015).
Politico (2015), 'The Most Exclusive Dining Club in Brussels', 18 June 2015, available at http://www.politico.eu/article/g5-brussels-most-exclusive-dining-club/ (accessed 13 March 2015).
Schimmelfennig, Frank (2015). 'What's the News in 'New Intergovernmentalism'? A Critique of Bickerton, Hodson and Puetter', *Journal of Common Market Studies*, 53:4, 723–30.
Schmitt, Hermann, Sara Hobolt, and Sebastian Adrian Popa (2015). 'Does Personalization Increase Turnout? Spitzenkandidaten in the 2014 European Parliament Elections', *European Union Politics*, 16:3, 347–368.
Shackleton, Michael (2015). 'Whither the Parliament and the Commission? Reflections on the First Year of the Juncker Commission', in Gerrit Voerman and Jan van der Harst (eds.), *De Commissie Juncker: Laatste Kans voor Europa?*. Den Haag: Montesquieu Instituut, 81–94.
Skocpol, Theda, and Paul Pierson (2002). 'Historical Institutionalism in Contemporary Political Science', in I. Katznelson and H.V. Milner (eds.), *Political Science: State of the Discipline*. New York, NY: W.W. Norton, 693–721.
Spiegel Online (2014a). 'Künftiger Kommissionspräsident: EU-Parlament stellt sich hinter Juncker', 27 May 2014, available at http://www.spiegel.de/politik/ausland/juncker-als-eu-kommissionspraesident-mehrheitssuche-im-europaparlament-a-971969.html (accessed 1 February 2015).
Spiegel Online (2014b). 'Gezerre um EU-Spitzenjobs: SPD verzichtet auf Kommissarsposten in Brüssel', 20 June 2014, available at http://www.spiegel.de/politik/deutschland/schulz-und-juncker-spd-ueberlasst-kommissarsposten-der-union-a-976317.html (accessed 1 February 2015).
Tagesschau (2014). 'EVP kürt ihren Kandidaten für Europa', 7 March 2014, available at https://www.tagesschau.de/ausland/evp104.html (accessed 1 November 2015).
Westlake, Martin (2016). 'Chronicle of an Election Foretold: The Longer-Term Trends leading to the Spitzenkandidaten Procedure and the Election of Jean-Claude Juncker as European Commission President', LSE Europe in Question Paper No.102/2016.

The Commission: boxed in and constrained, but still an engine of integration

Stefan Becker, Michael W. Bauer, Sara Connolly and Hussein Kassim

ABSTRACT
In the debate about the impact of the eurozone crisis on the EU's institutional balance, antagonists have often argued past each other. Supporters of the new intergovernmentalism contend that the European Council has supplanted the European Commission in policy leadership, while scholars who hold that the EU executive has been a winner of the crisis highlight the new management functions it has acquired. This article argues, first, that an accurate assessment of the institutional balance requires a more global evaluation of the Commission, acknowledging external and internal dynamics. Second, it contends that the crisis did not cause a Commission retreat but accelerated a process already underway that finds its origins in the presidentialisation of policy control. The adoption of fewer legislative proposals during the crisis was due to the ability and choice of a strong president to focus the attention on crisis-related areas. The broader lesson is that rather than marking a further step in the decline of the Commission, the crisis reveals how the centralisation of power within the institution and its expanded management duties have enhanced its capacity to take strategic action. The Commission's role as an engine of integration will therefore endure, but in a different guise.

At the very moment the Lisbon Treaty entered into force – and thereby brought a decade of constitutional debate in the European Union to an end – the eurozone crisis put the new institutional balance to the test. Widely viewed as one of Lisbon's losers, the European Commission immediately faced a critical moment that questioned its institutional role (Laffan 2016). The EU's handling of the crisis raised serious questions about the Commission's role in economic governance and EU policy-making in general.

Although the debate about the Commission's influence over EU policy is as old as European integration itself (e.g. Haas 1958; Lindberg 1965), the focus over the last two decades has been on its apparent decline, challenged by the growing role of the European Council, the empowerment of the European Parliament, and the creation of new regulatory agencies (e.g. Kassim and Menon 2010; Kassim *et al.* 2013: 131–5). More recently, this argument has been extended by advocates of a 'new intergovernmentalism' who emphasise the increased use of decision-making processes beyond the Community method,[1] the reluctance of member states to delegate further competences to the 'traditional' supranational institutions, and the emergence of the European Council as *the* central actor in EU policy-making (Bickerton *et al.* 2015a). The new intergovernmentalism seeks to 'recast' the role of the Commission and the Court of Justice 'in a new mould', arguing that these institutions are now 'more circumspect about the pursuit of ever closer union' (Bickerton *et al.* 2015b: 39). In the era of new intergovernmentalism, which began with the Maastricht Treaty, they 'are no longer the "engines of integration" that they once were' (Bickerton *et al.* 2015a: 717). Authors writing from this perspective about the crisis depict the Commission as the 'little engine that wouldn't' (Hodson 2013). More modestly, Peterson (2015: 207) argues that, despite the trend towards an intergovernmentalist dynamic, the Commission 'mostly gets on with its work', which mainly 'is focused on closer European policy cooperation'. It might even represent 'an oasis of calm within the storm' in the disequilibrium that is the current EU. Bauer and Becker (2014), by contrast, have challenged the view that the Commission's role has been diminished as a result of the crisis and contend, to the contrary, that the Commission emerged stronger with important new managerial tasks in economic governance.

This article argues that the impact of the crisis on the Commission is considerably more complex than is suggested by the current debate and contests key elements of the new intergovernmentalist approach. First, any assessment of the effects of the crisis on the Commission in the institutional balance needs to look beyond either policy-making as highlighted by the new intergovernmentalism or management responsibilities. A more global examination, acknowledging external and internal dynamics, is necessary. The Commission's role as an engine of integration that seeks to provide leadership and impetus for EU policy-making, its own traditional interpretation of its mandate to 'promote the general interest of the Union' (Art. 17 TEU), needs to be reconsidered. Entrepreneurship - i.e. aiming 'to induce authoritative political decisions that would not otherwise occur' - by the Commission has long been based on 'favoring more ambitious schemes for further institutional and substantive integration' (Moravcsik 1999: 271). It is now more subtle and versatile.

Second, although the number of proposals adopted by the Commission – and, correspondingly, the volume of EU legislation – did fall when the eurozone crisis broke in 2010, the crisis was a *catalyst* rather than a *cause* of the decline in legislative proposals. The crisis did not initiate the change, but altered the speed of a process of change that had already been underway for a number of years. Moreover, contrary to claims that the Commission had retreated or been eclipsed by the European Council, the analysis shows that far from abandoning the field, the Commission concentrated its attention on aspects of economic governance and provided leadership in areas that pertained directly to the eurozone crisis.

Third, the explanation for a reduction of the Commission's policy activism is to be found in an intra-organisational process rather than the inter-institutional dynamic highlighted by the new intergovernmentalism. The downward trend in the Commission's decisional outputs was the result of concerted action on the part of its eleventh President, José Manuel Barroso, to strengthen presidential control over the Commission's policy activism, especially during his second term, not displacement of the Commission by the European Council. Indeed, the crisis accelerated the process of presidentialisation that had begun during Barroso's first term. Both Barroso after 2010 and Jean-Claude Juncker, his successor, have used the enhanced powers and resources available to the office to take personal control over the Commission agenda and to end the expansionist policy activism that historically characterised the organisation. As a result, a new model of Commission intervention has emerged – top-down managed, measured, restrained and strategic – that contrasts with the unprogrammatic and piecemeal approach of the past.

Drawing on new empirical evidence – two large-scale surveys in the Commission,[2] interviews with high-level officials, and legislative data from EUR-Lex – to support these contentions, the article proposes a new interpretation of the impact of the crisis on the Commission and a new assessment of the organisation's post-crisis position. It contends that the Commission may face increased constraints, but its capacity to legislate, even in controversial areas such as economic governance, is still important. Moreover, its expanded management duties mean new opportunities to provide impetus for EU policy-making. Finally, the emergence of presidentialised leadership has equipped the Commission with a new strategic ability, enabling it to act more programmatically and with greater focus than previously.

The Commission on the eve of the crisis

In order to assess the changes in the role of the Commission during the crisis, it is essential to revisit the point of departure. The Commission had already undergone several transformations by the time the eurozone crisis unfolded in 2010. This section reviews its condition before the crisis, at the end of 2009, to provide a benchmark against which to assess subsequent change.

Institutional and political environment

The Commission has historically been an embattled institution (see e.g. Lindberg 1965). Since the early 1990s, however, it had come under particular pressure. Successive treaty changes – Maastricht, Amsterdam and Nice – had encroached upon the Commission's institutional position by strengthening the European Parliament, limiting the Commission's power in new EU competences, and delegating regulatory tasks to other executive bodies (Kassim and Menon 2004). Shortly before the crisis, the entry into force of the Lisbon Treaty further undermined its centrality. First, although the European Council already played an influential role in setting the EU's political agenda, the formalisation of its position was of practical and symbolic significance. The wording of Article 15 (1) Treaty on European Union (TEU) – namely, that the European Council 'shall provide the Union with the necessary impetus for its development and shall define the general political directions' – overlaps with the Commission's mission to promote the Union's general interest. As well as acknowledging the European Council's long-standing leadership role, the Lisbon Treaty established a full-time presidency. This strengthened the European Council's capacity by enabling it to develop more focused working methods (Puetter 2012). It has thus become an even stronger challenger for the Commission in setting the agenda and formulating answers to strategic problems. Second, the Lisbon Treaty further empowered the European Parliament by the expansion of co-decision. Although the Commission kept its sole right of initiative in most policy areas and remained the crucial actor for policy formulation,[3] its role of delivering policy proposals grew more complex due to an additional veto player and a more heterogeneous set of preferences. This made Commission policy entrepreneurship in the classic sense – i.e. formulating and pushing for hard law in the Community method – more difficult.

In addition to the Lisbon reforms, the political environment of the pre-crisis years also affected the Commission. Although European integration was never acclaimed by ordinary citizens, European elites were relatively unrestricted when negotiating EU matters. This 'permissive consensus' had all but vanished; political actors now operated under a 'constraining dissensus' (Hooghe and Marks 2008: 5). European integration was heavily politicised and closely scrutinised (for a recent account, see Hutter and Grande 2014). Blame games and general complaints about 'Brussels' being too powerful and interventionist were common. Positive views on EU membership among its citizens frequently dipped below the 50 per cent level since Maastricht; and although public opinion fluctuates, such dips had not happened before (for an overview, see European Commission 2014a). This growing hostility effectively limited the Commission's ability to propose bold integration proposals, and even modest initiatives often attracted negative responses. Furthermore, enlargement made policy entrepreneurship for the Commission more complicated; by now, it had to accommodate the preferences of 28 member states when developing policy proposals. At the same time, its responsibilities as the guardian of the treaties had expanded in scale, scope and complexity. As a consequence, the Commission's task portfolio had shifted towards management (Bauer 2006; Laffan 1997; Metcalfe 1992; Kassim and Menon 2004, 2010). Finally, some policy fields were by now almost saturated; the main legislative work had been done. The governance of the single market had, for instance, broadly moved from development to management (see also Pelkmans 2016). In general, the Commission was now more concerned with implementation, better regulation and improving the quality of existing legislation than promulgating new laws. The combined effect of the institutional and political environment for the Commission was thus a stronger focus on management rather than policy entrepreneurship.

Internal organisation

The presidentialisation of the Commission was also a key factor in the pre-crisis years. Starting from a low base (Campbell 1983: 181), the Commission presidency has become increasingly powerful since the 1990s and especially since 2004 (Kassim 2012; Kassim *et al.* 2016). Acutely aware of growing Euroscepticism, wariness if not hostility about intervention from 'Brussels' on the part of national capitals, and seeking to combat the perception of the Commission as a remote bureaucracy driven by a relentless desire to regulate 'every matter under the sun', Barroso used the constitutional powers available to the office to strengthen the Commission Presidency as a means to control policy activism within the institution. He believed that the Commission could only succeed if it concentrated on issues where the EU could demonstrably add value, showed greater sensitivity to member governments, and made more use of options other than 'hard' law (Kurpas *et al.* 2008). Strengthening the Commission Presidency, he used the enhanced resources of the office to promote a more discriminating, disciplined and measured approach to policy, established quality control systems and implemented a better regulation agenda. He also took personal charge of certain policy areas, as well as putting his name to key initiatives.

Historically, the Commission had been a fragmented institution, where power was widely dispersed within the College and between the services (Coombes 1970; Kassim *et al.* 2013: chs. 6, 7). In the absence of a central capacity to orchestrate or promote a coherent or unified programme, individual Commissioners and policy Directorates General had considerable autonomy to pursue their own policy agendas. Since the 1990s and especially since 2004, however, the powers of the Commission Presidency have been significantly enhanced. Not only is the policy leadership of the Commission President now unchallenged, but the incumbent has been able to bring policy activism within the Commission under control. Strong presidentialism is no longer an exception that is based on personal qualities, such as in the case of Delors, but underpinned by formal organisation.

This presidentialisation can be explained in terms of three main factors. The first is the differentiation of the Commission President from other members of the College. Beginning with the Treaty of European Union, which provided for a separate selection procedure for the Commission President, successive treaties have steadily strengthened the incumbent's personal mandate. In terms of policy leadership, the primacy of the Commission President was first established by the Treaty of Amsterdam. Successive treaties also granted the Commission President powers to appoint other Commissioners, decide on their portfolios, and to dismiss them.

Second, new administrative capacities, established within the Secretariat General as part of the Kinnock reforms that were enacted under the Prodi Commission in response to the crisis that led to the resignation of the Santer Commission, were an important step in developing an administrative platform at the centre of the institution enabling policy coordination and oversight. The most important was Strategic Planning and Programming (SPP), a system of priority-setting and resource allocation. The introduction of impact assessment procedures was also significant.

Political entrepreneurship on the part of Barroso is a third factor. Barroso mobilised the formal powers granted by the treaties both to reaffirm the pre-eminence of the Commission Presidency and to extend the procedural and administrative resources of the office, with the aim of establishing detailed presidential control over the College and the wider organisation (Kassim *et al.* 2016, Kurpas *et al.* 2008). His transformation of the Secretariat General, historically the guardian of collegiality and the representative of the Commission administration at the political level, into a personal service of the Commission Presidency was a key element. Since the Secretariat General is the Commission's central coordinating body and process manager, its conversion dramatically extended the Commission President's reach into the administration and grip over policy. Moreover, since the Secretariat General was the locus of SPP, the Commission President gained important control over policy coordination and internal gatekeeping.

Survey responses and data from interviews with Commissioners, cabinet members and managers as part of 'The European Commission in Question', carried out in 2008 and 2009 at the end of Barroso I (and reported in Kassim *et al.* 2013: 6) testify both to the increased power of the Commission President and to his control over the policy agenda. Three of the five Commissioners interviewed for that project characterised Barroso I as presidential rather than collegial. Giving their answers to the online survey distributed to policy officers and members of cabinet in 2008 as part of 'The European Commission in Question', respondents rated Barroso as strong on 'setting a policy agenda' and 'managing the house'. These views were expressed especially strongly by cabinet members and senior managers. In interviews, senior managers in particular testified that Barroso closely controlled the policy agenda at all levels of the policy process. Cabinet members highlighted how in meetings of 'special chefs', the President's chef de cabinet had shaped, delayed or effectively vetoed policy proposals.

They noted that Barroso kept a much tighter rein on the Commission's policy programme than his immediate predecessors (see Kassim *et al.* 2013: ch. 6).

It would be surprising if such a dramatic reorientation had been welcomed positively by staff. Most theoretical perspectives on bureaucratic change, including sociological institutionalism and historical institutionalism – public choice accounts are an exception – suggest that bureaucrats are conservative and wary about, if not hostile to, administrative reform (Kassim 2008). In the case of the Commission, concentration of power in the hands of the President was at odds with the principle and practice of collegiality (Dimitrakopoulos 2008) and the assertion of presidential control over policy was likely to offend not only other members of the College, but Directors General who had been powerful and important policy-making figures (Coombes 1970; Kassim *et al.* 2016). Coming immediately after the Kinnock reforms, which had sought to give the Commission a stronger organisational steering capacity and to strengthen management, but on which staff were divided (Kassim 2008; Kassim *et al.* 2013: ch. 8), the presidentialisation of policy-making authority was likely to be interpreted as a further step away from the Commission's traditional mission.

Evidence from 'The European Commission in Question' shows that there was indeed strong ambivalence among Commission staff about both presidentialisation and the emergence of a more interventionist Secretariat General that had accompanied it (Kassim *et al.* 2013: chs. 6, 7). They were also divided on whether coordination from the centre was a good thing and on the new emphasis on management. Although recognising that the introduction of processes such as SPP had been intended to make the overall administration more systematic, effective and accountable, many doubted its effectiveness and value. Moreover, for many officials, 'managerialism' ran counter to the Commission's culture, which prized policy formulation far above policy management and implementation. Although 49 per cent of respondents to the online survey administered as part of the 'European Commission in Question' agreed or strongly agreed with the proposition that 'The Commission is increasingly more involved in policy management and coordination, and less in policy conception or initiation', there was little evidence that there had been an accompanying change in the Commission's administrative culture. In the same survey fully 79 per cent of respondents disagreed with the proposition, 'The Commission should focus primarily on managing existing policies rather than developing new ones'. The 38 per cent who merely disagreed were outnumbered – albeit marginally – by the 41 per cent who *strongly* disagreed.

Legislative activity

The institutional and organisational transformations of the Commission preceding the crisis are clearly reflected in its output of the time. In line with his ambitions, Barroso succeeded in shifting the Commission towards a more

Table 1. Annual average of Commission preparatory acts by type in five-year intervals.

	Regulations	Directives	Decisions	Communications	Reports	Total
1985–1989	456	106	106	58	67	793
1990–1994	392	122	140	54	56	764
1995–1999	262	103	201	104	115	785
2000–2004	227	82	238	167	115	829
2005–2009	190	69	211	231	120	821

Note: Rounded numbers.
Source: EUR-Lex. Search query: Preparatory acts, date of document, excludes corrigenda.

programmatic, disciplined and sensitive approach. It has not become less active but more and more diversified in the use of legislative instruments and increasingly opting for less intrusive measures. Analysis of data from EUR-Lex, the EU's database of legislation, preparatory acts and other public documents, reveals that the EU executive reduced the number of hard law proposals after a peak of legislative activity in the late 1980s and early 1990s (see also Kurpas *et al.* 2008). In 2009, on the eve of the crisis, the Commission issued proposals for 145 regulations and 30 directives. Exactly 20 years earlier, it proposed 418 regulations and 133 directives. The numbers thus dropped by 65 per cent and 77 per cent respectively. During the same period, the number of decision proposals increased by 88 per cent, from 140 to 263. This attenuates the overall decrease in hard law proposals, but it still amounts to 37 per cent.

At the same time, the Commission produced an increasing amount of soft law. In 1989, communications and reports added up to a total of 100; in 2009, there were already 360 such documents. The ratio of hard law to these forms of soft law thus changed from 1/0.16 to 1/0.82. Annual numbers are subject to some fluctuation, but a comparison of averages of preparatory acts in five-year intervals from 1985 to 2009, broadly representing Commission terms, yields similar results (Table 1). The overall output thus remained fairly constant over the years, but its composition changed considerably.

There have also been significant shifts between policy fields.[4] These can again be illustrated by comparing the numbers for 1989 and 2009. Agriculture and fisheries, previously hot spots of Commission activity, have witnessed a decrease of roughly two-thirds in preparatory acts, from 301 to 91. The progress in the integration of the single market led to an over 90 per cent drop in the field of customs, from 112 to 19. The most significant increase in output is related to the gradual integration of justice and home affairs in the new millennium. Previously not a concern for EU action, the Commission issued 82 preparatory acts in this field in 2009. The field of environment, customers and health has also experienced strong growth. Respective Commission output more than doubled, arriving at over 100 preparatory acts per year shortly before the crisis. Furthermore, outputs in general, financial and institutional matters as well as in economic and monetary policy, starting with minimal Commission activity, more than tripled, arriving at 59 and 45 preparatory acts respectively.

Finally, a moderate increase of 20 per cent can be observed in the field of external relations – i.e. common commercial policy and bilateral agreements. By 2009, the Commission therefore proved to be an institution with a broad sphere of action. This diversity can also be interpreted as a lack of focus: of all internal policy fields, not a single one accounted for more than 10 per cent of all preparatory acts.

In sum, on the eve of the crisis the Commission was already in a process of transformation. Institutionally, the Lisbon Treaty had increased the powers of the European Council and the European Parliament, while politically the Commission faced an increasingly sceptical climate. The response of the Commission under Barroso's first term had been to enact a major departure from previous practice. Building on the expanded formal prerogatives to further strengthen the office, Barroso used the political, procedural and administrative resources of the Commission Presidency to take a more disciplined, limited and sensitive approach to policy-making. In particular, there was a marked shift from hard to soft legislation. A substantial focus had, however, not yet materialised.

The Commission and the crisis

When the eurozone crisis unfolded in 2010, it threw the EU into political and institutional turmoil. In regard to the Commission, however, the crisis mainly served as a catalyst that reinforced trends in its institutional and political environment, internal organisation and legislative activity.

Institutional and political environment

In line with its new status accorded by the Lisbon Treaty, the European Council emerged as the main venue for debating how the EU should respond to the eurozone crisis (Puetter 2012). Although it has no legislative function under Article 15 TEU, in what might be interpreted as a deliberate move to pre-empt discussions of strong supranational solutions, the European Council not only defined the broad strokes of the crisis response but also put forward policy details. As Fabbrini (2013: 1011) argues, at the onset of the crisis 'the EU intergovernmental constitution enjoyed the support of a powerful constellation of political leaders and public opinions'. Indeed, important national leaders, such as Nicolas Sarkozy and Angela Merkel, quickly made it known that they preferred intergovernmental decision-making and outcomes to supranational alternatives, which included empowerments of the Commission (see also Dehousse 2015). This sentiment also corresponded with public opinion. Trust in the Commission among EU citizens dropped by 10 percentage points in the first two years of the crisis, from 46 per cent trusting the institution in autumn 2009 to 36 per cent in autumn 2011 (European Commission 2013: 50–70).

Talks of a new 'Union method' as an alternative to the 'Community method', Commission proposals that went nowhere, such as the Eurobonds (Hodson 2013), and the first institutional outcomes – i.e. lending facilities outside the EU's legal system – all highlight the intergovernmental character of early crisis management.

However, the institutional responses to the crisis have actually strengthened the Commission (Bauer and Becker 2014).[5] The Commission's involvement in economic policy surveillance is now broader and deeper. As a result of the 'six-pack' legislation, the Commission became responsible for monitoring the overall public debt and developments in national expenditure. Its assessments and recommendations also carry additional weight due to 'reversed qualified majority' voting for fines and sanctions. The Commission is also responsible for managing the new Macroeconomic Imbalance Procedure, in which it is able to conduct quantitative and qualitative analyses of national trade balances. Under the 'two-pack' legislation, the Commission is further entrusted with assessing – in an advisory capacity – the conformity of draft national budgets with EU rules, while as part of the intergovernmental Fiscal Compact, aimed at further strengthening fiscal discipline and intensifying surveillance, the Commission has a role in developing policy principles and monitoring compliance.

The coordination procedures for national policies in areas of common interest, including social security and employment, have also been upgraded during the crisis. Both the Europe 2020 process, the successor of the Lisbon Strategy, and the Euro Plus Pact, which was adopted in 2011 by the eurozone members and six other states to promote competitiveness, employment and sustainable public debt, have broadened the Commission's responsibilities. Its role is to gather and synthesise information and recommend paths of action. Finally, even the intergovernmental arrangements in the field of financial stability support involve the Commission in a number of capacities. Along with the European Central Bank, the Commission assesses the financing needs of applicants and subsequently proposes decisions on granting assistance. As part of the troika, which also features the European Central Bank and the International Monetary Fund, the Commission then negotiates conditionality agreements and monitors compliance afterwards.

The crisis has thus reinforced, at least in economic governance, the Commission's shift from policy entrepreneurship to management. Rather than weakening its position, however, this has strengthened the Commission, as the delegated tasks are not purely administrative matters. On the contrary, these coordination, negotiation and monitoring duties come with some discretion in highly political matters. The crisis and its institutional outcomes have therefore created new opportunities for the Commission to influence policy-making in the EU, even if they are less obvious than the classic entrepreneurship through hard law proposals.

Internal organisation

The crisis served to reinforce presidential leadership, first under Barroso II and second with the election of Jean-Claude Juncker. At the outset of his second term in 2010, which followed the entry into force of the Lisbon Treaty the preceding year, Barroso reinforced the Commission President's leadership role. Symbolising his pursuit of his aim of a more programmatic approach to policy, Barroso introduced a State of Union speech, to be given by the Commission President each September – the first was delivered in 2010 – that would set the main policy priorities not only of the Commission, but of the EU more generally, for the coming year. The speech would inform the policy agenda set out in the Commission's annual work programme. Moreover, Barroso took the decision that in the prevailing climate of austerity the Commission should focus its attention on crisis-related areas of policy only. Intervention in other areas would be seen as an unnecessary distraction. In the words of a senior manager in the Secretariat General: 'the legislative activity of the Commission was put on the backburner or in the freezer for a while'.[6]

Evidence from 'European Commission: Facing the Future' attests to the presidentialism of Barroso II. When asked their opinion on the propositions, 'Some people argue that the College under the current President is a presidential body; others that it is collegial', all eight members of the Commission in the sample expressed the view that the Commission was presidential. There was also consensus among the eight that College discussion was limited. Similarly, in face-to-face interviews conducted in 2014, 75 per cent of managers (total n = 110), 80 per cent of Directors General (total n = 18) and 92 per cent of cabinet members (total n = 17) characterised the Barroso Commission as 'more presidential' rather than 'more collegial'.

When he succeeded Barroso, Juncker further reinforced presidentialisation. The *Spitzenkandidaten* process by which he was elected Commission President gave Juncker a unique claim to personal authority (Christiansen 2016). Having won the EPP's primary contest, he became the party's official candidate in the 2014 elections to the European Parliament. Then, following his nomination by the European Council and his election by a majority of MEPs in the new Parliament, Juncker could claim that he had a mandate to put into effect the policy programme on which he had campaigned. That platform identified a number of policy priorities, but Juncker also argued that in the post-crisis climate the Commission urgently needed to deliver. It was in this context that as nominee Commission President Juncker spoke of the 'last chance Commission'.

The radical restructuring of the College undertaken by Juncker was designed not only to institutionalise the pre-eminence of the Commission President, but to address a number of weaknesses, old and new, in the Commission.[7] A first aim was to ensure that Commissioners were collectively mobilised behind the implementation of his policy programme. Departing from tradition, Juncker looked to recruit seven Vice Presidents. A largely honorary title in previous Commissions,[8] Juncker wanted Vice Presidents to play a 'hands on' role either in coordinating designated policy groups of portfolio Commissioners or managing institution-wide functions. The creation of a tier of Vice Presidents, subject to the authority of the Commission President, was a strategy intended to establish shared leadership and responsibility to 'ensure a dynamic interaction of all Members of the College' (European Commission 2014b).

Second, a complaint of the leadership during the Barroso era, particularly in the second term, had been that individual Commissioners often 'went missing' at moments of stress.[9] Appointing senior politicians – former Prime Ministers, deputy Prime Ministers and Foreign or Finance Ministers – to the position of Vice President was intended to ensure that political responsibility could spread among a team of experienced individuals, used to dealing with the media. Third, the restructuring was intended to ensure implementation of the Commission's policy programme. Juncker had made clear that only policy proposals relating to his 'ten priorities' would be adopted. Allowing Vice Presidents alone the right to submit agenda items for discussion at meetings of the College created a mechanism for policing this rule.

A final aim of the new structure was to give the Commission the powerful political leadership it had lacked for much of its history and especially to overcome its administrative fragmentation. In addition to the lack of shared purpose among Commissioners (Coombes 1970), the asymmetry between career politicians and permanent civil servants had been particularly marked in the Commission's case. The new organisation of the College was intended to prevent 'divide and rule' strategies on the part of Directors General and to ensure that, faced by a united political leadership, '[t]he directors-general, all highly competent, have to obey their Commissioners and not the other way round' (Juncker 2014). As Juncker explained: 'They will work together in a spirit of collegiality and mutual dependence. I want to overcome silo-mentalities and introduce a new collaborative way of working in areas where Europe can really make a difference' (European Commission 2014b).

This new model was radical, first, because it appeared to depart from the convention that all Commissioners are equal. However, Juncker denied this was the case: 'In the new Commission, there are no first or second-class Commissioners – there are team leaders and team players'. Second, although groups of Commissioners were nothing new – Hallstein had used them in the first College, as had Prodi and Barroso in the more recent past – the idea of flexible, fluid and overlapping teams was an innovation. Third, it raised issues of command and accountability. Since Vice Presidents would not be responsible for particular services, the new structure appeared to break the link between the Commissioner and his or her department. Interviews conducted with senior officeholders in the Juncker Commission emphasise the top-down character of decision-making, which is even more personal and presidential than under

Barroso. Proposals are rigorously screened first by the Vice Presidents, then by First Vice President Timmermans, and the catalogue, to which items not on the Commission work programme were added, has been all but abolished. In reporting on its first 100 days, the Juncker Commission proudly plotted Commission actions in terms of the implementation of the President's 10 priorities.

Legislative activity

The crisis years brought further shifts in legislative activity by the Commission. Existing trends continued and partly accelerated. Overall, the output of the Commission fell during Barroso II, even compared to Barroso I. However, the reduction was only indirectly due to the crisis and more an effect of the mechanisms introduced to increase the Commission President's control over policy-making. The role played by the Secretariat General and procedures such as impact assessment and the advance notice required by SPP to allow entry to the Commission work programme were effective in the development of a more programmatic approach and to dampening policy activism.

The pattern of sectoral differentiation between 2010 and 2014, however, reflects the decision of Commission President Barroso to focus on crisis-related areas. Economic governance is front and centre. Excluding external relations, the plurality of preparatory acts (70) issued by the Commission in 2014 was in the field of 'Economic and Monetary Policy and Free Movement of Capital'. In the three years before the crisis, from 2007 to 2009, this category only ranked tenth in the list of the most dynamic internal policy fields. Much of this increase can be attributed to the Commission's strengthened role in the European Semester, in particular the reinforced surveillance of macroeconomic policy and the new standing of country-specific recommendations since 2012. But even before, the Commission proved quite active in this field, especially in administering balance-of-payments assistance to Hungary, Latvia and Romania. It comes as no surprise then that in the period from 2010 to 2014, 'Economic and Monetary policy and Free Movement of Capital' was the fourth most dynamic field of Commission activity, close behind 'General, Financial and Institutional Matters', 'Industrial Policy and Internal Market' and 'Environment, Consumers and Health Protection' (see Table 2). In comparison with the immediate pre-crisis years, it not only surpassed the declining output in agriculture and fisheries, but also the most upcoming field in the first decade of the new millennium, that is justice and home affairs.

Furthermore, these numbers only include the Commission's role in financial stability support in regard to supranational lending facilities - i.e. the balance-of-payments assistance and the European Financial Stabilisation Mechanism. The important roles it plays in the intergovernmental facilities (the European Financial Stability Facility and the European Stability

Table 2. Commission preparatory acts in ten most active internal policy fields, 2010–2014.

Policy field	2010	2011	2012	2013	2014	Total 2010-2014	Total 2005-2009	Change in per cent
General, Financial and Institutional Matters	126	100	51	73	55	405	384	+5
Environment, Consumers and Health Protection	90	88	75	83	43	379	538	–30
Industrial Policy and Internal Market	88	106	65	52	46	357	527	–32
Economic and Monetary Policy, Free Movement of Capital	77	41	71	94	70	353	181	+95
Area of Freedom, Security and Justice	61	77	52	66	54	310	323	–4
Freedom of Movement for Workers and Social Policy	64	58	50	39	42	253	239	+6
Fisheries	42	42	47	38	45	214	203	+5
Transport	29	40	37	52	49	207	298	–31
Agriculture	58	46	32	38	24	198	340	–42
Taxation	20	24	29	30	21	124	135	–8

Note: Percentages rounded. Categories according to directory code.
Source: EUR-Lex. Search query: preparatory acts, date of document, excludes corrigenda.

Mechanism) – analysing financing needs, negotiating memoranda of understanding and monitoring implementation – are not represented in this data. For the second Greek bailout alone the Commission produced, in liaison with the European Central Bank and the International Monetary Fund, 12 informal documents, including four 300-page reviews. The actual increase of Commission activity in economic governance is therefore even higher. And it was not stopped by the incoming President Juncker's strategy of legislative self-restraint. While this decision applied to all policy fields, economic governance was among the least affected. In fact, roughly half of the 23 new initiatives in the Commission work programme for 2015 were more or less explicitly economic policy issues (European Commission 2015).

This quantitative expansion is accompanied by qualitative assertiveness. Respective evidence can be found in different areas of economic governance. As regards general institutional development, Copeland and James (2014: 12) provide an account of how the outbreak of the crisis has enabled the Commission 'to secure agreement on an important series of reforms which established a new governance architecture of economic surveillance' when steering the discussion on the reform of the Europe 2020 strategy. As was shown earlier, the Commission gained significant competences when this governance architecture later materialised. It then quickly emerged that, in practice, the Commission followed a clear mission when using its discretion in rule application, showing significant lenience towards member states struggling to meet the new criteria. As Schmidt (2016) argues, the Commission proved 'flexible and accommodating, given that [the member states] were encouraged to find ways to ameliorate their balance sheets while avoiding pro-cyclical measures'. Belgium, France and

Italy were the states that most openly benefited from this approach. While the member states are ultimately decisive in these proceedings, it is obvious that the Commission recommendations effectively steer the decision-making phase. In 2015, the incoming Juncker Commission underlined its willingness to further pursue the applied flexibility by issuing a communication (COM/2015/012) on the application of the existing rules in the Stability and Growth Pact. It set out to re-interpret exceptions for states implementing structural reforms. This document and the preceding lenience clearly run counter the preferences of many member states, especially Germany, that preferred stricter adherence to the new rules. Indeed, this development represented 'one of the remarkable aspects of changes introduced in the economic governance of the EU in the wake of the economic and financial crisis' (Dehousse 2015: 2).

Further evidence for Commission assertiveness can be found in its exercise of coordination functions. Schmidt (2016) shows how the Commission slowly changed the direction of policy coordination in the Europe 2020 strategy from strictly economic – i.e. subordinating every policy field to fiscal consolidation – to a broader, increasingly social agenda. More broadly, the Commission has used the reformed architecture of the European Semester to bolster the effect of country-specific recommendations, which are in principle not binding, by symbolically coupling them with its monitoring results in macroeconomic surveillance. In managing the field of financial stability support, it also turned towards more social and growth-friendly policies. Again, the incoming Juncker Commission intensified these efforts. Juncker's efforts in brokering a deal for a third Greek bailout in the spring of 2015 incensed the German and like-minded governments. His ostensible sympathy for Greek demands led the German Finance Minister, Wolfgang Schäuble, to publicly reflect on curtailing the powers of the Commission by separating its political leadership from some administrative functions (Mussler 2015). These examples show that the Commission is both willing and able to influence EU policy-making in economic governance. To this end, it is no longer fully dependent on hard law proposals, but increasingly competent to pursue its agenda through the various management functions it has gathered during the crisis. By linking its outputs in the various monitoring and coordination procedures, it can provide quite some impetus in economic governance.

Conclusion: a new kind of engine?

Although the eurozone crisis severely tested the Commission, it was only the latest challenge for an institution that has been embattled since the Maastricht Treaty and arguably before. The Commission has been repeatedly challenged by empowered institutions - i.e. the European Council and the European Parliament - and since the 1990s has been constrained by a political climate that has been increasingly hostile to action on the part of 'Brussels'. Yet the crisis did not change the Commission. Rather, it acted as a catalyst for a process of transformation that was already underway. On taking office in 2004, Barroso argued for a more presidential Commission that would take a more measured, strategic and responsive approach to policy. The crisis strengthened his hand, leading him to limit Commission action to those areas of policy that required urgent action – economic and monetary policy, financial services, competition policy and trade.

Although the Commission is under pressure, it is not facing general decline. Rather, its approach and outlook has changed. A new more restrained model has emerged, with the expansionist and interventionist ways of the past firmly set aside. Policy entrepreneurship in the classic sense – i.e. formulating and pushing for hard law – may be increasingly difficult in the current EU, but the Commission can succeed if its efforts are strategic and focused. Moreover, its array of management duties ensures that it is able to exert influence on EU action in less intrusive ways. At the same time, the crisis accelerated the process of presidentialisation within the Commission, leaving the President with new powers and resources to take personal control over the policy agenda. In combination, increased management responsibilities and strong presidentialism allowed the Commission to be assertive in the crisis context. The lesson from the crisis years is therefore that, at least in economic governance, the Commission is still able to act as an engine of integration; yet it is an engine increasingly different from the traditional understanding.

It remains to be seen whether this transformation will take the same form and have the same effect in other areas. As the Commission's competences vary across policy areas, different sectoral modes of entrepreneurialism may emerge. Given the trend of presidentialisation, and along with it prioritisation, some policy areas will receive even less attention in the near future – a tendency evident in interviews with some outgoing Commissioners in 2014, who expressed disappointment that items from their portfolios rarely featured on the Commission's agenda. The Commission will not be able or willing to advance integration in all fields at all times or at the same pace.

Yet, although the Commission has been remodelled, it is not clear that it has been 'recast' 'in a new mould' (Bickerton *et al.* 2015b: 39) as suggested by the new intergovernmentalism. The argument that it is by now more circumspect about pursuing an ever closer union cannot be dismissed. Nor can the claim that supranational institutions act strategically depending on the level of support in the political environment. But the assertion that the Commission has abandoned any pretentions to leadership or any policy ambitions appears to be unwarranted. Not only has the Commission emerged from the eurozone crisis with expanded management functions, as Puetter (2015) has acknowledged, which it can and does use to provide less intrusive impetus for policy-making; classic Commission policy entrepreneurship also remains, as initiatives in the area of economic governance and beyond (financial services, energy, the environment and migration) make clear.

The changing institutional balance since the Lisbon Treaty and the eurozone crisis, in particular in the field of leadership, may go beyond the traditional dichotomy of integration theory. Crespy and Menz (2015: 765) have, for instance, argued that a 'new hybrid form of governance drawing from both political intergovernmentalism and technocratic supranationalism' has emerged in the wake of the latter. The role of the Commission appears to be a prime example. Far-reaching entrepreneurship has diminished to a large extent but many of the new technical duties in budgetary and macroeconomic monitoring have a strong political component, with leadership implications. The Commission has also shown historically that it can act as a 'purposeful opportunist' (Cram 1994: 214), employing various techniques beyond the proposal of hard law to eventually further integration. Now that it is more hierarchical in its internal organisation, the strategic use of different methods to realise this goal is even more feasible. The Commission's role as an engine of integration will therefore endure, but in a different guise.

Notes

1. The Community Method is mainly characterised by the sole right of the Commission to initiate legislation, the co-decision power between the Council and the European Parliament, and the use of qualified majority voting in the Council. It stands in contrast to intergovernmental decision-making processes where the Commission's and the European Parliament's roles are much weaker.
2. The surveys and interviews were conducted as part of two research projects. The first project ('The European Commission in Question', 2008–2009) comprised an online survey in the Commission (n = 1901) and interviews with Commissioners (n = 5), cabinet members (28) and managers (n = 119). It was led by Hussein Kassim (PI, principal investigator) and John Peterson, involved Michael W. Bauer, Sara Connolly, Renaud Dehousse and Liesbet Hooghe, and was funded by the UK Economic and Social Research Council (grant number RES-062-23-1188). For more information, see http://www.uea.ac.uk/psi/research/EUCIQ. The findings are presented in Kassim *et al.* 2013. The second project ('European Commission: Facing the Future', 2014) included an online survey (n = 5545) and interviews with Commissioners (n = 9), cabinet members (n = 25) and managers (n = 120), conducted between March and September 2014. The project was led by Kassim and Connolly, the research team included Michael W. Bauer, Renaud Dehousse and Andrew Thompson. For more information, see http://www.uea.ac.uk/political-social-international-studies/facingthefuture.
3. There are 'indirect' rights of initiative for the Parliament (Art. 225 TFEU), the Council (Art. 241 TFEU) and even the citizens via the European Citizens Initiative (Art. 11(4) TEU), who all can 'invite' the Commission to submit a legislative proposal. The Lisbon Treaty strengthened the Parliament's indirect right by codifying the obligation of the Commission to give reasons when not submitting a proposal following an invitation.

4. Some of these differences reflect cross-sectoral variation in the development of the acquis communautaire. In some areas, the regulatory regime was already mature. In others, EU legislative action was newer or had been less extensive.
5. There is some debate to what extent the Commission can generally be considered a winner of the euro crisis (Bauer and Becker 2016; da Conceição-Heldt 2016); however, there is agreement that in the field of macroeconomic and budgetary surveillance, this verdict does hold true.
6. Interview conducted by Hussein Kassim and Renaud Dehousse, Brussels, 6 May 2015.
7. Interview with cabinet member of Commission President Juncker, conducted by Hussein Kassim, 18 June 2015.
8. There are important exceptions. One example is Neil Kinnock, who led administrative reform in the Prodi Commission.
9. Interview with cabinet member of former Commission President Barroso, conducted by Sara Connolly and Hussein Kassim, 5 May 2015.

Acknowledgements

Without funding from the ESRC (RES-062-23-1188), Françoise Girard and David G. Knott, and the School of Politics, Philosophy, Language and Communication at UEA, the fieldwork on which this article draws could not have been conducted. Our greatest debt is to respondents in the European Commission who completed online surveys or participated in interviews or focus groups either as part of 'The European Commission in Question' or 'European Commission: Facing the Future'. We also thank the other members of both research teams and, finally, the participants of the two authors' workshops and the anonymous reviewers for their valuable comments.

Disclosure statement

No potential conflict of interest was reported by the authors.

References

Bauer, Michael W. (2006). 'Co-Managing Programme Implementation: Conceptualizing the European Commission's Role in Policy Execution', *Journal of European Public Policy*, 13:5, 717–35.

Bauer, Michael W., and Stefan Becker (2014). 'The Unexpected Winner of the Crisis: The European Commission's Strengthened Role in Economic Governance', *Journal of European Integration*, 36:3, 213–29.

Bauer, Michael W., and Stefan Becker (2016). 'Absolute Gains are Still Gains: Why the European Commission is a Winner of the Crisis, and Unexpectedly So. A Rejoinder to Eugénia Da Conceição-Heldt', *Journal of European Integration*, 38:1, 101–06.

Bickerton, Christopher J., Dermot Hodson, and Uwe Puetter (2015a). 'The New Intergovernmentalism: European Integration in the Post-Maastricht Era', *Journal of Common Market Studies*, 53:4, 703–22.

Bickerton, Christopher J., Dermot Hodson, and Uwe Puetter (2015b). 'The New Intergovernmentalism and the Study of European Integration', in Christopher J. Bickerton, Dermot Hodson and Uwe Puetter (eds.), *The New Intergovernmentalism: States and Supranational Actors in the Post-Maastricht Era*. Oxford: Oxford University Press, 1–48.

Campbell, John (1983). *Roy Jenkins: A Biography*. London: Weidenfeld and Nicolson.

Christiansen, Thomas (2016). 'After the Spitzenkandidaten: Fundemental Change in the EU's Political System?', *West European Politics*. doi:10.1080/01402382.2016.1184414

da Conceição-Heldt, Eugénia (2016). 'Why the European Commission is Not the "Unexpected Winner" of the Euro Crisis: A Comment on Bauer and Becker', *Journal of European Integration*, 38:1, 95–100.

Coombes, David (1970). *Politics and Bureaucracy in the European Community: A Portrait of the Commission of the E.E.C.* London: Allen and Unwin.

Copeland, Paul, and Scott James (2014). 'Policy Windows, Ambiguity and Commission Entrepreneurship: Explaining the Relaunch of the European Union's Economic Reform Agenda', *Journal of European Public Policy*, 21:1, 1–19.

Cram, Laura (1994). 'The European Commission as a Multi-Organization: Social Policy and IT Policy in the EU', *Journal of European Public Policy*, 1:2, 195–217.

Crespy, Amandine, and Georg Menz (2015). 'Commission Entrepreneurship and the Debasing of Social Europe before and after the Eurocrisis', *Journal of Common Market Studies*, 53:4, 753–68.
Dehousse, Renaud (2015). 'The New Supranationalism'. Paper presented at the 22nd Annual Conference of the Council for European Studies, Paris, 8–10 July 2015.
Dimitrakopoulos, Dionyssis G. (2008). 'Collective Leadership in Leaderless Europe: A Sceptical View', in Jack E.S. Hayward (ed.), *Leaderless Europe*. Oxford: Oxford University Press, 288–304.
European Commission (2013). *Standard Eurobarometer 80*. Brussels: European Commission.
European Commission (2014a). *40 Years Eurobarometer*. Brussels: European Commission.
European Commission (2014b). 'The Juncker Commission: A Strong and Experienced Team Standing for Change', Press Release, IP/14/984, 10 September 2014, available at http://europa.eu/rapid/press-release_IP-14-984_en.htm
European Commission (2015). *Communication from the Commission to the European Parliament, the Council and the European Economic and Social Committee and the Committee of the Regions. Commission Work Programme 2015*. COM/2014/0910 final.
Fabbrini, Sergio (2013). 'Intergovernmentalism and Its Limits. Assessing the European Union's Answer to the Euro Crisis', *Comparative Political Studies*, 46:9, 1003–29.
Haas, Ernst B. (1958). *The Uniting of Europe. Political, Social, and Economic Forces: 1950–1957*. Stanford: Stanford University Press.
Hodson, Dermot (2013). 'The Little Engine That Wouldn't: Supranational Entrepreneurship and the Barroso Commission', *Journal of European Integration*, 35:3, 301–14.
Hooghe, Liesbet, and Gary Marks (2008). 'A Postfunctionalist Theory of European Integration: From Permissive Consensus to Constraining Dissensus', *British Journal of Political Science*, 39:1, 1–23.
Hutter, Swen, & Grande, Edgar (2014). 'Politicizing Europe in the National Electoral Arena: A Comparative Analysis of Five West European Countries, 1970–2010', *Journal of Common Market Studies*, 52:5, 1002–18.
Juncker, Jean-Claude (2014). 'Time for Action – Statement in the European Parliament Plenary Session ahead of the Vote on the College', available at http://europa.eu/rapid/press-release_SPEECH-14-1525_en.htm (accessed 17 August 2015).
Kassim, Hussein (2008). '"Mission Impossible", but Mission Accomplished: The Kinnock Reforms and the European Commission', *Journal of European Public Policy*, 15:5, 648–68.
Kassim, Hussein (2012). 'The Presidents and Presidency of the European Commission', in Erik Jones, Anand Menon and Stephen Weatherill (eds.), *The Oxford Handbook of the European Union*. Oxford: Oxford University Press, 219–32.
Kassim, Hussein, and Anand Menon (2004). 'EU Member States and the Prodi Commission', in Dionyssis G. Dimitrakopoulos (ed.), *The Changing European Commission*. Manchester, NH: Manchester University Press, 89–104.
Kassim, H., and Anand Menon (2010). 'Bringing the Member States Back in: The Supranational Orthodoxy, Member State Resurgence and the Decline of the European Commission since the 1990s', paper presented at ECPR Fifth Pan-European Conference in Porto, Portugal, 23–26 June.
Kassim, Hussein, John Peterson, Michael W. Bauer, and Sara Connolly; Renaud Dehousse, Liesbet Hooghe, and Andrew Thompson (2013). *The European Commission of the Twenty-First Century*. Oxford: Oxford University Press.

Kassim, Hussein, Sara Connolly, Renaud Dehousse, Olivier Rozenberg, and Selma Bendjaballah (2016). 'Managing the House: The Presidency, Agenda Control and Policy Activism in the European Commission', *Journal of European Public Policy*. doi: 10.1080/13501763.2016.1154590

Kurpas, Sebastian, Caroline Grøn, and Piotr Maciej Kaczynski (2008). *The European Commission after Enlargement: Does More Add up to Less?* Brussels: Centre for European Policy Studies.

Laffan, Brigid (1997). 'From Policy Entrepreneur to Policy Manager: The Challenge Facing the European Commission', *Journal of European Public Policy*, 4:3, 422–38.

Laffan, Brigid (2016). 'Europe's Union in Crisis – Tested and Contested', *West European Politics*. doi:10.1080/01402382.2016.1186387

Lindberg, Leon N. (1965). 'Decision Making and Integration in the European Community', *International Organization*, 19:01, 56–80.

Metcalfe, Les (1992). 'After 1992: Can the Commission Manage Europe?', *Australian Journal of Public Administration*, 51:1, 117–30.

Moravcsik, Andrew (1999). 'A New Statecraft? Supranational Entrepreneurs and International Cooperation', *International Organization*, 53:2, 267–306.

Mussler, Werner (2015). 'Schäuble will EU-Kommission entmachten', *Frankfurter Allgemeine Zeitung*, http://www.faz.net/-gqu-866sz (accessed 17 August 2015).

Pelkmans, Jacques (2016). 'Why the Single Market Remains EU's Core Business', *West European Politics*. doi: 10.1080/01402382.2016.1186388

Peterson, John (2015). 'The Commission and the New Intergovernmentalism: Calm within the Storm?', in Christopher J. Bickerton, Dermot Hodson, and Uwe Puetter (eds.), *The New Intergovernmentalism*. Oxford: Oxford University Press, 185–207.

Puetter, Uwe (2012). 'Europe's Deliberative Intergovernmentalism: The Role of the Council and European Council in EU Economic Governance', *Journal of European Public Policy*, 19:2, 161–78.

Puetter, Uwe (2015). 'Deliberativer Intergouvernementalismus und institutioneller Wandel: die Europäische Union nach der Eurokrise', *Politische Vierteljahreszeitschrift*, 56:3, 406–29.

Schmidt, Vivien A. (2016). '"Reinterpreting the Rules 'by Stealth" in times of Crisis: The European Central Bank and the European Commission', *West European Politics*. doi:10.1080/01402382.2016.1186389

Reinterpreting the rules 'by stealth' in times of crisis: a discursive institutionalist analysis of the European Central Bank and the European Commission

Vivien A. Schmidt

ABSTRACT
This article examines the ways in which EU actors have engaged in incremental changes to the eurozone rules 'by stealth' – that is, by reinterpreting the rules and recalibrating the numbers without admitting it in their public discourse. Using the methodological framework of discursive institutionalism to focus on agents' ideas and discursive interactions in institutional context, the article links EU actors' reinterpretation of rules to their efforts to ensure greater legitimacy in terms of policy performance and governance processes as well as citizen politics. Using the normative theoretical framework of EU democratic systems theory, it analyses EU actors' considerations of legitimacy not only in terms of their policies' 'output' performance and citizens' political 'input' but also the 'throughput' quality of their governance processes. The article illustrates this by elaborating on the different pathways to legitimation of the European Central Bank and the European Commission.

At the onset of the eurozone crisis in 2010, EU actors responded after some delay with loan bailouts and bailout mechanisms in exchange for which they all agreed to reinforce the pre-existing rules and numerical targets of the Stability and Growth Pact (SGP) through legislative pacts (the 'six-pack' and the 'two-pack') and intergovernmental treaties and agreements (e.g. the European Stability Mechanism (ESM) and the 'Fiscal Compact').[1] In the absence of any deeper political integration that could provide greater democratic representation and control over an ever-expanding supranational governance, and in the face of major political divisions among EU actors over what to do and how, the EU ended up 'governing by the rules and ruling by the numbers' in the eurozone (Schmidt 2015). But as the crisis evolved from 2010 through 2014, and as EU actors were tested by continued poor economic performance and growing political volatility, they slowly began to reinterpret the rules and recalibrate the numbers 'by stealth' – that is, without admitting it in their communicative discourse to the public. Instead, they mainly continued to insist that they were sticking to the rules even as they incrementally altered them.

Not acknowledging up-front that the rules did not work meant that EU actors continued to operate under rules that were sub-optimal, and that constrained the range of possible solutions. Moreover, it left their actions open at any time to being contested as illegitimate. By the same token, however, not saying what they were doing gave EU actors the space necessary to reinterpret the rules incrementally – arguably until such a time as they could gain agreement to legitimate changing the rules more formally.

The challenge for EU actors, in short, has been how to get beyond the original rules to more workable ones in a context in which formal rule change has been difficult. This has not just been a question of how to get around the institutional constraints that make formally changing the rules very difficult (Scharpf 1999, 2012) or the political logics of divided member state perceptions of the crisis and diverging national economic interests (Schimmelfennig 2015). It has also been a question of how to build legitimacy for change in a context of institutional-legal constraints and politico-economic divisions. And for this, we also need to consider EU actors' legitimating ideas and discourse about their actions within the EU institutional context.

Explaining the legitimation of institutional change in terms of a disjunction between discourse and action demands a combination of methodological theory to explain institutional change and normative theory to define legitimacy. In what follows, I argue that although the main neo-institutionalist analytic frameworks used in the explanation of the eurozone crisis – rational choice and historical institutionalism – go a long way towards explaining the crisis response, discursive institutionalism provides a necessary complement. By focusing in on agents' cognitive and normative ideas about what to do and their discursive legitimation of what they did as they coordinated with one another and communicated to the public, discursive institutionalism helps explain the dynamics of change (and continuity) in the on-going crisis over time. Moreover, because discursive institutionalism sets any such action in an institutional context, it is able to use the other neo-institutionalist approaches as background information even as it helps to explain the (re)defining of interests and the (re)shaping of institutions (Schmidt 2008, 2012). Beyond this, by theorising about legitimacy in terms of EU systems concepts focused on the responsiveness of the 'input' politics, the effectiveness of the 'output' policies, and the quality of the 'throughput' processes (Scharpf 1999; Schmidt 2013), the article additionally offers an analysis of the constructivist logics of EU actors' ideational and discursive legitimation of their reinterpretation of the rules 'by stealth'.

To illustrate the discursive institutionalist dynamics of change, this article focuses on the cases of the European Central Bank (ECB) and the Commission.

The different pathways to legitimation of the ECB and the Commission can be explained not only by differences in their (rationalist and historical) institutional context, in which the ECB had much greater autonomy than the Commission, which was subject to an increasingly divided and politicised Council, but also in meaning and discursive context. The ECB benefited from a more open policy forum within which to develop new legitimating ideas through its coordinative discourse and to engage in a much more elaborate communicative discourse to the public than the Commission. While the ECB was able to hide its reinterpretation of the rules 'in plain view', through a discourse that claimed that everything it did was in keeping with its Charter, the Commission had to hide behind a discourse that claimed that it was rigidly following the rules, even as it interpreted them ever more flexibly.

The article begins with a discussion of the differences between rational choice, historical, and discursive institutionalist theories of institutional change, and how they apply to the eurozone crisis, followed by a sketch of the normative framework for the analysis of legitimacy, focused on EU systems theory. It then explores the legitimating ideas and discursive interactions of the ECB, followed by the Commission.

Theorising neo-institutional change (and continuity) in the crisis

Explanations of the eurozone crisis often tend to fit into one or another neo-institutionalist approach, including rational choice, historical, and discursive institutionalism. Rational choice institutionalist approaches tend to focus on the interest-based political and economic logics of EU member state actors in the crisis. Historical institutionalist approaches concentrate on the path dependencies of or incremental changes to formal rules and institutional regularities during the crisis. Discursive institutionalist approaches tend instead to look into EU agents' crisis-based ideas and discursive interactions as they reshape their institutions and redefine their interests.

In the eurozone crisis, rational choice institutionalist approaches tend to cast member state political leaders in the Council as the key actors in the crisis. They generally concentrate on member states' rationalist political calculations in interstate bargaining and the domestic political interests and/or economic motivations that inform member state positions.

The more political accounts focus on interstate hard bargaining and brinkmanship, often within a 'liberal intergovernmentalist' framework in which domestic politics determines member state bargaining positions with minimal winning coalitions (Moravcsik 1998; see also Jones *et al.* 2016). For example, the eurozone crisis response of 2010 to 2012 has been described as a game of chicken in which the strong preference to avoid the breakdown of the euro area was combined with efforts to shift the costs to the weaker euro members most in trouble (Schimmelfennig 2015). Similarly, the lopsided outcome of the

Greek crisis of 2015, during which the government achieved none of its stated goals, was attributed to the Greek government's nested games (Eurogroup and national constituency) and incomplete information (about Greece's bargaining room), confronted with the brinkmanship of the Eurogroup finance ministers, led by German Finance Minister Wolfgang Schäuble (Tsebelis 2016).

The more economic accounts additionally describe a structurally flawed euro that serves to benefit some member states and handicap others. This has created perverse incentive structures that helped to divide preferences while enabling Germany (with its Northern European coalitional allies) to impose its strategic preferences, aided by the decision rules (most notably the unanimity rule) that gave veto players extra clout while resulting in sub-optimal outcomes, in particular for Southern Europe (e.g. Scharpf 2012; see also Schimmelfennig 2014). Where EU supranational actors are considered at all, moreover, they are often cast as secondary players following member states' orders, motivated by self-interest, the push for bureaucratic power, or the cultivation of neo-functionalist spillover (see e.g. Niemann and Ioannou 2015: 209–12).

Historical institutionalist approaches are often seen to provide a corrective to the rational choice perspective. They embed events in a broader context traced over time and emphasise the endogeneity of institutions, because they set the rules and the boundaries within which individuals may choose their course of action, and point to the unanticipated consequences of decisions (Pierson 1996; Schimmelfennig 2015: 19–20). In the eurozone crisis, historical institutionalism emphasises the design of the pre-existing institutions, and uses the concept of path dependency to explain how the rules of the SGP were mainly reinforced through subsequent agreements such as the six-pack, the two-pack and the Fiscal Compact (Gocaj and Meunier 2013; Verdun 2015). That said, path dependence can be too general a tool, with a tendency to underplay the incremental changes through which old rules are reinterpreted, new policies layered onto the old, or old rules converted into new ones (Streeck and Thelen 2005). In the eurozone crisis, incrementalist historical institutionalism has been deployed to describe the layering of new elements onto existing rules or the creation of new institutions patterned on the old. Scholars have noted a 'redirection' of existing instruments, as in the case of the ECB's new supervisory responsibilities for banking union (Salines *et al.* 2012), the invention of new rules 'copied' from older institutions, as in the case of the European Financial Stability Facility (EFSF), and the 'replacement' of institutions, as with the substitution of the ESM for the EFSF (Verdun 2015: 226–8).

Historical and rational choice institutionalist approaches have also sometimes been combined to great effect to explain how successive (rational choice institutionalist) intergovernmental bargains have deepened European integration through processes of (historical institutionalist) incremental change. For example, the phenomenon of 'failing forward' has been used to illustrate the neo-functionalist (historical institutionalist) dynamic in which liberal intergovernmental bargaining led time and again to incomplete agreements that produced piecemeal, failed reforms which soon required new intergovernmental bargains that generated further European integration without solving the overall problem of the eurozone (Jones *et al.* 2016).

From a discursive institutionalist perspective, historical institutionalist approaches do very well in describing how the rules and institutions continue or change incrementally over time but not so well in explaining why. This is because they do little to elucidate how and why agents engage in layering, let alone inventing or reinterpreting the rules – other than to categorise them as change agents (as in Mahoney and Thelen 2009). In contrast, although rational choice approaches do deal with agents, theirs are rational actors with fixed preferences in stable institutions. From the discursive institutionalist point of view, although the resulting game-theoretic analyses may serve as useful depictions of strategic interests at any given point in time, they cannot deal with the complexity of real agents' changing ideas about their interests in incrementally developing institutions, as member state agents engage in a constant process of dialogue, deliberation, and contestation in their 'coordinative' discourses of policy construction and 'communicative' discourses of political legitimation (Schmidt 2008, 2012).

In other words, without denying the usefulness of the parsimony of rational choice approaches that attribute interests to actors, discursive institutionalism seeks to elucidate agents' own ideas about their interests across a much wider range than economic or political self-interest alone, while adding their value-based ideas. Thus, instead of attributing socioeconomic interests to 'rational' agents, discursive institutionalists elucidate real agents' competing ideas about interests and values that may be embedded in policy ideas and programmes that emerge from deep philosophies. For example, scholars attuned to the importance of ideas point to the very different stories about the causes of the eurozone crisis, with competing narratives about the problems resulting from government finances, household debt, lack of competitiveness, or a sudden-stop in market financing (Jones 2015). Alternatively, they show how EU actors' ideas about austerity are embedded in policy programmes that reflect deep philosophies (e.g. Blyth 2013), as in Germany's 'stability culture', with its view of debt as shameful and its belief in an ordo-liberal economic philosophy focused on monetary stability and rule by laws (e.g. Howarth and Rommerskirchen 2013). And they demonstrate that ideas may be so powerful as to go against (rationalist) material self-interests, as in the 'perverse logic' of Germany's ordo-liberal ideas and the problems these have caused for the eurozone and Germany's own economic interests (Matthijs 2016).

Moreover, rather than seeing the European Council solely as an arena of hard-bargaining liberal intergovernmentalism, scholars focused on discursive interactions instead cast the Council as a forum of 'deliberative intergovernmentalism' in which the member states seek to come to consensus-based agreements via processes of persuasion and deliberation (Bickerton *et al.* 2015; Puetter 2014: ch. 2). We could add that only by considering the interactive processes of contestation along with deliberation can we explain how and why incremental changes in the rules were agreed in the Council, as Germany conceded, over and over again, to things it had initially resisted, including new institutional instruments of euro governance such as Banking Union and new guidelines for euro governance such as growth beginning in 2012 and flexibility beginning in 2014 (Schmidt 2015). It is also mainly through agents' ideas and discursive interactions that we can explain how the ECB was able to persuade the more powerful members of the Council, and in particular Chancellor Merkel, to accept its many reinterpretations of its mandates, as well as to agree to Banking Union; or how the Commission was able to increase its discretionary powers while obscuring its increasingly flexible reinterpretations of the rules in the European Semester (Bauer and Becker 2014; Dehousse 2015).

In sum, the addition of discursive institutionalism to our neo-institutionalist tool-kit helps lend insight into how EU institutional actors have incrementally managed to overcome the stasis-reinforcing aspects of their institutional contexts. This is the case whether institutional context is understood in terms of the (rational institutionalist) logics of the EU's sub-optimal incentive structures and member states' divided preferences (Scharpf 1999; Schimmelfennig 2015) or the (historical institutionalist) constraints of the path dependencies stemming from change-resistant decision rules and the sunk costs of adaptation (Pierson 1996), even where incremental changes are instituted over time (Verdun 2015) and successive bargaining games deepen integration (Jones *et al.* 2016). EU actors have overcome stasis by developing and implementing cognitive and normative ideas for reinterpretation of rules in coordination with other policy actors and in communication with the public. Institutional context here therefore needs to be defined not only as the (historical) institutions and (incentive) structures within which agents find themselves but also as the 'meaning' context for their ideas as well as the discursive 'forums' in which actors articulate their ideas (Schmidt 2012; Toulmin 1958). As a result, different EU actors may follow different pathways not only because of their different institutional settings but also because of their different constructions of meaning and the different communities of interlocutors with which they engage.

Theorising legitimacy

Within this constructivist logic, it is important not only to consider agents' (re)construction of their interests over time but also how they manage to normatively legitimate their actions to one another as well as to the wider public. Most importantly, in particular in any crisis of politics and economics, real people do not just think strategically, they also think about what is legitimate and how they will legitimate their actions to others.

Although there are many different normative theoretical approaches to EU legitimacy (e.g. Beetham and Lord 1998; Bellamy and Weale 2015), this paper turns for definitions of legitimacy to the systems concepts often used in the EU studies literature. These include the 'output' effectiveness of EU policies, the EU's 'input' responsiveness to citizens' political concerns (Mair 2013; Scharpf 1999, 2012), and the 'throughput' quality of the EU's policy-making processes (Schmidt 2013). Throughput is judged by the efficacy of the decision-making processes, the accountability of those engaged in making the decisions (e.g. Harlow and Rawlings 2007), the transparency of the information (e.g. Héritier 2003), and the processes' inclusiveness and openness to consultation and deliberation with the interest groups of 'civil society' (e.g. Coen and Richardson 2009; Kröger 2008).

The first two such legitimising mechanisms are often seen to involve a trade-off, in which more *output* performance through effective policy outcomes can make up for less *input* responsiveness, or vice versa (Majone 1998; Scharpf 1999). There is no such trade-off for the third mechanism. Better quality throughput does not make up for either bad output or minimal input, whereas bad throughput – consisting of oppressive, incompetent, corrupt, or biased governance practices – can throw input and output into question by seeming to skew representative politics or taint policy solutions (Schmidt 2013).

Using these three mechanisms of legitimation to analyse EU actors' initial 'governing by rules and numbers' and their subsequent 'rules-reinterpretation by stealth' suggests particularly interesting ways of stylising our understanding of the eurozone crisis. Put succinctly, it could be said that initially EU actors assumed that reinforcing rules-based governance (throughput) would ensure good policy results (output) even in the absence of citizens' political involvement (input). But as EU actors themselves soon recognised, however good the quality of rules-enforcement (throughput), policy performance (output) did not improve as expected while political volatility (input) rose in response. Therefore EU actors subsequently began slowly to reinterpret the rules (throughput) in order to ensure better results (output) and to respond to the increasingly negative politics (input). But doing so 'by stealth' still skirts problems of legitimacy, in particular with regard to lack of (throughput) accountability and transparency.

In what follows, we look closely at the different pathways to ideational innovation and normative legitimation taken by the ECB and Commission. There can be no doubt that formal institutional context matters greatly for the pathways taken by these supranational actors – meaning not only the rules governing their institutional autonomy and bureaucratic discretion but also their perceptions of their relative power and strategic interests vis-à-vis other EU actors. But equally important are the ways in which supranational EU actors (re) conceived of their roles and responsibilities while seeking to build legitimacy for their changing ideas about what to do and how to do it.

The ECB: legitimising without admitting rules reinterpretation

As a non-majoritarian institution, the ECB has generally seen itself and been seen as legitimated by its output policy performance and, arguably, its throughput processes, with good output considered to act as a trade-off for any deficiencies in political input. All central banks in advanced industrialised countries have over the years become increasingly insulated from input politics for this reason, and the ECB is the example of this par excellence. It has autonomy without any significant or at least sufficient democratic control from the classic 'democratic circuit' of parliamentary oversight (Héritier and Lehmkuhl 2011: 138–9). But the ECB is therefore even more keenly aware of the need to succeed (and to be perceived as succeeding) in its (output) policy performance as well as to ensure the (throughput) quality of its governance processes. This also means managing the perceptions of a wide range of actors not only directly, through citizens' experience of monetary policy performance, but also indirectly, through the effectiveness of the ECB's communicative discourse and/or its coordination with the groups engaged with the ECB in building, implementing, or assessing the euro's effectiveness (see Scharpf 1999, and discussion in Jones 2009). With such discourse, the ECB sought to legitimate its own increasingly radical reinterpretations of the rules by carefully arguing that its actions remained within its remit as set out in its Charter.

From 'credibility' to 'stability' and 'never' lender of last resort to 'almost'

Initially, the ECB sought to manage perceptions with a communicative discourse focused on the quality of its throughput processes, by emphasising the importance of maintaining its 'credibility' through strict adherence to its (throughput) rules of inflation-fighting while resisting any (input) political pressures from member state leaders. This was the main mantra of ECB President Jean-Claude Trichet, whose discourse focused on 'credibility' as the financial crisis turned into a crisis of the real economy and then a sovereign debt crisis, and as his 'non-standard' bond-buying programme remained extremely modest (in particular compared to the FED or the Bank of England), as he insisted that the ECB was not and could never be a lender of last resort (LOLR) (Trichet 2009).

When first appointed head of the ECB, Trichet's successor Mario Draghi initially continued with the discourse of 'credibility' while denying that the ECB could be a LOLR (Draghi 2011). But by spring 2012, as the ECB engaged in more robust bond-buying programme, he switched his legitimising discourse to a focus on 'stability' (see Figure 1). In a randomised sampling of speeches and press conferences from Draghi's appointment in late 2011 through 2013 (see Figure 1), although 'credibility' appears in the first months of his mandate (winter 2011/spring 2012), it largely drops out of his vocabulary subsequently (with the exception of a small increase in spring 2013). In contrast, 'stability'

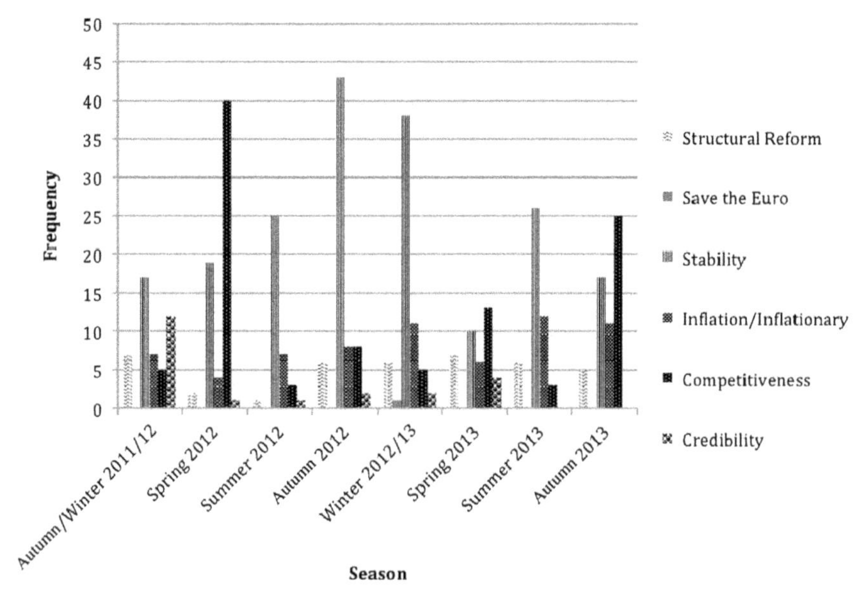

Figure 1. Word use frequency by ECB president Mario Draghi (autumn 2011 to autumn 2013). Source: Speeches and press conferences, randomised choice, 3–4 per season.

remains the most prevalent term from 2011 and 2013, rivalled only by the word 'competitiveness' – linked to the economic growth prospects of the eurozone – while 'inflation' was a low-level yet steady presence, as was 'structural reform' at an even lower level. 'Save the euro' appears only once, since Merkel's use of the phrase in 2010 to legitimate the Greek bailout to German citizens had panicked the markets. ECB Executive Board member Jörg Asmussen (2012) used that event explicitly in a speech to illustrate the problems of communicating to the people, with the markets listening (Schmidt 2014).

The shift from a discourse emphasising credibility to one focused on stability was not uncontroversial. The stability discourse was intended to help legitimate bond buying while overcoming the resistance of those who retained a narrow reading of the 'no-bailout clause'. Already with Trichet, the modest 'non-standard' bond-buying policies led to internal fights within the ECB, and even the resignation of the two German members of the ECB governing board, Axel Weber in April 2011, Jürgen Stark in September 2011, in protest (Matthijs 2016). This led to the appointment of the more moderate Jörg Asmussen to the governing board, which facilitated further discretionary policies by the ECB. But only once Draghi was appointed did the ECB move toward a more expansive view of its mandate. Even so, stability was not accepted as on a par with credibility until the euro itself was clearly in danger.

In using the word 'stability', the ECB sought to conjure up the 'stability paradigm' underlying EMU (Heipertz and Verdun 2010: 93), and thereby to reassure all that the ECB remained committed to its basic Charter philosophy. As ECB officials themselves explained, in a crisis the central bank 'must stand ready to back up the market while increasing its communication to explain that its primary objective has not changed in crisis mode' (Drudi *et al.* 2012: 890). Thus, at the same time they insisted that the Charter was correct to prohibit primary market purchases of public sector debt by central banks, to prevent the ECB and euro-system central banks from becoming lenders of last resort, they concluded that therefore 'it must be clear that an increased intermediation role for and outright purchases of the central bank are only justified on grounds of malfunctioning of the financial markets – and hence the exceptional measures are temporary in nature – to ensure price stability in the medium term' (Drudi *et al.* 2012: 894).

The switch from credibility to a stability discourse also opened up space for the ECB to engage in informal interactions with EU leaders in the Council. Unlike Trichet, Draghi sought to coordinate with Council leaders, including engaging in a concerted year-long 'charm offensive' to persuade Chancellor Merkel in particular that 'unorthodox' bond-buying programmes and banking union were essential. All the while, the bank was working to fashion policy packages acceptable (to Germany) and workable (for EMU) against Bundesbank opposition (Spiegel 2014). Draghi succeeded in getting around Bundesbank opposition largely via Merkel and after bypassing the objections of the German representative on the ECB board.

Importantly, however, while the ECB quickly switched its discourse from credibility to stability beginning in 2011, it continued to deny publicly that it would or could act as a LOLR despite slowly and incrementally layering on increasingly 'unorthodox' bond-buying policy that brought it closer to one (Buiter and Rahbari 2012). When Draghi was asked early in his term whether the bond buying was Europe's version of 'quantitative easing', his response was:

> Each jurisdiction has not only its own rules, but also its own vocabulary. [The bond-buying programmes] are certainly unprecedented. But the reliance on the banking channel falls squarely in our mandate, which is geared towards price stability in the medium term … We call them non-standard measures. (*Financial Times*, 19 December 2011)

Such measures did little to change the course of the crisis itself between 2010 and 2012, however, since the discourse of denial kept the markets worried and primed for panic and attack (Blyth 2013).

Only in July 2012, when Draghi pledged to do 'whatever it takes to preserve the euro', did the markets stop their massive attacks against Spanish and Italian sovereign debt, convinced that this constituted a pledge to act as LOLR (although the ECB never stated this – and qualified the statement by adding that it would do whatever it takes 'within our mandate'). The one significant difference from what central banks ordinarily do as LOLRs is that the ECB made its pledge conditional on the Italian and Spanish governments asking for it to purchase their debt and in exchange agreeing to a conditionality programme focused on austerity and structural reform. Conditionality made the programme more akin to an IMF-style lending programme, focused on dealing with insolvency, than a LOLR programme, focused on illiquidity (Mody 2015). Even German leaders largely accepted this shift in policy (Newman 2015), with the exception of the more orthodox Bundesbank, which supported the court case in the German Constitutional Court that opposed the ECB's right to institute OMT (Open Monetary Transactions).

Legitimising rules reinterpretation by hiding it in plain view

So how do we explain the ECB's remarkable reversals, in particular given the continual denials in the discourse? The answers require considering the policy programme and ideas on the one hand, the discursive interactions on the other. In terms of ideas, we could explain the ECB's slow, incremental shifts in bond buying as a search for solutions. The ECB's pre-crisis 'paradigm' on what to do in the event of a crisis did not cover all contingencies, and the ECB had to engage in a continual process of '*bricolage*' (see Carstensen 2011) in the context of emergency management via increasingly 'unorthodox' policies that were unimagined and arguably unimaginable prior to the crisis. These were the ad hoc responses of the ECB agents puzzling their way through a crisis rather than the result of 'wilful actors' seizing the moment (Braun 2013). Any reinterpretation of the rules was not easy because of very different ideas held initially by members of the ECB board between more pragmatic central bankers willing to take an increasingly more expansive interpretation of the rules and more orthodox ones insisting on following the rules as heretofore strictly defined.

In terms of discursive interactions, moreover, inside the ECB, member state representatives to the ECB governing board were engaged behind closed doors in processes of persuasion and contestation. Initially, the more orthodox bankers, mainly from Northern Europe, formed a blocking coalition around Germany, but this changed as more and more Northern European countries rallied around the ECB President. This left the Bundesbank increasingly on its own to espouse the most orthodox positions.

In terms of our normative theory of legitimacy, we could explain the standoff between the Bundesbank and the rest as a clash between the ECB and its increasing numbers of allies concerned about (output) policy results versus the Bundesbank's sticking to the (throughput) principles of accountability and its view that technical agents ought not to take decisions that are the domain of (input) politically legitimate political actors. This clash in views came out most clearly in the hearings of the German Constitutional Court. The ECB's executive board member Jörg Asmussen justified the unorthodox monetary policy measures as a (output) response to unusual circumstances, insisting that: 'We are in a situation of one size fits none, that is why we have extended these non-standard instruments'. Bundesbank President Weidmann instead vehemently opposed ECB intervention on the grounds that its (throughput) remit was to control inflation, and that only the politicians had the (input) legitimacy to deal with the rest (*Financial Times*, 12 June 2013).

Ideational entrepreneurship is an added factor in the explanation of the ECB's changing ideas and discourse over time. The switch in presidents of the ECB was of great significance, and needs to be added to the deliberative coordination of internal consensus among ECB bankers and the ECB's changing communicative discourse to the public. Trichet was the consummate civil servant whose career was focused on institution-building in financial and monetary affairs, and whose ideas about what to do remained conservative. Draghi was much more innovative, having had a more diverse background, beginning as an academic economist with stints in international institutions and private as well as public finance, in which he was often called in to reform institutions and innovate policies (Basham and Roland 2014). Draghi was also a bridge-builder. In the progressive reinterpretation of the rules to 'save the euro', not only did Draghi gain the trust and respect of fellow bankers, he also managed to develop sufficient rapport with Council leaders – and in particular Chancellor Merkel – to gain their trust and support as well. As such, Draghi could be seen as a highly successful 'policy entrepreneur' (Kingdon 2003) who was able not only to develop a new set of actionable ideas acceptable to the broader central banking community, but was also able to legitimate this to the satisfaction of political as well as technical actors in potential veto positions. The ECB itself, in fact, has been very successful as a policy entrepreneur overall. In banking union, for example, a dominant group in the ECB in 2012 took advantage of Council decision-makers' high uncertainty to help preferences converge around the idea of giving up national supervisory powers (de Rynck 2016; see also Dehousse 2015).

Thus, the ECB engaged in a constant process of reinterpretation of the rules to ensure better results. But however throughput legitimate the ECB's processes of reinterpretation may have been, questions related to the output legitimacy of the policies remain as regards their performance. Although the ECB remains the 'hero' of the crisis because it took action, one could nonetheless question its output performance. Most prominent among these is the question: did the ECB do enough soon enough? It took five years after the start of the euro crisis for its (throughput) reinterpretation of the rules to bring it the place where it began the kind of quantitative easing that the US has engaged in since 2008 – and only because deflation threatened.

The Commission: neither admitting nor legitimating reinterpretation of rules

During the crisis between 2010 and late 2014, the Commission incrementally also altered its interpretation of the rules without acknowledging it. But unlike the ECB, which has the autonomy to reinterpret its own rules, and chose constant communication to legitimate its reinterpretations by insisting that they remained true to the cardinal rules, the Commission had little independence of action, and therefore sought to hide its increasing flexibility with a discourse focused on austerity and structural reforms.

As befits a bureaucracy as opposed to an autonomous agency, the EU Commission depends for its legitimacy primarily on its carrying out of the (throughput) duties assigned it by the politically (input) legitimate bodies to which it must render accounts – the Council and increasingly over time the EP. With the onset of the eurozone crisis, however, the 'master' to which the Commission saw itself accountable was narrowed to the Council as a result of the massive increase in intergovernmental decision-making in this area and the sidelining of the EP (Fabbrini 2013). The Commission itself appeared to have lost much of its traditional power of initiative to the increasingly active European Council (Bickerton *et al.* 2015). That said, Council legislation focused on reinforcing the eurozone's 'governing by rules and numbers' – themselves mostly proposed by the Commission itself – further strengthened the Commission's role as enforcer in the European Semester. The Commission's own legislative proposals in fact vastly increased its powers of oversight as well as building in the discretionary authority that enabled it to reinterpret the rules – if only 'by stealth' (Dehousse 2015). But with such new powers, the Commission's legitimacy also became increasingly linked to the output performance of the policies it administered. As for input legitimacy, its (throughput) processes of oversight over national governments' budgets raised questions about whether this undermined the member states' own political input legitimacy.

From governing by rules and numbers to greater flexibility

Initially, the Commission was most concerned with the quality of its administration of the rules (throughput), and conceived of its autonomy rather narrowly, with a constant eye to possible Council response. As the crisis continued, however, in the absence of remedies the Commission was stuck with searching for solutions 'like the drunk who looks for his lost keys under the lamp post' because 'that is where the light is' (Mabbett and Schelkle 2014). As economic output performance deteriorated, the Commission made increasing numbers of exceptions and flexible adjustments for non-programme countries, in particular beginning in 2013. But it tried to avoid acknowledging this publicly not only because it lacked the independence of the ECB but also because it felt constant pressures from the member states in the Council either to make exceptions or to deny them. As a result, it maintained a harsh discourse focused on the necessity of austerity and structural reform so as to circumvent the political pressures from pro-austerity Council members.

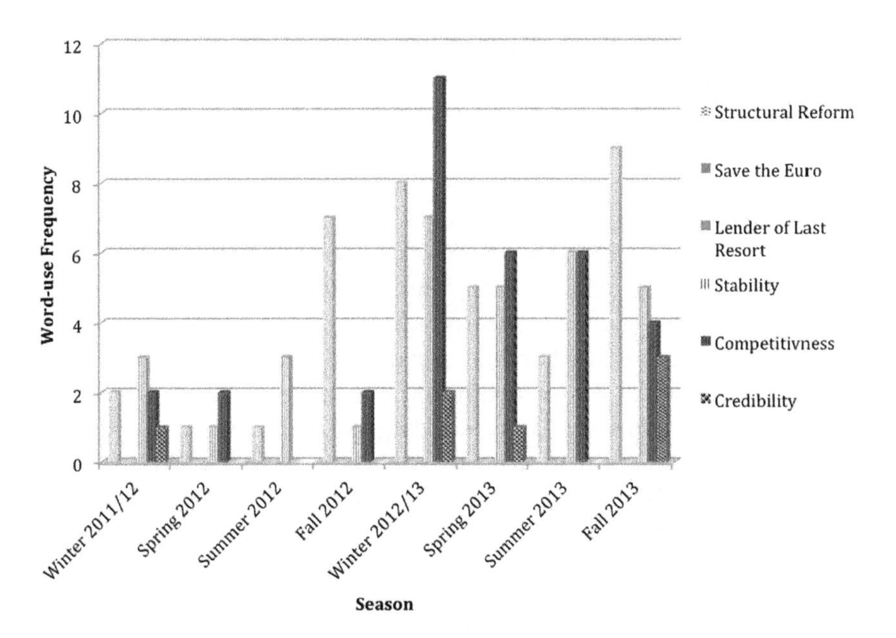

Figure 2. Word use frequency by Olli Rehn, EU vice president in charge of economic and monetary affairs and the Euro (autumn 2011 to autumn 2013).
Source: Speeches and remarks, randomised choice, 3–4 per season. *Note that the blank spaces left for 'save the Euro' and 'lender of last resort' indicate that no mention was made of these terms.

The Vice President of the Commission in charge of Economic and Monetary Affairs and the Euro, Olli Rehn, was the main public spokesperson for the Commission with regard to the European Semester between 2011 and 2014. His communicative discourse was all about fiscal consolidation and structural reform in order to bring down excessive deficits and address macroeconomic imbalances. Especially in the first few years, his speeches invariably referred to the need for consolidation along with structural reform. In terms of word use frequency between autumn 2011 and autumn 2013, Rehn's discourse was similar to that of ECB President Draghi, despite the differences in their responsibilities (see Figure 2). This was most apparent in the absence of considerations of inflation, lender of last resort, or even 'save the euro' in Rehn's public pronouncements. Moreover, although Rehn, like Draghi, repeatedly referred to the importance of stability, Rehn's discourse emphasised the 'stability culture' and/or the need for financial stability in the member states, not price stability.[2] Additionally, Rehn's focus on competitiveness was even more pronounced in his discourse than Draghi's, especially by late 2012 and into 2013. Competitiveness served as a justification for the push for structural reforms, which also appeared at an increasingly high level. Finally, interestingly enough, while Draghi largely dropped credibility as a reference point, Rehn continued to use it, but to different ends. It focused on the member states' regaining credibility by consolidating their finances,[3] or Europe regaining 'credibility on our road towards a stability union of both responsibility and solidarity', not on the institution's own credibility.[4]

Behind the discourse, credibility, and competitiveness were practices that were becoming incrementally more flexible in the application of the rules and calculation of the numbers. This is because the increasingly precise definition of rules and numerical targets, although limiting the Commission's room for manoeuvre, actually gave the Commission greater margin for flexibility. The six-pack regulations increased Commission discretion in evaluating a member state's fiscal position, since it was to take into account the 'range of relevant factors' when judging non-compliance, including mitigating or aggravating ones, along with 'exceptional circumstances' (Mabbett and Schelkle 2014: 12–13). Moreover, RQMV (Reverse Qualified Majority Voting) made it harder for the Council to reverse a Commission decision. This ensured the Commission a built-in discretion without any built-in input accountability, in particular with regard to the Macroeconomic Imbalance Procedure (MIP), where the Commission was essentially free to decide when to launch (or not) an MIP (Scharpf 2012). This was in contrast to the Excessive Deficit Procedure (EDP), where merely hitting a certain number would trigger the procedure.

But for both procedures, the actual calculations mattered, giving way to a 'politics of numbers' that raises questions about the 'accounting' end of flexibility (Mabbett and Schelkle 2014: 12–13) as well as the Commission's accountability. One such example was the change to calculating the deficit in terms of a 'primary' surplus (deficit minus interest payments). This enabled the Commission to allow countries that posted a primary surplus to delay rapid deficit reduction in order to propel growth, which is why France and Italy were given two-year delays to meet their targets, first in 2013 and again in 2015. In the case of Spain, moreover, the Commission ultimately agreed to delay deficit reduction by using a new calculation of the 'structural deficit' proposed by the Spanish government itself. But the Commission refused to generalise this calculation out of 'concern in some capitals' (read Germany) about the implications of using better estimates – which might ease up the pressures on programme countries (*Wall Street Journal*, 24 September 2013), thus raising questions about (throughput) fairness in the application of the rules.

The Commission's (throughput) flexibility came in for increasing criticism beginning in 2012, in particular from Northern European member states. Germany remained very much wedded to the 'stability culture' and ordo-liberal ideas (Howarth and Rommerskirchen 2013; Matthijs 2016), as did other Northern European countries like Finland and the Netherlands. Their increasing opposition to flexibility came to a head in 2014, with Germany and Finland making a frontal attack on the Commission in an eight-page memo in which they claimed that the Commission used 'a somewhat arbitrary approach' in granting budget flexibility, and went so far as to suggest that 'a separate pair of eyes' was needed to ensure that the rules were properly applied (*Financial Times*, 28 February 2014). In contrast, Southern European member states continued to complain that the Commission was too rigorous, and that without greater leeway in the application of the rules they were concerned that their economies' performance would deteriorate along with their legitimacy, as the voters turned increasingly to populist parties at the political extremes. Moreover, by 2014 Italian Prime Minister Renzi, supported by French President Hollande, had been pushing the Council – and Merkel in particular – to agree to greater flexibility in view of the need for growth (Schmidt 2015). Finally, lack of (throughput) inclusiveness in the internal Commission evaluation process was also an issue, in particular at first, since the Commission had initially shut out other Directorates-General which could have provided more nuanced information to moderate judgements about the numbers as well as to address the effects of any cuts (Zeitlin and Vanhercke 2014).

But whatever the criticisms, the Commission consistently claimed to be applying the rules and running the numbers as its mandate demanded, despite the fact that it reinterpreted the rules increasingly flexibly over time. And by 2013, although the Commission tacitly acknowledged the failure of fiscal consolidation policies by agreeing to ease the policy on rapid deficit reduction, Commission spokespeople stuck to a discourse that claimed that it was prior success in austerity measures, not failure, which had allowed for a more flexible policy. Rehn claimed that things were getting slightly better only because the crisis response offered 'a policy mix where building a stability culture and pursuing structural reforms supportive of growth and jobs go hand in hand' (Rehn 2013). In response to the Northern Europeans in particular, moreover, the Commission insisted that the increasing complexity of the rules constituted a 'methodological refinement', and was 'no change in policy, only a change in circumstances' since 'we now have more room for manoeuver' because cutting deficits was no longer such an urgent priority (*New York Times*, 17 May 2013).

Legitimising reinterpretation of rules by hiding behind a discourse of denial

While the Commission's communicative discourse remained largely the same across time, and outside analysts saw the Commission as deaf to the economic and social impact of numbers-targeting rules, the actual internal coordinative bureaucratic discourse, as contained in official reports, including the Annual Growth Surveys (AGSs) and the Country Specific Recommendations (CSRs) became incrementally more inclusive of such concerns. This resulted not only from Commission responsiveness to Council admonitions as output performance deteriorated but also to an internal opening by DG ECFIN to other

DGs as well as to the member states in the context of the sectoral advisory committees on employment and social policy.

The initial experiences confirmed critics' worst fears regarding a 'one size fits all' approach in the European Semester that subordinated social cohesion goals to fiscal consolidation and welfare retrenchment. This was clear in the first AGS and CSRs in the 2011 exercise (Pochet 2010; see also Zeitlin and Vanhercke 2014: 12–14). The AGSs' first priority was 'to set budgetary policies on a sound footing through rigorous fiscal consolidation'; the second priority was to engage in 'rapid reduction in unemployment through labour market reforms' focused on wage devaluation; and only the third proposed 'growth enhancing measures', while there was no mention of social concerns such as the increase in poverty (Annual Growth Survey (AGS) 2011 – COM 2011, 11 final, 12 January 2010: 9). Subsequent exercises of the European Semester were less narrowly targeted, however, at least on paper (see Zeitlin in this volume). But because fiscal consolidation remained the first priority of the AGS through 2014, changes in the content of AGS recommendations in the second and third priorities toward more social and employment friendly policies had little impact. Governments cut first, and then found that there was nothing left for poverty alleviation or employment promotion (Alcidi *et al.* 2014).

Only with a new Commission, in January 2015, have the practices and the discourse seemed to be coming into greater alignment. The Juncker Commission began presenting structural reform as a *quid quo pro* for greater flexibility through slower deficit reduction. It also pledged to do more to alleviate the social costs of the crisis, as well as to promote growth through an investment fund. And the Commission's AGS of 2015 for the first time put fiscal consolidation – now renamed 'fiscal responsibility' (defined as 'growth-friendly fiscal consolidation') – in third place, following investment for growth in first place, and structural reform in second place – now with a much wider set of recommendations, instead of the narrow focus on labour market flexibility of the AGS of 2011 (AGS COM (2014) 902 final, 28 November). As Commission President Jean-Claude Juncker declared in his first State of the Union speech to the EP on 9 September 2015: 'You cannot run a single currency on the basis of rules and statistics alone. It needs constant political assessment, as the basis of new economic, fiscal and social policy choices'. The Commission's first step in getting beyond the contradictions between its discourse and its actions was to publish a set of rules on flexibility in January 2015 – only to get push-back from the ECB and the Council.

Conclusion

Increasingly over the course of the eurozone crisis between 2010 and 2015, both the ECB and the Commission sought to improve policy performance (output) by reinterpreting the rules by which they governed (throughput) more and more extensively. But they did this very differently.

The ECB had significant autonomy to reinterpret the rules set out in its Charter so long as it could build a sense of agreement about what to do in its coordinative discourse of policy construction. In addition, the ECB developed an elaborate communicative discourse to hide its reinterpretations of the rules 'in plain view', by seeking to persuade its interlocutors and the general public that its policies remained within the mandate set out by its Charter, even as it reinterpreted that mandate more and more broadly. As such, the ECB moved from a discourse of 'credibility' to one of 'stability' and from a discourse that pledged that it would 'never' be a lender of last resort like normal central banks to almost becoming one, while passing over this in silence.

The Commission had much less margin for manoeuvre than the ECB since the rules it devised and administered were decided by the Council (with the EP in certain instances) and pushed by the ECB. The Commission's lack of autonomy meant that although it also sought to build legitimacy with other EU actors for rules reinterpretation, the Commission had a rather thin communicative discourse through which it generally insisted that it was applying the rules with great vigour, via harsh austerity and structural reform, even as it actually applied the rules with increasing flexibility.

Notes

1. Many of the ideas discussed herein were developed during a part-time Research Fellowship (June 2014–June 2015) awarded by European Commission, Directorate General of Economic and Financial Affairs (DG ECFIN) to consult and produce a paper on 'Political Economy of EMU: Rebuilding Trust and Support for Economic Integration'. For the report, see DG ECFIN Economic Discussion Papers 15 (September 2015): http://ec.europa.eu/economy_finance/publications/eedp/dp015_en.htm.
2. See e.g. Rehn's speech at the European American Press Club, Paris, 1 October 2013; Debate in the European Parliament, Strasbourg, 13 June 2012; Speech at the European Economic and Social Committee public hearing/Brussels, 19 February 2013.
3. See e.g. Rehn's speech on the adoption by the Italian government of extraordinary fiscal and economic measures on 4 December 2011; at the Conference on the European Semester/Warsaw, 8 March 2013; at the European American Press Club, Paris, 1 October 2013; and his Press Conference in Strasbourg, 14 February 2012.
4. Speech at the EPC Policy Breakfast in Brussels, 11 January 2013.

Disclosure statement

No potential conflict of interest was reported by the author.

References

Alcidi, Cinzia, Alessandro Giovannini, and Sonia Piedrafita (2014). *Enhancing the Legitimacy of EMU Governance*, CEPS Special Report No. 98. Brussels (December).

Asmussen, Jörg (2012). 'Building Trust in a World of Unknown Unknowns: Central Bank Communication between Markets and Politics in the Crisis', Speech at the European Communication Summit 2012, Brussels, 6 July.

Basham, James and Roland, Aanor (2014). 'Policy-making of the European Central Bank during the Crisis: Do Personalities Matter?', Institute for International Political Economy Berlin. Working paper no. 38/2014.

Bauer, Michael, and Stephan Becker (2014). 'The Unexpected Winner of the Crisis: The European Commission's Strengthened Role in Economic Governance', *Journal of European Integration*, 36:3, 213–29.

Beetham, David, and Christopher Lord (1998). *Legitimacy and the European Union*. London: Longman.

Bellamy, Richard, and Albert Weale (2015). 'Political Legitimacy and European Monetary Union', *Journal of European Public Policy*, 22:2, 257–74.

Bickerton, Christopher J., Dermot Hodson, and Uwe Puetter (2015). 'The New Intergovernmentalism and the Study of European Integration', in J. Bickerton, Dermot Christopher Hodson, and Uwe Puetter (eds.), *States and Supranational Actors in the Post-Maastricht Era*. Oxford: Oxford University Press, 1–50.

Blyth, Mark (2013). *Austerity: The History of a Dangerous Idea*. Oxford: Oxford University Press.

Braun, Benjamin (2013). 'Preparedness, Crisis Management and Policy Change: The Euro Area at the Critical Juncture of 2008–2013', *British Journal of Political and International Relations*, 17:3, 419–41.

Buiter, Willem, and Ebrahim Rahbari (2012). 'The European Central Bank as Lender of Last Resort for Sovereigns in the Eurozone', *Journal of Common Market Studies, Annual Review*, 50, 6–35.

Carstensen, Martin B. (2011). 'Paradigm Man vs. the Bricoleur: An Alternative Vision of Agency in Ideational Change', *European Political Science Review*, 3:1, 147–67.

Coen, David, and Jeremy Richardson (2009). *Lobbying in the European Union: Institutions, Actors, and Issues*. Oxford: Oxford University Press.

Dehousse, Renaud (2015). 'The New Supranationalism'. Paper prepared for presentation at the Council for European Studies Annual Meetings (Paris, July 8-10).

De Rynck, Stefaan (2016). 'Banking on a Union: The Politics of Changing Eurozone Banking Supervision', *Journal of European Public Policy*, 23:1, 119–35.

Draghi, Mario (2011) Press conference, Nov. 3, available at http://www.ecb.int/press/pressconf/2011/html/is111103.en.htm.

Drudi, Francesco, Alain Durré, and Francesco Paolo Mogelli (2012). 'The Interplay of Economic Reforms and Monetary Policy: The Case of the Eurozone', *Journal of Common Market Studies*, 50:6, 881–98.

Fabbrini, Sergio (2013). 'Intergovernmentalism and its Limits', *Comparative Political Studies*, 46:9, 1003–29.

Gocaj, Ledina, and Sophie Meunier (2013). 'Time Will Tell: The EFSF, the ESM, and the Euro Crisis', *Journal of European Integration*, 35:3, 239–53.

Harlow, Carol, and Richard Rawlings (2007). 'Promoting Accountability in Multi-Level Governance', *European Law Journal*, 13:4, 542–62.

Heipertz, Martin, and Amy Verdun (2010). *Ruling Europe: The Politics of the Stability and Growth Pact*. New York, NY: Cambridge University Press.

Héritier, Adrienne (2003). 'Composite Democracy in Europe. The Role of Transparency and Access to Information', *Journal of European Public Policy*, 10:5, 814–33.

Héritier, Adrienne, and Dirk Lehmkuhl (2011). 'New Modes of Governance and Democratic Accountability', *Government and Opposition*, 46:01, 126–44.

Howarth, David, and Charlotte Rommerskirchen (2013). 'A Panacea for all Times? The German Stability Culture as Strategic Political Resource', *West European Politics*, 36:4, 750–70.

Jones, Erik (2009). 'Output Legitimacy and the Global Financial Crisis: Perceptions Matter', *Journal of Common Market Studies*, 47:5, 1085–1105.

Jones, Erik (2015). 'Getting the Story Right: How You Should Choose between Different Interpretations of the European Crisis (and Why You Should Care)', *Journal of European Integration*, 37:7, 817–32.

Jones, Erik, Daniel Kelemen, and Sophie Meunier (2016). 'Failing Forward? The Euro Crisis and the Incomplete Nature of European Integration', *Comparative Political Studies*, 49:7, 1010–34.

Kingdon, John (2003). *Agenda's, Alternatives, and Public Policies*, 2nd ed. New York, NY: Pearson.

Kröger, Sandra (2008). 'Nothing but Consultation: The Place of Organized Civil Society in EU Policy-making across Policies', *European Governance Papers (EUROGOV)* No. C-08-03, available at http://connex-network.org/eurogov/pdf/egp-connex-C-08-08.pdf.

Mabbett, Debra and Waltraud Schelkle (2014). 'Searching under the Lamp-Post: The Evolution of Fiscal Surveillance', LEQS Paper No. 75/2014 (May).

Mahoney, James, and Kathleen Thelen (2009). *Explaining Institutional Change: Ambiguity, Agency, and Power*. Cambridge: Cambridge University Press.

Mair, Peter (2013). *Ruling the Void: The Hollowing of Western Democracy*. London: Verso.

Majone, Giandomenico (1998). 'Europe's Democratic Deficit', *European Law Journal*, 4:1, 5–28.

Matthijs, Matthias (2016). 'Powerful Rules Governing the Euro: The Perverse Logic of German Ideas', *Journal of European Public Policy*, 23:3, 375–91.

Mody, Ashoka (2015). 'Living Dangerously without a Fiscal Union', Bruegel Working Paper, available at http://www.bruegel.org/download/parent/875-living-dangerously-without-a-fiscal-union/file/1788-living-dangerously-without-a-fiscal-union/ (accessed 3 March 2015).

Moravcsik, Andrew (1998). *The Choice for Europe*. Ithaca, NY: Cornell University Press.

Newman, Abe (2015). 'The Reluctant Leader: Germany's Euro Experience and the Long Shadow of Reunification', in Matthias Matthijs and Mark Blyth (eds.), *The Future of the Euro*. New York, NY: Oxford University Press, 117–35.

Niemann, Arne, and Demosthenes Ioannou (2015). 'European Economic Integration in Times of Crisis: A Case of Neofunctionalism?', *Journal of European Public Policy*, 22:2, 196–218.
Pierson, Paul (1996). 'The Path to European Integration: A Historical Institutionalist Analysis', *Comparative Political Studies*, 29, 123–63.
Pochet, Philippe (2010). 'What's wrong with EU2020?', *European Trade Union Institute Policy Brief, European Social Policy*, 2, 1–7.
Puetter, Uwe (2014). *The European Council and the Council: New Intergovernmentalism and Institutional Change*. Oxford: Oxford University Press.
Rehn, Olli (2013). *Recovery is Within Reach*, available at http://blogs.ec.europa.eu/rehn/recovery-is-within-reach/.
Salines, Marion, Gabriel Glöckler, and Zbigniew Truchlewski (2012). 'Existential Crisis, Incremental Response: The Eurozone's Dual Institutional Evolution 2007-2011', *Journal of European Public Policy*, 19:5, 665–81.
Scharpf, Fritz W. (1999). *Governing in Europe*. Oxford: Oxford University Press.
Scharpf, Fritz W. (2012). 'Monetary Union, Fiscal Crisis and the Pre-emption of Democracy', *Zeitschrift für Staats- und Europawissenschaften*, 9:2, 163–98.
Schimmelfenig, Frank (2014). 'European Integration in the Euro Crisis: The Limits of Postfunctionalism', *Journal of European Integration*, 36:3, 321–37.
Schimmelfennig, Frank (2015).'Liberal Intergovernmentalism and the Euro Area Crisis', *Journal of European Public Policy*, 22:2, 177–95.
Schmidt, Vivien A. (2008). 'Discursive Institutionalism: The Explanatory Power of Ideas and Discourse', *Annual Review of Political Science*, 11, 303–26.
Schmidt, Vivien A. (2012). 'Discursive Institutionalism: Scope, Dynamics, and Philosophical Underpinnings', in Frank Fischer, and Herbert Gottweis (eds.), *The Argumentative Turn Revised: Public Policy as Communicative Practice*. Durham, NC: Duke University Press, 85–113.
Schmidt, Vivien A. (2013). 'Democracy and Legitimacy in the European Union Revisited: Input, Output and 'Throughput', *Political Studies*, 61:1, 2–22.
Schmidt, Vivien A. (2014). 'Speaking to the Markets or to the People? A Discursive Institutionalist Analysis of EU Leaders' Discourse during the Eurozone Crisis', *British Journal of Politics and International Relations*, 16:1, 188–209.
Schmidt, Vivien A. (2015). 'Forgotten Democratic Legitimacy: 'Governing by the Rules' and 'Ruling by the Numbers', in Matthias Matthijs, and Mark Blyth (eds.), *The Future of the Euro*. New York, NY: Oxford University Press, 90–116.
Spiegel, Peter (2014). 'If the Euro Falls, Europe Falls', *Financial Times*, (May 15).
Streeck, Wolfgang, and Kathleen Thelen (2005). *Beyond Continuity: Institutional Change in Advanced Political Economies*. Oxford: Oxford University Press.
Toulmin, Stephen (1958). *The Uses of Argument*. Cambridge: Cambridge University Press.
Trichet, Jean- Claude (2009). 'Introductory Comments with Q and A', European Central Bank, Press Conference, (May 7), available at http://www.ecb.europa.eu/press/pressconf/2009/html/is090507.en.html)
Tsebelis, George (2016). 'Lessons from the Greek Crisis', *Journal of European Public Policy*, 23:1, 25–41.
Verdun, Amy (2015). 'A Historical Institutionalist Explanation of the EU's responses to the Euro Area Financial Crisis', *Journal of European Public Policy*, 22:2, 219–37.
Zeitlin, Jonathan, and Bart Vanhercke (2014). 'Socializing the European Semester? Economic Governance and Social Policy Coordination in Europe 2020', Draft Report prepared for the Swedish Institute of European Studies (SIEPS).

Europe's crises and the EU's 'big three'

Ulrich Krotz and Richard Maher

ABSTRACT
This article examines the impact and significance of the Crimea–Ukraine–Russia and the eurozone crises on relations among and between the EU's three biggest member states – Britain, France and Germany – as well as their individual influence and roles within the EU. The Ukraine and eurozone crises have revealed and intensified three longer-term developments in contemporary European politics: Germany's rise as the EU's most powerful member state and its role as Europe's indispensable policy broker; the resilience and centrality of Franco-German bilateralism, despite the growing power imbalance separating the two; and Britain's diminished and diminishing role in EU affairs. To put the current period of turmoil in perspective, this article also aims to contribute to a better understanding of the operating logic of crisis, continuity and change in the relations of the EU's big three member states.

The European Union today faces a set of crises that threaten its historic achievements of the past six decades. Russia's annexation of Crimea and de facto invasion of eastern Ukraine represent direct challenges to the post-Cold War European security order and the principles that have defined it, including territorial integrity and the inviolability of national borders. A revanchist and revisionist Russia complicates European security affairs in ways many Europeans hoped and expected had disappeared with the end of the Cold War. The debt and banking crisis in the eurozone has exposed serious flaws in the design and implementation of monetary union and the single currency. The euro was intended to unite Europeans and EU member states economically and politically. Instead, it has driven them further apart and has become a growing source of tension and division. While independent of each other, these two predicaments pose deep and fundamental questions about the nature, shape and future of the European project and of European affairs more broadly.

While various studies have analysed the implications of these two crises for the EU's polity and its policies, this article directly addresses the impact and significance of the Ukraine and eurozone crises on relations among and between the EU's three biggest member states – Britain, France and

Germany – as well as their individual influence and roles within the EU. As the member states with the deepest reserves of power and influence, these three historically have had the greatest ability to shape outcomes and find solutions to common EU problems. When some combination of the trio leads, other member states often fall into line, whereas when they do not – or when they cannot agree on how to lead – paralysis and gridlock often result. Whether the EU emerges from these crises as a stronger and better functioning polity, therefore, or as a weakened and hobbled giant, will depend in large part on the choices, actions and policies of the EU's big three member states.[1]

Relations between the big three comprise various formulations, including one trilateral relationship (Britain-France-Germany) and three bilateral ones (Britain-France, France-Germany and Britain-Germany) – as well as the ebb and flow of national policies, roles and strategies. A trilateral 'concert of powers' or 'directorate' has never emerged within the EU. Much more important for the shaping of European affairs and EU politics and policies have been the various bilateral relationships. In addition to frequently being central in security and defence initiatives, the Anglo-French partnership has at times aimed to serve as an informal hedge or balance against German power and influence within the EU.[2] While Anglo-German bilateralism has never been central to the politics of European integration or to EU affairs more generally, Britain and Germany are often reliable allies in promoting free trade and market-oriented economic policies within the EU, and serve as a counterweight to the statist initiatives often preferred by France and other member states (Parker and Peel 2012).[3]

The Franco-German partnership has played by far the deepest and most fateful role of the three bilateral relationships in shaping the scope, depth and pace of European integration.[4] Franco-German reconciliation – the ability to overcome centuries of rivalry, war and mistrust to build a constructive and functioning bilateral relationship – has been the very core, and a sine qua non, of the European project. While differences and disagreements have always existed between Paris and Bonn/Berlin, the Franco-German partnership has become deeply institutionalised, emerging as an integral part of both the political and public life in both countries and generating its own type of bilateral order.[5]

To evaluate the Ukraine and eurozone crises' impact on the roles, relations and influence of the EU's big three member states, this article addresses three main questions: What is the nature and character of these crises' impact on their relations, and particularly on how power and authority is distributed among them? Are we witnessing a painful and lasting rupture in their relations, a revitalisation of their commitment to Europe and to their common fate, or to a settled arrangement that lies somewhere between these two extremes? And finally, why and how do the answers to these two questions matter for European politics and EU affairs?

This article argues that the Ukraine and eurozone crises have revealed and intensified three longer-term developments in European politics today. The crises have affirmed and hastened Germany's rise as the EU's most powerful member state and its role as Europe's indispensable policy broker; shown the resilience and centrality of Franco-German bilateralism, despite the growing power imbalance separating the two; and displayed Britain's diminished and diminishing role in EU affairs. This article does not aim to provide an exhaustive analysis or review of these two crises or their long-term consequences. Instead, it seeks to clarify and evaluate the three developments listed above and their implications for European politics.

This article also shows how the Ukraine and eurozone crises, which are different in many obvious and important respects – the one primarily an issue of regional security and the other primarily an issue of political economy and monetary affairs – and which are usually considered separately (except, perhaps, as two sources of stress and tension on European politics and decision-making today), do in fact exhibit several distinct and surprising underlying similarities, most notably revealing the same three broad trends in European politics today listed above.

In addition to analysing the impact and significance of the Ukraine and eurozone conflicts on the EU's big three member states, we also hope to better understand the operating logic of crisis, continuity and change in their relations. Doing so will not only help to put the current period of turmoil in perspective, but will also allow us to fill a gap in our understanding of the operation of the EU political system. Even after six years of turbulence, concepts such as crisis, continuity and change remain incompletely understood by scholars of EU politics.

This article proceeds as follows. The first section introduces an analytical framework to study continuity and change within the EU political system, and the broader implications for EU affairs that they entail. The next two sections analyse in turn the Ukraine and eurozone crises and how they have affected the distribution of power and authority among the EU's big three member states and their individual political roles and orientations. The conclusion reflects on this article's main findings and the implications for and study of European and EU politics.

Crisis, continuity and change in big three relations

From their beginnings, the Ukraine and eurozone crises have generated various disagreements and disputes over policy and strategy among British, French and German policy-makers, from the scope and severity of Russian sanctions, to the proper way to stabilise and reform the eurozone. Quarrels and squabbles among the three have existed since the beginning of the European integration process, of course, and have notably included de Gaulle's veto of Britain's membership application to the European Economic Community (EEC), the fear and anxiety Germany's post-Cold War unification instilled in London and Paris, and

Britain's controversial opt-out of the Franco-German plan for monetary union. Ultimately new bargains, new rules and new institutions resolved these and other periods of crisis, and integration either consolidated or moved forward.[6]

Scholars, policy-makers and pundits today reflect on whether the EU's big three member states will be able to overcome the current period of crisis and avoid a fundamental rupture in their relations – or if the twin shocks of Russia's undeclared war against Ukraine and the protracted eurozone turmoil might slowly pull the EU apart (Soros 2014). The Ukraine and eurozone crises have also prompted scholars to think more deeply about the management and resolution of political conflict within the EU, institutional and political cohesion in periods of crisis, and the dynamics of continuity and change in member state relations.[7]

Crises are important historical junctures – 'extraordinary moment[s] when the existence and viability of [a] political order are called into question' (Ikenberry 2008: 12).[8] Within a political order like the EU, crises lead to one of three possible outcomes: breakdown, transformation or adaptation. *Breakdown* involves the disappearance of the old system. Fundamental disagreements arise over the political order's basic underlying bargains, norms and principles. The old order does not reconstitute itself. New institutions, rules and structures do not replace the old ones. Instead, disorder replaces order.

At the extreme, balance of power politics and strategic competition may return when the old order falls apart. Few observers seriously imagine that this could be the fate of Britain, France and Germany today, even if the bonds of political or economic integration further weaken or unravel – whether through a British exit from the EU, growing tension over economic policy in the eurozone, or some other, unanticipated development.[9] The form breakdown would take between the three would be different, but nonetheless significant and far-reaching. Breakdown most likely would involve the collapse of the single currency, a broad repatriation of power and authority from Brussels, or perhaps even a German–Russian rapprochement that would come at the expense of EU goals and policies. Breakdown would lead to a significant downgrade in relations between the big three and a lasting reluctance to embark again on projects of economic, social or political integration. To date, big three relations – and the EU political order more broadly – have shown no inclination toward this outcome.

Crisis can also lead to a *transformation* of the system (or policy sub-systems), which leaves the order in a fundamentally different state. In this scenario the political order is maintained but restructured in basic ways, leading to new political and institutional arrangements. States, perhaps together with EU-level entities, develop new governance structures. The basic rules and norms of the order are renegotiated, and new bargains replace old ones.

Transformation would involve a serious and sustained effort by the three to create a more cohesive polity, probably with further transfer of power and authority from national to supranational institutions and bodies. The Ukraine crisis could serve as a catalyst for the creation of a more robust European security and defence framework, for example, either among the three or embedded within EU structures and institutions. To overcome the problems of monetary union and the single currency, the three (or, more likely, France and Germany) would lead efforts toward clearer and more robust rules, or more fiscal or political integration. Such transformative steps have not yet been taken, and, given the current political climate, appear unlikely in the near future.

The third outcome is *adaptation*, which is in between breakdown and transformation. Adaptation constitutes a continuation of the political order in its fundamental respects. The old order is not completely replaced, but the formal mechanisms of the old order are altered or modified. New rules and institutions are added to cope with new challenges, disagreements and problems.

At times inelegant and often muddled, ad hoc responses to crises or other unsettled situations, adaptation would include incremental yet meaningful modifications to eurozone governance, such as tighter fiscal and budgetary rules; clear mechanisms for state bankruptcy, eurozone exit, or bailouts; or yet further enhanced policy tools for the European Central Bank (ECB). Regarding the Ukraine crisis, adaptation would involve further development of common EU policy instruments and capabilities in foreign and security policy, including on the rules and mechanisms that govern the imposition of sanctions and other coercive measures against third-party countries.

As the next two sections show, to date both the Ukraine and the eurozone crises have led to adaptation rather than to breakdown or transformation of big three relations and the EU political order more broadly.

The Ukraine crisis: the return of geopolitics to Europe

Russia's seizure of Crimea in March 2014 and its ongoing proxy war in eastern Ukraine directly challenge the post-Cold War European political and security order. The conflict has already claimed over 9000 lives and has derailed more than two decades of fitful efforts to pull Russia closer to the West. The crisis not only threatens to reverse Ukraine's post-Communist economic and political gains, but has also created a level of uncertainty over Russia's intentions and behaviour unmatched since the days of the Cold War.[10]

The crisis also represents a serious setback to the Eastern Partnership (EaP), the EU's signature initiative to build closer ties with Ukraine and five other post-Soviet states. Moscow still views these territories as part of its privileged sphere of influence, despite repeated Western warnings and admonitions that such behaviour belongs to Europe's past. Geopolitics and security competition have thus returned to the European continent, with an increasingly revisionist, nuclear-powered Russia openly challenging the post-Cold War status quo (Legvold 2016; Lo 2015).

Though violence has abated since the signing of the February 2015 Minsk II ceasefire agreement, the situation in Ukraine remains dire.[11] The country is facing economic and financial collapse, its military forces stand no chance of retaking territory seized by the Russian-backed separatists in the east, and there is growing concern across European capitals that eastern Ukraine is moving toward becoming a 'frozen conflict', marked by interminable violence and the absence of a lasting and stable peace.

Rather than leading to breakdown or transformation, however, the Ukraine crisis has led to the adaptation of the EU political order. Individual EU countries have not abandoned the pursuit of European unity for the potential of enhancing their own privileged ties with Russia. Nor have they taken decisive steps toward greater integration, especially in defence, to counter the Russian threat. Instead, Britain, France and Germany have coalesced around a common approach toward Russia's actions in Ukraine. This strategy has mainly included trying to prevent a more serious deterioration of the security situation in Ukraine's eastern Donbas region, dissuading Russia from pursuing any steps that might lead to further instability, either in Ukraine itself or at points further west, and raising the costs Russia must pay for bullying its neighbours. Shared concern that Russia may destabilise Ukraine if Kiev pursues a deeper economic and political relationship with the West, indignation over Russia's flagrant breach of international law, and Germany's ability to coordinate a common approach amid disparate attitudes and interests among EU member states have bolstered this consensus.

The Ukraine crisis has also revealed and sustained three bigger trends in European politics today: a more visible and important leadership role for Germany, the resilience of Franco-German bilateralism (though marked by a reversal of traditional roles in crisis diplomacy), and Britain's growing disengagement from EU affairs.

Germany: bound to lead

The Ukraine conflict marks the first time Germany has played a leading role in a major international security crisis since the end of World War II (Speck 2015). German Chancellor Angela Merkel was instrumental in negotiating the 13-point 'Minsk II' ceasefire agreement in February 2015, and Germany has been at the forefront of designing and implementing EU sanctions against Russia, the principal policy instrument EU countries have used to punish Russia for its actions in Ukraine and to deter it from taking yet more provocative steps.[12]

The conflict has coincided with an effort by some German policy-makers to see their country take a more active role on regional and global security issues. Speaking at the 2014 Munich Security Conference, for example, German President Joachim Gauck called for greater German engagement in international affairs. Germany at times uses its National Socialist past as an excuse, he said, to not contribute to pressing global problems and concerns (Bundespräsidialamt 2014). Still, Berlin has assumed its new leadership role in the Ukraine crisis more by default and necessity than by deliberate choice or design. Neither other EU member states nor the EU itself are able or willing to lead, and the United States has largely left it to its European allies to manage the crisis, thereby forcing Germany to coordinate the Western response.

Another reason Germany has taken a leadership role in the Ukraine crisis is because it has more at stake than do to its British and French partners. It is not clear, for example, that Germany would have adopted a similarly active response had a crisis of similar scale and magnitude appeared on the EU's southern rather than its eastern periphery. Russia is both a major energy provider for Germany and an important export market for German goods. And since Germany has more interests at stake in Eastern Europe than do Britain or France, Russia has the greatest potential to threaten German rather than British or French security and welfare, as it did for more than four decades during the Cold War.

Given its extensive commercial and energy ties with Russia, Germany also has more leverage over Moscow than any other European country (Szabo 2015). Germany is Russia's biggest trading partner and source of investment, while Germany imports more natural gas from Russia than any other EU country. Some analysts speculated that this expansive commercial and energy relationship might make Germany the principal obstacle to a unified EU response toward Moscow (Kundnani 2015b). Merkel has consistently and sharply condemned Russian actions, however, and has emerged as one of Russia's fiercest critics in the EU. She has described the annexation of Crimea as 'criminal and illegal', and has called on Russia to abandon the 'politics of the nineteenth and twentieth centuries' (Myers and Smale 2014). She has also voiced concerns that, without a strong and unified Western response, other post-Soviet states, and possibly even Serbia, may be the next victims of Russian aggression (Smale 2014).

While the conflict has demonstrated a new German foreign policy activism, it has also revealed the limits of Germany's power and influence. As observers inside and outside the country have pointed out, Berlin still lacks a military dimension to its power projection capability. Germany is, furthermore, both unwilling and unable to issue security guarantees to countries in Eastern Europe that feel threatened by Russia, such as Poland and the Baltic states. Instead, these countries continue to look to the United States as the ultimate guarantor of their security.

The conflict has also underscored some of the continuities in German foreign policy, such as its reluctance to rely on military power as an instrument of its foreign policy. Merkel has ruled out a military response of any kind, for example, including arms shipments to Ukrainian forces fighting anti-government rebels.[13] And fearing that Moscow would view such a step as a provocation,

Germany has rejected proposals to establish a permanent NATO deployment in Eastern Europe, instead favouring the creation of a rapid-response force that can respond to crisis situations as they arise.

While Germany has had the biggest impact on the timing and scope of EU sanctions on Russia, the longer the conflict continues the harder it will be for Berlin to maintain EU unity. Two examples reveal the challenges of maintaining long-term economic and political pressure on Russia. London, home to many Russian oligarchs who store their wealth in City financial institutions, has been reluctant to impose measures that might jeopardise this lucrative arrangement. France, whose arms sales to Russia are the highest among European countries, was forced to cancel a Russian order for two Mistral-class amphibious warships as a result of pressure from its EU and NATO allies (Smith 2015).[14]

As sanctions increasingly damage their own commercial, financial and industrial interests, and as they seem to have at best a limited impact on Russian behaviour with respect to eastern Ukraine, political leaders and interest groups in Britain, France, Germany and other EU countries will question the utility and wisdom of maintaining sanctions over the longer term. Germany will then be forced to decide how much pressure, if any, to impose on its own EU partners to continue to isolate and punish Russia.

Franco-German bilateralism: role reversal and crisis diplomacy

The Ukraine crisis has revealed a reversal of the traditional roles in crisis diplomacy for France and Germany. Capturing the reality but also the political and moral constraints of German power after World War II, de Gaulle once described Europe as 'a coach with horses, with Germany the horse and France the coachman' (quoted in Eddy and Erlanger 2013). Or, as Gunther Hellmann put it more recently, in the decades after World War II, 'For France to be in the lead was politically necessary, morally justified, and dutifully acknowledged by German elites' (Hellmann 2016).

During the Ukraine crisis, however, Merkel rather than French President François Hollande has played the pre-eminent role in formulating and implementing the EU response to Russia. But while the Ukraine crisis reversed their traditional roles in foreign policy and security, Germany's unfamiliar leadership role has not replaced, rendered obsolete, or come at the expense of Franco-German bilateralism. In fact, there are compelling reasons why Germany will seek to further strengthen its bilateral relationship with France as its own power expands.

Merkel was eager to have Hollande by her side during the negotiations in February 2015 that produced the 'Minsk II' ceasefire agreement, for example, and to include France in the so-called 'Normandy Quartet' – the four-power group composed of France, Germany, Russia and Ukraine. Despite Hollande's participation in the ceasefire talks and France's formal presence in the Normandy

Quartet, however, there is little doubt that Merkel is leading while Hollande is following when it comes to formulating and implementing policy responses toward the crisis (Pond 2015). This marks a major departure in their traditional post-war bilateral relationship.

Germany wants to have France by its side for two main reasons. First, Germany is still deeply reluctant to be seen to be pursuing a unilateral role in foreign policy, especially on such sensitive and important political and security questions as those raised during the current Ukraine crisis. Having France by its side gives Germany cover and endows its initiatives with greater legitimacy, both at home and abroad. Second, having France on board generally makes it easier to get other EU member states also on board. French and German positions – whether in economic, political or security affairs – are often seen to be at opposite ends of the spectrum of available European policy responses. Historically, if France and Germany are able to reconcile their policy differences and arrive at a common position, other EU member states are likely to do the same.[15]

The Ukraine crisis has thus shown that German leadership and Franco-German bilateralism are not mutually exclusive. Moreover, the desire to maintain at least the appearance of Franco-German bilateralism is not for idealistic or sentimental reasons, but rather because both countries continue to understand that they are better able to achieve their individual and common goals when they work together.

Britain: bystander to crisis

Despite traditionally being one of the EU's two main diplomatic and military actors, Britain has played a comparatively small role in the Ukraine crisis. Prime Minister David Cameron did not take part in the February 2015 Minsk ceasefire negotiations, for example, leading some influential British voices to accuse him of being a bystander to the crisis.[16] Also absent have been any major Anglo-French initiatives similar to those during previous security crises, such as the 2011 Libyan intervention. Nor have there been any major Anglo-German or Anglo-American initiatives or coordination.

Like other foreign policy establishments across Europe and the United States, the crisis caught British policy-makers off-guard. The British Parliament released a report in February 2015 stating that Britain and the EU had made a 'catastrophic misreading' of Russia and of Putin's intentions before the crisis. Britain and other European countries 'sleepwalked' into the conflict, the report concluded, treating it as if it were only a trade matter rather than a foreign policy and security issue.[17]

Combined with the small role it has played in trying to resolve the eurozone crisis, Britain's relative absence in the Ukraine turmoil signals a broader retrenchment for Britain in EU and even global affairs (LSE Diplomacy

Commission 2015; Menon 2015). If this trend continues, the EU's ability to become a potent foreign policy and security actor will be seriously impaired. Among EU member states, Britain and France have the most capable military forces and the most experience in security and defence operations. And as permanent members of the UN Security Council, they also hold significant diplomatic experience and clout.

Eurozone crisis: dashed hopes and an uncertain future

The crisis at the heart of the eurozone constitutes one of the most serious and fateful trials in the six decades of European integration. The vicissitudes of the past six years have not yet precipitated a breakdown or transformation of the mechanisms that govern the eurozone. Instead, the turmoil has led to an at times muddled adaptation or bending of some of the eurozone's main rules, norms and institutions. Since the onset of the crisis, a number of new institutions and initiatives have been created and implemented, including the European Financial Stabilization Facility (EFSF), European Stabilization Mechanism (ESM), a rudimentary banking union, new policy instruments for the ECB, and greater oversight and supervisory powers over eurozone members' economic and budgetary policies for the European Commission.[18] These steps, among others, while falling far short of constituting a true fiscal or political union, have helped to prevent a collapse of the common currency.

Such incremental reforms seem to be the upper limit that the vast majority of elected officials, national parliaments and electorates across Europe will currently tolerate. While no high-ranking elected official in Europe has openly advocated an unravelling of the eurozone in its current form, there is also no desire for decisive steps toward full fiscal or political union, which would require new treaties that would need unanimous approval by all 28 EU member states, a feat appearing to be beyond the realm of the possible in the current political climate (Moravcsik 2012).

Like the Ukraine crisis, the eurozone turmoil has revealed and intensified three deeper developments in European politics today: Germany's growing clout, the resilience and centrality of Franco-German bilateralism (despite Germany's emergence as the eurozone's and the EU's indisputably pivotal player), and Britain's growing disengagement from EU affairs.

Germany: primus inter pares

The eurozone crisis has highlighted the power and continued importance of national capitals, Berlin above all. Britain's status outside the common currency and France's comparative economic weakness has magnified German primacy during the six years of near-constant eurozone summitry. Despite

Merkel's regular consultations with French officials on the proper response to the various problems facing the eurozone and France's pivotal role in any lasting solution to the plight at the heart of the common currency, Germany has been the driving force behind the various initiatives and programmes since the beginning of the crisis.

While Merkel has declared that if the euro fails 'then not only the currency fails. Europe will fail, and with it the idea of European unity', German officials have also made clear that there are limits to putting an institutionally shaky euro over its own fiscal position. Concerned that responsibility to bail out struggling eurozone economies would fall disproportionately on itself, Germany has stated that the eurozone must be governed by clear and enforceable fiscal rules. Since the beginning of the crisis, creditor countries and institutions, led by Germany, have insisted on fiscal responsibility and structural reforms in exchange for financial assistance. If countries fail to follow these stipulations, the German Finance Ministry has said, they must suffer the consequences.

One of the main paradoxes of the eurozone crisis is that Germany today finds itself as the key member state in a currency union that it never would have entered had it known how it would turn out. Germany has at stake not only vast sums of money – according to some estimates Germany would be liable for more than €90 billion in the event of a Greek default – but also the cohesion, good will and stability it has carefully cultivated over the past several decades.

Franco-German bilateralism: divisions, but not divided

While tensions and disagreements between France and Germany over basic questions of economic and monetary policy are nothing new, the current crisis has revealed a number of sharp policy differences.[19] French officials, for example, have had a stronger desire than their German counterparts to keep Greece in the eurozone, believing that a Greek exit would do irreparable damage to the single currency and to the European project more broadly. A Greek exit would show that membership in the euro area – and perhaps in the EU – is not irrevocable, but rather contingent on the inclination of other member states. German officials such as Finance Minister Wolfgang Schäuble, on the other hand, have made clear that a Greek exit from the eurozone is a possibility, and perhaps even necessary to maintain a fiscally sound and prosperous monetary union (Geithner 2014: 483–4; Smale 2015; *Spiegel* 2015).

France has also been uncomfortable with what it sees as Germany's rigid approach toward countries with fiscal imbalances. With its own budget deficits, stubbornly high unemployment and tepid economic growth, France dreads German economic orthodoxy becoming further entrenched in the eurozone. But lacking the ability to alter Berlin's position, Paris has had little choice but to reluctantly follow German prescriptions for fiscal and structural reforms across the eurozone (Vail 2015).

France's struggle to implement domestic reforms to revitalise its economy – as well as having the least popular President in the history of the Fifth Republic currently in office – has also helped thrust Germany into the eurozone's leadership position. Though France has struggled to keep up with its partner across the Rhine, Germany's enhanced role in eurozone crisis management has not come at the expense of, or the perceived desire or necessity for, Franco-German coordination. Despite differences in economic performance and sharp disagreements over economic policy and the future direction of the eurozone, Franco-German bilateralism has proved resilient, and remains essential to any lasting solution to the eurozone's current problems (Schild 2013).

Britain: on the outside looking in

Britain's position outside the eurozone has meant that it has been absent from many of the discussions and decisions on how to quell the turmoil at the heart of the crisis. London has called on eurozone countries to move toward more fiscal integration, but has no intention of joining the currency union itself. At an EU summit in November 2011, for example, Britain vetoed a treaty proposing a so-called EU fiscal compact – the first time Britain has vetoed an EU treaty since joining the EU's precursor, the EEC, in 1973. As a result, other member states were forced to move ahead separately (Lyall 2011).

While Britain has no interest in seeing the eurozone in perpetual turmoil, the present crisis has nonetheless provided Britain with some economic and political benefits. The euro's weakness makes the pound sterling stronger on global currency markets; continental Europe's muddle gives Britain greater latitude to exert independence, especially in the debate over the future shape of the EU; uncertainty over the future of the euro has allowed Britain to put off a decision on what kind of relationship to have with it; and the eurozone's current plight makes Britain's domestic politics less contentious, since there are fewer political battles between Labour and Conservatives over Britain's proper relationship with its Continental partners (Marsh 2013: chapter 18).

The crisis has confirmed and strengthened many Britons' opposition to any further power sharing with Brussels institutions. The crisis has provided traditional British Eurosceptics with plenty of ammunition on the supposed dangers of closer economic and political integration, and any possibility that Britain might someday join the common currency has most likely evaporated. There is in Britain today a groundswell of support to renegotiate the status of Britain's relationship with the EU. Partly as a result, Cameron has scheduled a referendum for 23 June 2016 on whether Britain should stay in or leave the EU.

As Britain's role in EU policy-making becomes progressively smaller, there is likely to be even more support among many Britons to renegotiate their country's membership status. As one observer noted, 'In Britain, the case for staying in the EU has been complicated by the fact that, as a non-euro country, it will never be part of the inner sanctum of power, the German-dominated eurozone' (Cohen 2015). A two-tier (or 'two-speed') Europe is emerging, with Britain increasingly on the outside (Piris 2012).[20]

Conclusion

The Ukraine and eurozone crises are different in many important respects, but both reveal three deeper developments in European politics today: Germany's growing clout, the resilience of the Franco-German axis despite the widening power imbalance between the two, and Britain's disengagement from EU affairs. Each development is important for the future prospects and direction of European integration. The three happening simultaneously suggests that the European project may be entering a new phase. Yet despite the problems and challenges outlined in this article, to date these two crises have led neither to a breakdown nor to a transformation in big three relations, nor to truly fundamental changes in their individual roles. Instead, the adaptation of EU rules, procedures, institutions, and of their individual influence and orientation have been the main outcomes.

The shift in power toward Germany and away from France is not just a reflection of their divergent economic performances since the onset of the global financial crisis. Combined with the inability of French leaders to implement comprehensive economic reforms over the past decade and Germany's comparatively robust economic growth during the same period, it also reflects less hesitancy among many of today's German political leaders compared to their predecessors over asserting and pursuing a narrower conception of the country's interests and responsibilities.

Rather than embracing its enhanced and more visible role in Europe, however, Germany has yet to show that it is willing or able to provide the leadership and vision that Europe currently needs. Berlin has avoided supplying key public goods within the EU, for example, such as maintaining a web of security commitments and guarantees or serving as the lender of last resort for eurozone countries facing balance of payments crises. And on foreign policy issues beyond Ukraine, Germany has yet to embrace the security and defence role Britain and France have traditionally held, as well as the burdens and responsibilities that come with it.[21]

A stronger Germany and weaker France, however, has not rendered obsolete or come at the expense of Franco-German bilateralism.[22] Despite the current crises and their at times divergent policy preferences, the relationship remains resilient due to ideational reasons (both French and German leaders continue to believe in the importance of the symbolism of the Franco-German partnership); instrumental reasons (the two countries continue to believe that they are more likely to get what they want when they work together rather than at cross-purposes); and the deep institutional fabric of the bilateral relationship developed over six decades. One lesson of both the Ukraine and eurozone crises has been that a more active, confident and powerful Germany on the one hand, and a resilient Franco-German bilateralism on the other are not mutually exclusive. It is true that France is weaker today relative to Germany than perhaps at any time since the end of World War II, but this has not extinguished the need or desire for bilateralism. Claims that France and Germany are 'decoupling', or that the Franco-German axis is on the verge of collapse, are therefore not just premature – they fail to fully grasp the resilience of the relationship.

And as this article has also shown, Anglo-French and Anglo-German bilateralism, or a meaningful unilateral role for Britain, have been largely absent in the Ukraine and eurozone crises. Nor has a British-French-German triumvirate emerged as a serious possibility to overcome the present turmoil.

It is too soon to fully understand the lasting effects of the Ukraine and eurozone crises, and whether eventually they will lead to deep and transformative changes in big three relations, in their individual preferences and orientations, or the future prospects of European affairs. Europe could go in a number of different directions over the next several years. But what is certain is that how big three member states emerge from the current period of crisis, and the trajectory of their relations and individual roles, will be crucial in shaping Europe's future course. These crises and the broader trends that they illuminate will also encourage or perhaps even force scholars of European and EU politics to focus on new or different questions, and to re-examine some of their basic assumptions.

First, if Germany's enhanced standing, France's relative weakening, and Britain's disengagement persist or become even more pronounced, scholars will have to think more about the role of hierarchy within the EU.[23] Will Germany gradually take on more responsibility in the EU, with all the attendant costs and risks, or will it continue to operate as a 'reluctant hegemon'? Or might Germany increasingly move toward a third option, in which it displays more ambivalence and far greater reluctance in leading the EU than it has shown over the past five years? And as a corollary, will France be able to revitalise its economic prospects and its position in European policy-making? Or will its cherished 'rank' and grandeur further erode?

Second, if inner and outer circles of membership further solidify within the EU – with Britain firmly entrenched in the outer ring – it will be necessary to better understand the operating logic and implications of what some scholars have called 'differentiated integration', 'variable geometry', or a 'multi-speed' Europe (see for example Leuffen *et al.* 2012). How will the core and periphery relate to one another? Will it resolve some of the contradictions at the heart of European integration today or accentuate them? And will Britain accept membership in an organisation in which it has less and less influence over crucial questions of governance and authority, or will it decide to downgrade its formal status within the EU or leave altogether?

Finally, scholars probably will devote more attention to the impact and significance of crises and other forms of political conflict, politicisation and contestation on big three relations and EU affairs more broadly, and in particular when and why crises lead to a breakdown, transformation or adaptation of the European political order. The current period of crisis affirms that scholars are just starting to understand these dynamics. These and other questions suggest that debates over Europe's future are just beginning.

Notes

1. On the importance of the big three member states in shaping the grand bargains that have propelled the process of European integration forward, see Moravcsik (1998). Historically, France and Germany have taken the lead in shaping the economic, political and institutional development of Europe, while the Anglo-French duo has traditionally led on foreign policy and security issues. On the Franco-German role in Europe, see Krotz and Schild (2013). On Anglo-French cooperation in EU security affairs, see Howorth (2007: 33–7). In recent years Anglo-French security and defence cooperation has centred on the areas of procurement and of joint missions and operations (see Burns 2010; UK Foreign & Commonwealth Office 2010).
2. Upon German unification in 1990, for example, British Prime Minister Margaret Thatcher raised the possibility of an Anglo-French entente that would serve as a de facto hedge against German hegemony, but French President François Mitterrand never embraced this initiative (see Bozo 2010: 168–70). On the post-war Anglo-French relationship, see Tombs and Tombs (2007: chapters 13 and 14).
3. On Anglo-German relations in the EU, see Larres and Meehan (2000).
4. Accordingly, the Franco-German partnership has received ample scholarly attention (note, for example, Calleo and Staal 1998; Krotz and Schild 2013; Simonian 1985; Webber 1999). On Franco-German bilateralism in security and defence affairs, see Krotz (2011). For a historical overview of France and Germany in Europe from the nineteenth to the twenty-first centuries, see Krotz (2014).
5. On the bilateral Franco-German order as part of the European polity, see Krotz and Schild (2013: chapters 1–4).
6. These and other times of friction are ably captured in Dinan (2014). For classic long-standing differences within the 'Franco-German couple' across a variety of policy domains, see Krotz and Schild (2013: 37–42). On frequently diverging French and German actions and orientations in foreign policy, security, and, especially, defence, see Krotz (2015, chapters 5–8).
7. Among a rapidly growing literature on the problems at the heart of Europe today, see Giddens (2013), Majone (2014),and Offe (2015).
8. The discussion in this section draws from Ikenberry (2008).
9. On how EU disintegration could transpire, see Vollaard (2014) or Webber (2014). For a debate on the future prospects of the European project, see Krotz and Maher *et al.* (2012).

10. For early appraisals of the Ukraine crisis and its implications, see Menon and Rumer (2015) and Wilson (2014).
11. The first ceasefire, agreed in September 2014 and, like the second, also in the Belarussian capital, quickly broke down. The February 2015 accord requires, among other stipulations, both government forces and separatists to pull back heavy artillery out of range of each other, the withdrawal of 'foreign' fighters and equipment, and allows for Ukraine to regain full control over its borders following local elections in rebel-held territory and constitutional changes that would grant these regions greater autonomy. See *Financial Times* (2015b) for the full text of the protocol.
12. The EU first imposed sanctions on Russia in March 2014, shortly after the seizure of Crimea. The sanctions have targeted Russia's financial, energy and defence sectors. In June 2015, with Russia continuing to support its proxy forces in eastern Ukraine, EU leaders announced that sanctions would remain in place until a peace agreement is reached and fully implemented by the Russian-backed rebels. See http://europa.eu/newsroom/highlights/special-coverage/eu_sanctions/index_en.htm (accessed 15 October 2015).
13. Here Merkel is firmly in line with German public opinion, which strongly opposes any kind of military intervention in Ukraine. Regardless of the wisdom of the policy, however, Merkel's categorical rejection of arming government forces deprived her of an important bargaining chip in negotiations.
14. Under intense pressure, France suspended the sale indefinitely in November 2014. The order was cancelled in August 2015, with France refunding Russia's initial deposit (Tavernise 2015).
15. On that logic, see Krotz and Schild (2013: 8–11).
16. General Sir Richard Shirreff, for example, who served as NATO's second most senior military officer, described Cameron as 'a bit player' and a 'foreign policy irrelevance' in the crisis (*Financial Times* 2015a).
17. See House of Lords (2015) for the full report.
18. The literature on the eurozone crisis is now voluminous. Among the best works are Peet and La Guardia (2014), Pisani-Ferry (2014) and Sandbu (2015).
19. For long-standing differences between France and Germany across policy domains and their ways of dealing with them, see Krotz and Schild (2013: 37–42); on differences over economic and monetary policy specifically, see Krotz and Schild (2013: chapter 8).
20. While some scholars have claimed that a common European identity has emerged, Britain's identity has remained strongly nationalist (Risse 2010). On Britain's often acrimonious relationship with its EU partners, see Wall (2008).
21. On Germany's status as a 'reluctant' hegemon, see Bulmer and Paterson (2013); Paterson (2011); Schönberger (2012); and Schönberger (2013). Also note Garton Ash (2013) and Kundnani (2015a).
22. On Franco-German 'embedded bilateralism' in European politics from the 1950s, see Krotz and Schild (2013).
23. On 'hierarchy' in international relations, see Lake (2009) and Wendt and Friedheim (1995).

Acknowledgements

We wish to thank Brigid Laffan, the other members of this special issue, and two anonymous reviewers for helpful feedback on an earlier version of this article. We also thank Katharina Meißner for valuable research assistance.

Disclosure statement

No potential conflict of interest was reported by the authors.

References

Bozo, Frédéric (2010). *Mitterrand, the End of the Cold War, and German Unification.* Susan Emanuel, trans. New York, NY: Berghan.

Bulmer, Simon, and William E. Paterson (2013). 'Germany as the EU's Reluctant Hegemon? Of Economic Strength and Political Constraints', *Journal of European Public Policy*, 20:10, 1387–405.

Bundespräsidialamt (2014). 'Germany's Role in the World: Reflections on Responsibility, Norms, and Alliances', Speech by Federal President Joachim Gauck at the Opening of the Munich Security Conference, 31 January 2014, Munich, available at http://www.bundespraesident.de/SharedDocs/Downloads/DE/Reden/2014/01/140131-Muenchner-Sicherheitskonferenz-Englisch.pdf?__blob=publicationFile (accessed 15 October 2015).

Burns, John F. (2010). 'Britain and France Expand Their Military Cooperation', *New York Times*, 2 November.

Calleo, David P., and Eric R. Staal, eds. (1998). *Europe's Franco-German Engine.* Washington, D.C.: Brookings Institution Press.

Cohen, Roger (2015). 'The German Question Redux', *International New York Times*, 14 July.

Dinan, Desmond (2014). *Origins and Evolution of the European Union*, 2nd ed. Oxford: Oxford University Press.

Eddy, Melissa and Steven Erlanger (2013). 'Europe's Odd Couple, France and Germany, 50 Years Later', *New York Times*, 23 January.

Financial Times (2015a). 'Britain's Drift to the Foreign Policy Sidelines', 6 February.

Financial Times (2015b). 'Full Text of the Minsk Agreement', available at http://www.ft.com/cms/s/0/21b8f98e-b2a5-11e4-b234-00144feab7de.html#axzz3ipsVodcS (accessed 15 October 2015).

Garton Ash, Timothy (2013). 'The New German Question', *New York Review of Books*, 60: 13.

Geithner, Timothy F. (2014). *Stress Test: Reflections on Financial Crises*. New York, NY: Crown.

Giddens, Anthony (2013). *Turbulent and Mighty Continent: What Future for Europe?* Cambridge: Polity.

Hellmann, Gunther (2016). 'Germany's World: Power and Followership in a Crisis-Ridden Europe', *Global Affairs*, 2:1, 3–20.

House of Lords (2015). *The EU and Russia: Before and Beyond the Crisis in Ukraine*. London: The Stationery Office Limited, available at http://www.publications.parliament.uk/pa/ld201415/ldselect/ldeucom/115/115.pdf (accessed 15 October 2015).

Howorth, Jolyon (2007). *Security and Defence Policy in the European Union*. Basingstoke: Palgrave Macmillan.

Ikenberry, G. John (2008). 'Explaining Crisis and Change in Transatlantic Relations: An Introduction', in Jeffrey J. Anderson, G. John Ikenberry, and Thomas Risse (eds.), *The End of the West? Crisis and Change in the Atlantic Order*. Ithaca, NY: Cornell University Press, 1–27.

Krotz, Ulrich (2011). *Flying Tiger: International Relations Theory and the Politics of Advanced Weapons*. Oxford: Oxford University Press.

Krotz, Ulrich (2014). 'Three Eras and Possible Futures: A Long-Term View on the Franco-German Relationship a Century after the First World War', *International Affairs*, 90:2, 337–50.

Krotz, Ulrich (2015). *History and Foreign Policy in France and Germany*. London: Palgrave Macmillan.

Krotz, Ulrich, and Joachim Schild (2013). *Shaping Europe: France, Germany, and Embedded Bilateralism from the Elysée Treaty to Twenty-First Century Politics*. Oxford: Oxford University Press.

Krotz, Ulrich and Richard Maher, David M. McCourt and Andrew Glencross, Norrin M. Ripsman, Mark S. Sheetz and Jean-Yves Haine, and Sebastian Rosato (2012). 'Correspondence: Debating the Sources and Prospects of European Integration', *International Security*, 37:1, 178–99.

Kundnani, Hans (2015a). *The Paradox of German Power*. Oxford: Oxford University Press.

Kundnani, Hans (2015b). 'Leaving the West Behind: Germany Looks East', *Foreign Affairs*, 94:1, 108–16.

Lake, David (2009). *Hierarchy in International Relations*. Ithaca, NY: Cornell University Press.

Larres, Klaus, and Elizabeth Meehan, eds. (2000). *Uneasy Allies: British-German Relations and European Integration since 1945*. Oxford: Oxford University Press.

Legvold, Robert (2016). *Return to Cold War*. Cambridge: Polity Press.

Leuffen, Dirk, Berthold Rittberger, and Frank Schimmelfennig (2012). *Differentiated Integration: Explaining Variation in the European Union*. Basingstoke: Palgrave Macmillan.

Lo, Bobo (2015). *Russia and the New World Disorder*. Washington, D.C.: Brookings Institution Press.

LSE Diplomacy Commission (2015). *Investing for Influence*. London: LSE Ideas, available at http://www.lse.ac.uk/IDEAS/publications/reports/pdf/LSE-IDEAS-InvestingforInfluence.pdf (accessed 16 February 2016).

Lyall, Sarah (2011). 'Cameron Says His Veto on Europe Treaty Protects Britain', *New York Times*, 13 December.

Majone, Giandomenico (2014). *Rethinking the Union of Europe Post-Crisis: Has Integration Gone Too Far?* Cambridge: Cambridge University Press.

Marsh, David (2013). *Europe's Deadlock: How the Euro Crisis Could Be Solved – and Why It Won't Happen*. New Haven, CT: Yale University Press.
Menon, Anand (2015). 'Littler England: The United Kingdom's Retreat from Global Leadership', *Foreign Affairs*, 94:6, 93–100.
Menon, Rajan, and Eugene B. Rumer (2015). *Conflict in Ukraine: The Unwinding of the Post-Cold War Order*. Cambridge, MA: The MIT Press.
Moravcsik, Andrew (1998). *The Choice for Europe: Social Purpose and State Power from Messina to Maastricht*. Ithaca, NY: Cornell University Press.
Moravcsik, Andrew (2012). 'Europe After the Crisis: How to Sustain a Common Currency', *Foreign Affairs*, 91:3, 54–68.
Myers, Steven Lee and Alison Smale (2014). 'Russian Troops Mass at Border in Ukraine Rift', *New York Times*, 14 March.
Offe, Claus (2015). *Europe Entrapped*. Cambridge: Polity.
Parker, George, and Quentin Peel (2012) 'UK and Germany: Exasperated Allies', *Financial Times*, 6 November.
Paterson, William E. (2011). 'The Reluctant Hegemon?: Germany Moves Centre Stage in the European Union', *Journal of Common Market Studies*, 49:1, 57–75.
Peet, John, and Anton La Guardia (2014). *Unhappy Union: How the Euro Crisis – and Europe – Can Be Fixed*. London: The Economist.
Piris, Jean-Claude (2012). *The Future of Europe: Towards a Two-Speed EU?* Cambridge: Cambridge University Press.
Pisani-Ferry, Jean (2014). *The Euro Crisis and Its Aftermath*. Oxford: Oxford University Press.
Pond, Elizabeth (2015). 'Germany's Real Role in the Ukraine Crisis', *Foreign Affairs*, 94:2, 173–6.
Risse, Thomas (2010). *A Community of Europeans? Transnational Identities and Public Spheres*. Ithaca, NY: Cornell University Press.
Sandbu, Martin (2015). *Europe's Orphan: The Future of the Euro and the Politics of Debt*. Princeton: Princeton University Press.
Schild, Joachim (2013). 'Leadership in Hard Times: France, Germany, and the Management of the Eurozone Crisis', *German Politics & Society*, 31:1, 24–47.
Schönberger, Christoph (2012). 'Hegemonie wider Willen: Zur Stellung Deutschlands in der Europäischen Union', *Merkur: Deutsche Zeitschrift für Europäisches Denken*, 66:1, 1–8.
Schönberger, Christoph (2013). 'Nochmals: Die deutsche Hegemonie', *Merkur: Deutsche Zeitschrift für Europäisches Denken*, 67:1, 25–33.
Simonian, Haig (1985). *The Privileged Partnership: Franco-German Relations in the European Community 1969–1984*. Oxford: Clarendon Press.
Smale, Alison (2014). 'Merkel Issues Rebuke to Russia, Setting Caution Aside', *New York Times*, 18 November.
Smale, Alison (2015). 'Minister in Germany Discusses Greece Role', *New York Times*, 19 July.
Smith, Ben (2015). 'Sanctions over the Ukraine Conflict', SNIA 6951, available at http://researchbriefings.files.parliament.uk/documents/SN06951/SN06951.pdf (accessed 20 October 2015).
Soros, George (2014). *The Tragedy of the European Union: Disintegration or Revival?* with Gregor Peter Schmitz. New York, NY: PublicAffairs.
Speck, Ulrich (2015). 'German Power and the Ukraine Conflict', *Carnegie Europe*, available at http://carnegieeurope.eu/2015/03/26/german-power-and-ukraine-conflict (accessed 15 October 2015).

Spiegel (2015). 'Interview with Wolfgang Schäuble', available at http://www.spiegel.de/international/germany/interview-with-german-finance-minister-wolfgang-schaeuble-a-1044233.html (accessed 15 October 2015).
Szabo, Stephen F. (2015). *Germany, Russia, and the Rise of Geo-Economics*. London: Bloomsbury Academic.
Tavernise, Sabrina (2015). 'Canceling Deal for 2 Warships, France Agrees to Repay Russia', *New York Times*, 6 August.
Tombs, Robert, and Isabelle Tombs (2007). *That Sweet Enemy: The French and the British from the Sun King to the Present*. New York, NY: Vintage.
UK Foreign & Commonwealth Office (2010). 'Treaty between the United Kingdom of Great Britain and Northern Ireland and the French Republic for Defence and Security Co-operation', in London: The Stationery Office, available at https://www.gov.uk/government/uploads/system/uploads/attachment_data/file/238153/8174.pdf (accessed 15 October 2015).
Vail, Mark (2015). 'Europe's Middle Child: France's Statist Liberalism and the Conflicted Politics of the Euro', in Matthias Matthijs and Mark Blyth (eds.), *The Future of the Euro*. New York, NY: Oxford University Press, 136–60.
Vollaard, Hans (2014). 'Explaining European Disintegration', *Journal of Common Market Studies*, 52:5, 1142–59.
Wall, Stephen (2008). *A Stranger in Europe: Britain and the EU from Thatcher to Blair*. Oxford: Oxford University Press.
Webber, Douglas, ed. (1999). *The Franco-German Relationship in the European Union*. London: Routledge.
Webber, Douglas (2014). 'How Likely Is It That the European Union Will Disintegrate? A Critical Analysis of Competing Theoretical Perspectives', *European Journal of International Relations*, 20:2, 341–65.
Wendt, Alexander, and Daniel Friedheim (1995). 'Hierarchy and Anarchy: Informal Empire and the East German State', *International Organization*, 49:4, 689–721.
Wilson, Andrew (2014). *Ukraine Crisis: What It Means for the West*. New Haven: Yale University Press.

EU experimentalist governance in times of crisis

Jonathan Zeitlin

ABSTRACT
This paper analyses the evolution of EU governance since the financial and eurozone crisis from an experimentalist perspective. It argues that EU governance in many key policy domains continues to take the form of an experimentalist decision-making architecture, based on a recursive process of framework goal-setting and revision through comparative review of implementation experience in diverse local contexts, which is well adapted to the Union's turbulent and polyarchic environment. The first part of the paper presents a synoptic theoretical account of the characteristics of experimentalist governance, and summarises the empirical evidence on its incidence and operation within the EU before the crisis. The second part of the paper examines two 'hard cases' from an experimentalist perspective, namely financial regulation and the European Semester of socio-economic policy coordination. The paper concludes that both cases illustrate the limits of centralised hierarchical governance under the diverse and polyarchic conditions of the EU, together with the continuing attraction of experimentalist approaches for tackling complex, uncertain problems like financial regulation and reform of national employment and welfare systems.

Over the decade prior to the onset of the global financial crisis in 2008, governance in the EU came increasingly to be characterised by a new experimentalist architecture, as a growing body of empirical research has documented (Sabel and Zeitlin 2008, 2010, 2012a; Zeitlin 2015). In this iterative, multi-level architecture, open-ended framework goals and metrics for assessing their achievement are established jointly by the EU institutions and the member states, typically following consultation with relevant civil society stakeholders. 'Lower-level' units (like national ministries and regulatory authorities) are then given substantial discretion to advance these goals in ways adapted to their local contexts. But in return for this autonomy, such units must report regularly on their performance and participate in a peer review in which their results are compared with those of others following different means towards the same ends. Where lower-level units are not making good progress, they are expected to take corrective measures, based on a plausible plan for improvement informed by the experience of their peers. The goals, metrics and decision-making procedures are then periodically revised in response to the problems and possibilities revealed by the review process, and the cycle repeats (for a diagram, see Zeitlin 2015: 2).

Such governance architectures have a number of fundamental advantages. First, they accommodate diversity by adapting common goals to varied local contexts, rather than seeking to impose one-size-fits-all solutions. Second, they provide a mechanism for coordinated learning from local experimentation through disciplined comparison of different approaches to advancing the same general ends. Third, because both the goals themselves and the means for achieving them are explicitly conceived as provisional and subject to revision in light of experience, problems identified in one phase of implementation can be corrected in the next iteration. For each of these reasons, experimentalist governance architectures have emerged as a widespread response to turbulent, polyarchic environments, where pervasive uncertainty about the nature of current and emerging problems means that policy-makers cannot define ex ante their precise goals or how best to achieve them, while a multi-polar distribution of power means that no single actor can impose their preferred solution without taking into account the views of others. These scope conditions and the governance architectures they encourage are by no means confined to the EU. But because the Union has had to face problems of rising strategic uncertainty under conditions of deep internal diversity and firm polyarchic constraints, it appears to have found its way more quickly and consistently than other polities to experimentalist solutions (Sabel and Zeitlin 2012a, 2012b).

Experimentalist architectures of this type have become pervasively institutionalised in the EU across a broad range of policy domains. Well-documented examples include: regulation of competition, energy, telecommunications, and finance; food, drug, chemicals, and maritime safety; environmental protection; employment promotion and social inclusion; justice, security, and crisis management; data privacy, anti-discrimination, and fundamental rights (Sabel and Zeitlin 2008, 2010; Zeitlin 2015). These architectures also play a growing part in EU external governance, where the revisable framework rules they generate are frequently extended through a variety of channels to third-country actors, both public and private, many of whom also participate in the Union's governance processes (Zeitlin 2015).

Such experimentalist architectures encompass a variety of organisational forms, including European agencies, networks of national regulators, open methods of coordination (OMCs), and operational cooperation among front-line officials, often in combination with one another. A typical pattern in many domains in the years preceding the crisis was the progressive formalisation and reinforcement of European regulatory networks while avoiding supranational centralisation, as in the case of the Third Energy Package (2009), which empowered a new Agency for Cooperation of Energy Regulators (ACER) to co-design framework guidelines and binding network codes for European gas and electricity markets in collaboration with transmission system operators and the Commission (Anderson and Sitter 2015).

Such governance architectures are neither ubiquitous nor universal across the EU.[1] In some domains, like Justice and Home Affairs, experimentalist practices such as revisable framework goals, multi-annual programme targeting, and mutual evaluation by front-line national officials coexist with hierarchical enforcement of detailed rules on certain sensitive issues (Monar 2010). In others, like chemicals, concern for the integrity of the internal market has led to the creation of a single set of harmonised rules which member states at any given moment have limited discretion to alter. But as in the experimentalist architectures described above, to accommodate the strategic uncertainty facing decision-makers in complex and rapidly changing environments, these harmonised rules are explicitly defined as provisional and contestable, subject to revision on the basis of new information and implementation experience, through review processes involving not only national and European officials, but also business and civil society actors from within and beyond the EU (Biedenkopf 2015).

Analogous governance architectures combining synchronic uniformity of rules and procedures with rapid diachronic revisability based on learning from their implementation in different contexts can be found in a variety of settings beyond the EU, from public service provision in the US (Sabel and Simon 2015) to production systems in multinational firms (Herrigel 2015). As with their EU counterparts, the crucial point that distinguishes such experimentalist architectures from conventional hierarchical governance is their contestability, whereby local actors have the autonomy to report problems with existing rules and explore alternatives, while the organisational centre is obliged to take account of such local experience in reconsidering and revising the rules (de Búrca *et al.* 2013: 772–3).

As the examples cited above indicate, experimentalist governance is not confined to fields where the EU has weak competences and produces mainly non-binding guidelines, action plans, scoreboards, and recommendations. It is also well developed in domains where the Union has extensive legislative and regulatory powers. In many such cases, EU experimentalist architectures regularly result in the elaboration of revisable standards mandated by law and new principles which may eventually be given binding force. A noteworthy example is the revision of the EU procedures for integrated permitting and control of pollution introduced by the 2010 Industrial Emissions Directive, which requires member states to adopt 'Best Available Techniques' (BAT) standards developed by multi-stakeholder working groups in defining permissible emissions levels, or justify departures from them according to agreed criteria (Koutalakis *et al.* 2010). Often, too, these experimentalist architectures are underpinned by 'penalty defaults': destabilisation mechanisms that induce reluctant parties to cooperate in framework rule-making and respect its outcomes, while stimulating them to propose plausible and superior alternatives, typically by threatening to reduce the actors' control over their own fate. In the EU context, such penalty defaults frequently involve judgments by the European courts or (threats of) Commission decisions, which oblige member states and/or private actors to explore how to pursue their own preferred goals in ways compatible with fundamental principles of EU law, without imposing a specific hierarchical solution (Sabel and Zeitlin 2008: 305–8; 2010: 13–16; 2012b: 413–14).

The eurozone crisis as a break point in EU governance?

If experimentalist architectures had become increasingly characteristic of EU governance during the first decade of the twenty-first century, the Union's responses to the financial and eurozone crises might appear as a break point, inflecting its trajectory towards more centralised and hierarchical forms. A number of developments could be adduced in support of this view, at least on the surface. Many crucial decisions during the eurozone crisis were taken on an emergency basis by the European Council, the Eurogroup, and the European Central Bank (ECB), stretching the powers of these institutions under the EU Treaties and creating new bodies outside their formal framework, such as the Troika and the European Stability Mechanism (ESM). EU financial regulation has arguably become significantly more centralised, through the creation of new European Supervisory Authorities (ESAs) and especially the Single Supervisory Mechanism (SSM) for eurozone banks. The hierarchical character of EU economic governance has likewise been deliberately strengthened through a succession of crisis-inspired measures such as the Six-Pack, Fiscal Treaty, and Two-Pack, which subject member states' fiscal, budgetary, and macroeconomic policies to increasingly close scrutiny by the Commission and the Council through the new 'European Semester' of policy coordination, backed up by stronger and putatively more 'automatic' sanctions for persistent failures to correct excessive deficits and imbalances. Such developments have been widely viewed as a substantial increase in executive power within the EU (Chalmers 2012; Crum 2013; Curtin 2014), whether understood as the ascendancy of intergovernmentalism (Bickerton *et al.* 2015), the reinforcement of supranationalism (Bauer and Becker 2014), or a combination of the two (Dawson 2015).

There is much to be said for this interpretation, which overlaps with the perspectives of some of the key players in EU decision-making during the crisis (van Middelaar 2015). But it does not capture the full story. In most policy domains, EU experimentalist governance remains highly resilient, and continues to function much as it did before the crisis, demonstrating a robust capacity to revise and improve existing regulatory frameworks, as for example in the cases of energy and industrial emissions discussed above. In other policy fields, such as trade, experimentalist principles serve as the basis for new initiatives like the Transatlantic Trade and Investment Partnership (TTIP), where practices of 'regulatory equivalence assessment' developed in domains such as food safety and data privacy underpin the Commission's proposals for regulatory cooperation with the US (European Commission 2013-2015; Zeitlin 2015: 7-8, 352-4).

But even in the policy fields within the EU most strongly affected by the crisis, it is essential to analyse carefully not only the institutional design of the revised governance arrangements but also their practical operation, in order to understand to what extent they mark a genuine shift towards hierarchical centralisation, and how far the persistence of polyarchy and strategic uncertainty may instead foster the (re)emergence and elaboration of more experimentalist approaches. The next sections of this paper accordingly examine through this lens two of the most important cases: financial regulation and the European Semester.

Financial regulation

In the early 2000s, the EU introduced an ambitious new governance architecture for financial regulation, known as the 'Lamfalussy Process'. At its heart was a networked, multi-level structure of decision-making, based on collaboration between EU institutions and member state administrations on the one hand and between national financial supervisors on the other. In this design, framework principles for financial regulation would be defined in EU legislation, following wide consultations (level 1); detailed rules for their implementation would be developed by the Commission under comitology procedures (level 2); new sectoral committees of national supervisors (for banking, securities markets, and insurance and occupational pensions respectively) would develop interpretative guidelines and standards, monitor and review implementation, and advise the Commission on new and revised rules (level 3); while the Commission, in cooperation with national supervisors, would be responsible for enforcement of EU law (level 4). The affinities of this process with a classic experimentalist governance architecture were evident (Posner 2010; Sabel and Zeitlin 2008: 296-8).

The Lamfalussy Process produced a number of positive results, including from an experimentalist perspective. Its novel approach to regulatory governance facilitated the rapid adoption of a large body of directives aimed at integrating EU financial markets, which had previously been blocked by inter-institutional conflicts and disputes between member states, even if the sharp distinction between framework legislation and detailed rule-making turned out to be difficult to sustain in practice. The new level 3 committees quickly proved able to feed front-line technical expertise into the rule-making process, to elaborate an extensive body of standards and guidelines for national implementation, and to develop original practices of consultation, benchmarking, and peer review. They also demonstrated significant capacity to revise their decision-making procedures and working methods in response to problems and criticism; to identify areas for necessary revision of EU rules; and to develop innovative cross-border governance arrangements, such as colleges of supervisors for multinational firms (Ferran 2012: 116–30; Moloney 2014a: 866–80, 952–8; Posner 2010, 2015).

But there were also fundamental flaws in the Lamfalussy architecture, which the onset of the global financial crisis threw into sharp relief. Foremost was the imbalance between the 'single passport' for financial institutions and the relative weakness of European arrangements for supervisory cooperation, information sharing, and crisis management (above all in banking). But the crisis also underscored the risks of regulatory arbitrage arising from the incomplete harmonisation of financial rules and supervisory practices across EU member states, which the guidance and peer review activities of the level 3 committees had failed to overcome. A further weakness exposed by the crisis, in common with other jurisdictions around the world, was the limited capacity of both European and national supervisory bodies to effectively monitor and assess the risk-management strategies of large, systemically important firms in rapidly changing financial markets (Black 2012; Ferran 2012: 122–5, 128–9; Moloney 2014a: 880–82; 956, 958–60).

Based on this diagnosis, articulated by the influential de Larosière report (2009), the EU undertook a far-reaching set of reforms to its financial regulatory governance. Foremost was the transformation of the Lamfalussy level 3 committees into ESAs with enhanced powers as part of a new European System of Financial Supervision (ESFS) alongside National Competent Authorities (NCAs). These ESAs were designed to help create a 'single rulebook' for each area of financial regulation, as well as to promote stronger convergence of national supervisory practices and improve coordination among NCAs, especially at moments of crisis. The ESAs were empowered to propose Binding Technical Standards (BTS) for the elaboration and implementation of EU financial regulation, which the Commission must endorse or present compelling reasons not to do so. They were likewise empowered to develop a body of non-binding guidelines, opinions, and recommendations on the implementation of EU financial regulation, with which both NCAs and market participants are required to 'make every effort' to comply, or explain why they do not, subject to intensive peer review of national practice. Under a tightly specified set of conditions, ESAs may issue instructions to NCAs and market participants to tackle breaches of EU law and emergency situations, for example as regards short selling, as well as to resolve disputes between NCAs through binding mediation. Finally, the new European Securities and Markets Authority (ESMA) has been given direct supervisory powers over pan-European credit rating agencies and trade repositories (Ferran 2012: 132–55; Moloney 2014a: chs. X–XI).

These new powers of the ESAs to formulate uniform binding rules, override NCAs, and issue direct instructions to market actors have been widely seen as a 'great leap forward' towards centralised hierarchical authority in EU financial governance (e.g. Grossman and Leblond 2012). But a closer look at these authorities' governance and operation reveals a more nuanced picture. The ESA's supervisory boards are composed of the heads of the NCAs themselves, who collectively take all key decisions by majority vote. Thus, as Eilís Ferran observes, the European Banking Authority (EBA) 'does not, and cannot, impose "its" view against the collective view of the national competent authorities. Rather, their (majority) view is its view' (Ferran 2016: 8-9, 23; on ESMA see Moloney 2015: 556-7). Such collective decision-making is subject to extensive requirements for prior consultation with other EU institutions and external stakeholders, as well as to formal procedures for challenge and appeal as it affects third parties (Ferran 2016: 26-7; Moloney 2014a: 898-939, 973-86). The ESAs' powers to impose decisions on NCAs are designed for use in exceptional circumstances, and are hedged round with conditions, constraints, and appeal procedures, especially where they may have fiscal consequences for member states. So far these powers have scarcely been used, with both ESAs and NCAs preferring to tackle problematic issues through peer review, comply-or-explain, and voluntary mediation procedures (Ferran 2016: 31-6, 41-3; Moloney 2015: 15-19, 31-3; 2014a: 973-86, 1004-9).

Examining the practical operation of the ESAs reveals not only the persistence of experimentalist features of the Lamfalussy Process, but also their deepening and extension in some areas. The ESAs have proved adept not only at mobilising the expertise of front-line supervisors to develop BTSs and interpretative guidelines for the huge raft of new financial legislation enacted in response to the crisis, but also at deploying their experience of these 'rules in action' to propose revisions addressing unintended consequences of measures adopted under conditions of high uncertainty (Ferran 2016: 14-23; Moloney 2014a: 897-8, 920-29). Compared to the Lamfalussy level 3 committees, the ESAs have stepped up their capacity for surveillance of both NCAs and financial institutions, 'drilling down' more deeply into national practices through benchmarking and peer review procedures aimed at ensuring supervisors' capacity to achieve high-quality outcomes, while also developing a battery of tools for monitoring, assessing, and reporting on micro-prudential and systemic risks (Ferran 2016: 38-40; Moloney 2014a: 987-92). While the ESA's production of 'Single Supervisory Handbooks' is undoubtedly intended to promote convergence of practices and culture across NCAs (Moloney 2014a: 974, 989-90), the EBA, which is furthest along in this process, emphasises that 'the aim is to "assist" supervisors and to "support" the practical application of technical standards and guidelines and not to "restrict judgment-led supervision"' (Ferran 2016: 38). In securities markets, where the complexity of the regulatory environment and the pace of innovation are greater than in banking, while the focus on conduct 'requires close proximity to market actors', there is little sign that ESMA's efforts to promote supervisory convergence have reduced the NCAs' capacity for local experimentation (Moloney 2014a: 989-92, 1003-5; 2015: 535-7). A striking example is consumer protection, where recent research shows that national authorities are pursuing a variety of novel approaches to overseeing and intervening in firms' internal processes for developing and marketing new financial products (Svetiev and Ottow 2014).

Summing up these developments, one highly knowledgeable observer concludes that the emerging post-crisis system of EU financial regulation may be regarded

> as a broadly functional combination of an open-textured approach with experimentalist traits (in particular participative decision-making in which actors responsible for implementation at the local level have a central role, and a dynamic regulatory framework in which periodic review and adjustment in the light of 'on the ground' experience is embedded) ... with the disciplines and efficiencies of an administrative agency operating within an established EU framework. (Ferran 2016: 27)

In this view, both the Commission's ability to adopt binding technical standards if their production by the ESAs deadlocks and the reserve powers of the ESAs to override NCA decisions can be understood as penalty default mechanisms for ensuring ongoing participation by reluctant parties in cooperative rule-making and implementation, rather than a decisive step towards hierarchical centralisation (Ferran 2016: 27-8, 32). In this sense, the ESAs form part of a broader trend towards the progressive formalisation and reinforcement of EU networked regulation, as in the case of energy discussed earlier (Moloney 2014a: 997).

The same cannot be said of the SSM, created in 2012-2014 as an authoritative supranational supervisor for eurozone banks attached to the ECB. The SSM was explicitly designed to break up the 'cosy relationships' between banks and national supervisors, which were deemed to have contributed through lax oversight to the financial crisis, as well as to cut the 'doom loop' between bank and sovereign debt, which had become a key source of negative contagion in the eurozone crisis (Moloney 2014b: 1622-5; Veron 2015: 14-16). It was likewise a response to the failure of the initial stress tests conducted by the EBA to flag the parlous state of Irish and Spanish banks, which had to be bailed out soon thereafter, even if the sources of this failure lay primarily in the Authority's limited powers to extract information from individual financial institutions, which have since been reinforced (Ferran 2016: 43-4).

The SSM is designed as a more centralised and hierarchical institution than the ESAs. Foremost among its powers is the final authority to grant and withdraw banking licences in the eurozone. The SSM supervises directly the 123 largest and most systemically important eurozone banks, accounting for some 85 per cent of total banking assets. The SSM can also take over supervision of the remaining 3500 or so less significant institutions (LSIs) from national authorities where it deems this necessary to ensure consistent application of high prudential standards, and can demand any information it requires from these institutions via their supervisors. To carry out these tasks, the SSM has rapidly built up a substantial central organisation employing some 1000 staff, mostly recruited from national supervisors and the ECB (ECB 2015: 38-9; Moloney 2014b: 1630-33; Veron 2015: 10-13, 23-4).

By its own account, the SSM is committed not only to implementing the single banking rulebook 'diligently and assertively' through 'intrusive and hands-on supervision' of significant financial institutions, but also to promote further harmonisation of EU regulation and convergence of supervisory approaches (ECB 2015: 5, 8, 23). Thus, for example, the SSM is reviewing the numerous options and discretions available to national authorities under EU capital adequacy requirements legislation with the aim of reducing variations across the eurozone which could dilute banks' loss-absorbing capacity (ECB 2015: 7, 51; Veron 2015: 26-7). It has already developed a harmonised Supervisory Manual describing 'common processes, procedures and methodologies' for overseeing both significant and less significant institutions, as well as for cooperation with NCAs (ECB 2015: 33-4, 66). At the heart of this Manual are the methodologies for the annual Supervisory Review and Evaluation Process (SREP), which assesses the adequacy not only of the capital and liquidity of directly supervised banks, 'but also their internal governance, strategies and processes', and prescribes corrective actions to be undertaken; together with the Supervisory Examination Programme (SEP), which defines for each bank 'the main supervisory activities [to be] carried out to monitor risks and address identified weaknesses' over the coming year (ECB 2015: 34, 36-7, 51-4; Veron 2015: 26).

To ensure close interaction with regulated entities throughout this process, ongoing oversight of each significant bank is carried out by a Joint Supervisory Team (JST), including staff from the relevant NCAs as well as the SSM. Each JST is coordinated by an ECB employee, who is normally 'a national of a different member state from that in which the bank is headquartered, and who has the final say in making proposals for decisions to the Supervisory Board, [though] any dissenting opinions from national supervisors are reported' (Veron 2015: 24-5; and see Das 2014: 34-5; ECB 2015: 5, 6-7, 22, 34-7). The JSTs are supported in carrying out these tasks by the SSM's horizontal services, which benchmark individual banks' capital, liquidity, and use of internal models against common standards. These horizontal services are likewise responsible for monitoring and reviewing NCA supervisory practices and developing methodologies for identifying high-priority LSIs requiring more intensive supervision (ECB 2015: 23, 37, 44, 52-3, 59-60, 67-70).

Despite this emphasis on harmonisation, the SSM is not seeking to impose a single 'one-size-fits-all' approach to supervision of banks across the eurozone or to homogenise their business models. The aim instead, as Supervisory Board Chair Danièle Nouy explains, is to 'ensure consistency across institutions and supervision tailored to [their] specificities ... by balancing uniform supervisory anchor points with constrained supervisory judgement', thereby accommodating banking diversity, which remains 'very desirable for financial stability' (Nouy 2015b). To achieve this goal, the SSM oversight model is explicitly designed to combine the 'deep specific knowledge of national supervisors' with 'common methodologies' and the 'broad-ranging experience of the ECB', not only for the wide variety of LSIs, but also for significant banks, where the JSTs are mandated to 'drill ... down from the governance structures into the business units' (Das 2014: 36–7; ECB 2015: 5, 8, 35).

Interviews with participating officials as well as SSM reports reveal that the formation of the JSTs has involved an intensive process of cross-fertilisation and mutual learning between supervisors from different national systems, who 'look with different eyes and different perspectives' on each other's entrenched practices, while simultaneously ensuring that the SREPs and SEPs are enriched by 'bottom-up information' from local contextual knowledge about each institution's specific risk profile (Das 2014: 39–40; ECB 2015: 52–3). The SSM Supervisory Manual, which has been 'developed by the ECB and the national supervisors together', similarly seeks to build on and combine the 'best practices' of all participating member states, rather than adopting a single off-the-peg model, for example for onsite inspections or banks' remuneration practices. As with the annual risk assessment and oversight programmes for individual institutions, there is a strongly recursive dimension to this Manual, which both EU and national officials understand as 'a living document', 'subject to continuous review and improvements on the basis of internal evaluations, internationally accepted benchmarks and international regulatory developments' as well as 'new market developments and supervisory practices'. The Manual has already been comprehensively revised once, following field tests covering half the significant banks in the eurozone, aimed at identifying and correcting problems in the SREP methodology, promoting 'learning by testing' on the part of the JSTs, and identifying further supervisory best practices (Das 2014: 39–42; ECB 2015: 33–4, 36–7, 52–7; Nouy 2015a).

This remarkable combination of uniform rules and processes, contextually adapted to banks' individual risk profiles by mixed teams of European and national supervisors, and regularly revised on the basis of central benchmarking and comparative review, supports the conclusion that, at least for now, experimentalist practices are flourishing beneath the SSM's hierarchical veneer (Das 2014). In this respect, there are close analogies to recent developments in other domains where concern for the integrity of the internal market under conditions of strategic uncertainty has given rise to uniform but rapidly updatable rules, such as the harmonised but contestable procedures for chemical regulation discussed earlier.

But the SSM leadership remains ambivalent about the diversity of approaches among national supervisors, even when the outcomes they produce are very similar, looking forward to the development of a 'common supervisory culture'. On the one hand, as its Chair observes, such diversity 'can be an advantage, because it opens up different options for getting something done'. But it can also be a source of conflicts and delays, 'as when the coordinator of a Joint Supervisory Team has to reconcile the views of nine ECB staff, 20 national supervisors from a bank's home country and a few dozen other supervisors from other countries in which the bank operates' (Nouy 2015b). Hence it is conceivable that after the initial phase of innovation and cross-fertilisation, the SSM's hierarchical constitution and powers could gradually lead to an ossification of rules and routinisation of supervisory practices, through the socialisation of staff into a homogeneous organisational culture and the reduction of space for 'learning from difference' through comparison of alternative approaches.

A potential bulwark against such developments, above and beyond strategic uncertainty generated by turbulent financial markets, is the polyarchic setting of the SSM, which obliges the ECB to take account of the views of a wide range of other actors. National supervisors comprise 19 of 25 members of the SSM Supervisory Board, a majority of whose votes is needed for all decisions, while consumer protection, anti-money laundering, and macro-prudential regulation, as well day-to-day supervision of LSIs, remain in their hands. Decisions about the winding up or restructuring of failing institutions will be taken together with the Single Resolution Board (SRB), a separate EU agency dominated by the national resolution authorities of participating member states, which makes recommendations for adoption by the Commission and the Council, with expedited procedures for use in crisis conditions. The EBA remains responsible for developing both the single EU banking rulebook and the Supervisory Handbook, including the stress test procedures, while a double majority procedure has been introduced to ensure that the interests of non-euro member states are not overridden by SSM countries voting as a bloc. The ECB/SSM must also reckon with the views of the other ESAs within the ESFS and the European Systemic Risk Board, as well as those of foreign regulators within international standard-setting bodies like the Basel Committee (Ferran 2015: 62–3, 68–85; 2016: 14–23, 38; Nouy 2015b; Veron 2015: 10–11, 27, 32–3, 45–8). Taken together, these polyarchic features of the SSM's internal and external decision-making environment seem likely to serve as a powerful mechanism for destabilising emergent tendencies towards regulatory monoculture and bureaucratic routinisation.

The European Semester

Since the onset of the eurozone crisis, the EU has introduced a series of far-reaching changes to its institutional architecture for socio-economic governance.[2] At its centre is the 'European Semester' of policy coordination, through which the Commission, the Council, and the European Council set priorities for the Union in the Annual Growth Survey (AGS), review Commission Country Reports and National Reform Programmes (NRPs), and issue Country-Specific Recommendations (CSRs) to member states, backed up in some cases by the possibility of financial sanctions. The European Semester brings together within a single annual cycle a wide range of EU governance instruments with different legal bases and sanctioning authority, from the Stability and Growth Pact (SGP), the Macroeconomic Imbalance Procedure (MIP), and the Fiscal Treaty to the Europe 2020 Strategy and the Integrated Economic and Employment Policy Guidelines. This process in turn gives the EU institutions a more visible and intrusive role than ever before in scrutinising and guiding national economic, fiscal, and social policies, especially within the eurozone.

The rapid evolution of the European Semester since its inception in 2010 raises important questions about its nature as a governance process. Should it be understood as a more effective framework for enforcing national compliance with EU rules and policy recommendations, aimed at redressing the pervasive implementation deficits that had undermined the SGP and the Lisbon Strategy before the crisis, as many economic policy-makers claimed (e.g. Ioannou and Stracca 2011)? Or does the Semester's new governance architecture offer opportunities for joint exploration and recursive learning among member states about how to pursue multi-dimensional objectives and provisional solutions to uncertain problems in diverse national contexts, as an experimentalist approach would recommend? The remainder of this section approaches these questions by examining the social dimension of the European Semester, both for reasons of tractability and because debates about the scope for national policy autonomy and learning within the Semester have been particularly salient in this field.[3]

Initial experiences under the European Semester seemed to confirm fears that the new policy coordination framework would result in the subordination of social objectives to fiscal discipline, budgetary austerity, and welfare retrenchment imposed by economic policy actors, buttressed by legally binding CSRs and threatened financial sanctions (see Pochet and Degryse 2012). Thus the AGS and CSRs for 2011 focused primarily on fiscal consolidation, while emphasising the need for financial reform of pensions and healthcare systems to relieve pressure on national budgets, together with increased benefit conditionality to 'make work pay' and boost employment rates.[4] More generally, the first European Semester followed a prescriptive 'one-size-fits-all' approach, with limited adaptation of the CSRs to the specific situations of individual member states. The Commission explicitly sought to use multilateral surveillance by national officials in EU economic and employment policy committees as a mechanism for peer pressure towards implementation of top-down structural reforms. Social policy actors at both EU and national level found themselves largely excluded from preparation and review of the NRPs and CSRs (Zeitlin and Vanhercke 2014: 27–30).

But as the sovereign debt crisis within the eurozone morphed into a broader economic and employment crisis, a significant rebalancing between social, economic, and employment objectives became visible in the policy orientation of successive European Semesters. The 2011 AGS had set three overarching priorities for the EU: 'rigorous fiscal consolidation for enhancing macroeconomic stability', 'labour market reforms for higher employment', and 'growth-enhancing measures'. The 2012 AGS replaced these with a broader and more socially balanced set of priorities, including 'tackling unemployment and the social consequences of the crisis', which were reaffirmed in subsequent years. Similar developments occurred in the CSRs, whose social scope and content expanded progressively from year to year, placing increasing stress on the need for member states to ensure the adequacy, accessibility, and effectiveness of their social security, pension, and healthcare systems; to combat poverty and social exclusion on a variety of dimensions; and to improve their education, training, and activation services (Zeitlin and Vanhercke 2014: 19–20).

The substantive reorientation of the European Semester towards a more socially balanced policy stance from 2011 to 2014 was accompanied by organisational and procedural developments which have reinforced the role of social and employment policy actors in its governance, while at the same time expanding the scope for deliberation and mutual learning about how to adapt common European objectives to diverse national contexts. Both the Social Protection Committee (SPC) and the Employment Committee (EMCO) of national officials advising the Employment, Social Affairs, Health and Consumer Affairs (EPSCO) Council have established themselves as key players in monitoring, reviewing, and assessing national reforms within the European Semester. Together, they have developed a Joint Assessment Framework for the implementation of the Employment Guidelines, whose results feed into separate Employment and Social Protection Performance Monitors for identifying and comparing emerging challenges and outcomes across member states. Both committees are committed to using these indicator-based monitoring tools to underpin multilateral surveillance and support member states in establishing their reform priorities, identifying good practices, and stimulating mutual learning, as well as feeding into the broader EU policy debate. (Zeitlin and Vanhercke 2014: 37–8).

This extended social and employment policy monitoring has gone hand-in-hand with an intensification of multilateral surveillance and peer review in both committees. This includes thematic as well as country-specific reviews of CSR implementation and reform plans to facilitate horizontal debate and comparison across member states. The SPC's thematic reviews are particularly aimed at fostering mutual learning and stimulating multilateral discussion on how to tackle specific policy challenges identified as common negative 'trends to watch' in its performance monitor. Commission officials as well as committee members see this review process as a 'game changer', making exchanges within the committees less 'cosy' and more incisive than in the past, while transforming 'the bilateral discussion on the CSRs between Member States and the Commission into a multilateral decision making process' (Zeitlin and Vanhercke 2014: 39–43).

Such intensified monitoring, multilateral surveillance, and peer review in turn forms the basis for enhanced input by EMCO and the SPC into the adoption of the CSRs, the culmination of the Semester. In the first European Semester of 2011, the SPC (and Ministers of Social Affairs more generally) were largely excluded from the review and adoption of the CSRs. Beginning in 2012, however, the social players began to acquire a more influential place in the CSR process, drawing on the expertise gained through the monitoring, surveillance, and review activities described above, as well as through explicit political challenges by the EPSCO Council to the jurisdiction of economic policy actors over social and employment issues. The 2012 European Semester catalysed a vigorous push back by member states against the Commission's increasingly prescriptive approach to the CSRs, along with its reluctance to deliberate over proposed amendments with national representatives (Zeitlin and Vanhercke 2014: 44–5).

These conflicts over the organisation of the European Semester gave rise to a substantially revised procedural framework beginning with the 2013 cycle, based on a clearer allocation of responsibilities and cooperation in reviewing and amending the CSRs in areas of overlapping competences between the various committees and Council formations involved. Underlying this revised procedural framework were new decision-making processes and working methods within as well as between the participating committees. In each case, amendments to the CSRs were supported by qualified majority voting (QMV) to test the support among member states for changes to the Commission's proposals. Multilateral surveillance within the committees is likewise crucial to the review and amendment of the CSRs. Only issues that have been extensively discussed by member states during the multilateral surveillance process stand a chance of securing the necessary qualified majority within the committees. Both EMCO and SPC draw extensively on evidence from their multilateral surveillance in negotiating with the committees advising the Economic and Financial Affairs (ECOFIN) Council and the Commission over amendments to the CSRs. Since under the 'comply or explain' rules of the European Semester, the Council is expected to provide a written explanation of its reasons for modifying the Commission's recommendations, both committees also refer explicitly to these multilateral reviews in the formal reports justifying their amendments (Zeitlin and Vanhercke 2014: 46–9).

The revised procedural arrangements for reviewing and adopting the CSRs had a significant impact on the frequency of amendments. Most of these amendments concerned points of detail, focusing on better contextualisation of individual CSRs in relation to national challenges and reform measures. But it was also sometimes possible to obtain 'horizontal' amendments to multiple CSRs addressing broader issues, notably in the case of pension reform, where the comply-or-explain text emphasised the importance of allowing member states to choose among alternative paths to reach the underlying objective of raising the effective retirement age. This broader message was endorsed by the rotating Council Presidency, which urged the Commission to 'ensure that its CSR proposals are sufficiently precise as regards policy outcomes but not overly prescriptive as regards policy measures so as to leave sufficient space for … national ownership' (Lithuanian Presidency 2013; Zeitlin and Vanhercke 2014: 49–51).

Thus over the life of the second Barroso Commission, a progressive 'socialisation' of the European Semester took place. This shift was visible at the level of substantive policy orientations, in terms of a growing emphasis on social objectives in the AGS and especially the CSRs. It was equally visible at the level of governance procedures, in terms of an enhanced role for social and employment policy actors in monitoring, reviewing, and amending the CSRs.

Through this process, member state representatives were also able to push back against what they perceived as 'over-prescriptive', 'one-size-fits-all' recommendations from the Commission, which sought to lay down not only reform objectives, but also the specific way of reaching them, without taking sufficient account of national contexts and competences. By demonstrating their ability to amend the Commission's draft CSRs through QMV, these committees were also able to force the latter to engage more deliberatively with member states in both multilateral and bilateral fora.

Many prominent actors within both the Commission and the Council still view the European Semester first and foremost as a framework for enforcing national compliance with EU rules and recommendations. The Semester has undoubtedly been used by the EU institutions to put pressure on member states to address the specific policy challenges flagged by the CSRs, especially under the SGP and MIP. But no sanctions have yet been imposed on any member state within the Semester, including under the MIP, and given the political and legal hurdles involved this seems likely to occur, if at all, only under very exceptional circumstances. While recommendations under the European Semester typically receive greater national political and media attention than those of previous EU policy coordination processes, interview evidence suggests that there are still wide differences between member states in how seriously they take the CSRs, depending on a variety of domestic considerations, including public attitudes towards European integration, the political sensitivity of the issues at stake, the national fiscal and macroeconomic situation, and the weight of the structural funds, as well as the quality and persuasiveness of the analysis behind them (Zeitlin and Vanhercke: 56–8).

If there is little consensus on the effectiveness of the European Semester as a top-down compliance mechanism, EU-level interviewees were remarkably positive about the extent of joint exploration and mutual learning developing through the Semester process, especially within EMCO and the SPC. Participants in the review process emphasise that its iterative character has produced a strong learning and consensus-building effect within the committees. An added impetus to mutual learning in recent years has come from the innovative *ex ante* reviews piloted by both committees, where member states present planned reforms before their enactment and receive 'experience-based feedback' from other countries 'wh[ich] had implemented similar reforms in the past', together with 'concrete advice on how to improve the[ir] policy design' (SPC 2014; Zeitlin and Vanhercke 2014: 58–60).

In contrast to the post-crisis evolution of EU financial regulation, it would be exaggerated to claim that these developments have transformed the European Semester into an experimentalist governance process. But at least in the social and employment policy fields, there are clear signs of a growing focus on joint exploration and recursive learning about how to address common European objectives and challenges in diverse contexts through monitoring, surveillance, and peer review of national reforms. The intensification of these 'learning by monitoring' activities between 2011 and 2014 was accompanied by a vigorous pushback by member states against the Commission's perceived efforts to impose uniform, over-prescriptive recommendations insufficiently adapted to national circumstances, which gave rise not only to successful amendments of the CSRs, but also to revisions of the broader governance procedures of the Semester itself that have made it less hierarchical and more interactive.

The new Juncker Commission, which took office in November 2014, introduced a further round of procedural revisions to the 2015 European Semester. Building on plans initiated by its predecessor and responding to member state demands, the new Commission sought to 'streamline' the Semester process by integrating the In-Depth Reports prepared as part of the MIP with the Staff Working Documents supporting the CSRs into a single Country Report, setting out its analysis of the main national reform challenges and measures taken to address them. These Country Reports were the subject of intensive bilateral discussions with member states both before and after publication, giving the latter an opportunity to challenge and in some cases correct the Commission's assessment. The Commission also released both the Country Reports and CSRs earlier in the cycle, in order to leave more time for review and debate within the EU committees. But the most fundamental change was the Juncker Commission's own decision to reduce drastically the number and scope of the CSRs, concentrating on key priority issues identified as actionable and monitorable within a 12- to 18-month timescale. In most cases, this new generation of CSRs focused more on challenges and outcomes than on specific policy measures – 'the what rather than the how', as one high Commission official put it (European Commission 2015; Vanhercke and Zeitlin 2015).

These changes in the organisation of the European Semester, which the Commission presented as a means of increasing 'national ownership' of the reform process, were broadly welcomed by member states as well as other EU institutions. But the dramatic reduction in the number, detail, and scope of the CSRs meant that many significant policy challenges flagged in the Country Reports did not figure in the recommendations. The selection among these issues, which was decided at the highest levels within the Commission, thus appeared less transparent and more self-consciously 'political' than in previous years. The amendment process likewise appears to have been more politicised and less evidence-based than in preceding years, with member states in similar situations obtaining different results on the same issues (e.g. pensions) depending on lobbying and coalitional voting. It remains uncertain how these revised features of the Semester process will develop in subsequent years, particularly as regards how challenges identified in the Country Reports but not addressed by the CSRs would be monitored and reviewed. Both EMCO and the SPC are currently revising their multilateral surveillance arrangements to ensure ongoing coverage of the full range of social and employment policy issues reviewed in past years, along with new trends to watch flagged by their monitoring instruments (EMCO 2015; SPC 2015; Vanhercke and Zeitlin 2015).

The future of the European Semester likewise remains open in the longer term. The 'Five Presidents' Report' on Completing Europe's Economic and Monetary Union (Juncker *et al.* 2015) has proposed using a stronger and more integrated European Semester to promote convergence of economic, social, and employment performance among eurozone member states, based on 'common high level standards' eventually defined in EU legislation, including a 'social protection floor'. In some areas, this would involve 'further harmonisation', while in others, 'where different policies can lead to similarly good performance', it would mean 'finding country-specific solutions'. Progress towards these standards would be monitored and followed up through the CSRs and an expanded version of the MIP. In the first stage of this process, eurozone member states would continue to receive 'concrete and ambitious' CSRs focused on priority reforms, especially as regards expected outcomes and timeframe, but would retain 'a degree of freedom concerning the exact measures to be implemented', subject to more systematic reporting, peer review, and 'comply or explain' requirements. The Eurogroup could already play 'a coordinating role in cross-examining performance, with increased focus on benchmarking and pursuing best practice', accompanied by a fuller use of the MIP, including in dealing with necessary reforms 'in countries accumulating large and sustained current account surpluses' (Juncker *et al.* 2015: 7–9, 22).

It remains far from clear for now how these proposals might work in detail, and still less how far eurozone member states would be prepared to embrace them. But the experience of the European Semester to date strongly suggests that centralised efforts to impose one-size-fits-all policy templates are unlikely to prove effective in the diverse and polyarchic conditions of the EU, as the Five Presidents' Report itself acknowledges. This experience likewise suggests that a more intensive process of joint exploration and experimental learning would be required to support convergence of performance among eurozone member states by discovering contextually appropriate solutions to complex, uncertain challenges such as those involved in reforming national employment and welfare systems.

Conclusion

Tested by the crisis like the Union itself, EU experimentalist governance has proved remarkably resilient. In most policy domains, it continues to function much as before the crisis, displaying a robust capacity to revise and improve existing regulatory frameworks, as for example in fields like energy and industrial emissions. In others, like trade, experimentalist principles and practices have served as the basis for ambitious new initiatives, such as the regulatory equivalence assessment proposals in the TTIP negotiations. Even where the EU's responses to the crisis have appeared to move decisively towards centralised hierarchical authority, as in financial regulation, front-line supervisors retain a key role in the new ESAs, with responsibilities for drafting binding European rules, monitoring and reviewing national implementation, and proposing revisions in light of on-the-ground experience. In the SSM, whose institutional design is more explicitly centralised, experimentalist practices of 'learning from difference' in joint teams of European and national supervisors, contextual adaptation of common rules and processes to banks' individual risk profiles, and recursive revision of supervisory methods on the basis of comparative benchmarking and review appear to be flourishing, at least for now, under a hierarchical veneer. The case of the European Semester is more ambiguous and its future more open. But at least in the social and employment policy fields there are clear signs of a growing emphasis on joint exploration and mutual learning about how to address common European objectives and challenges in diverse national contexts, coupled with a vigorous pushback by member states against the Commission's perceived efforts to impose uniform, over-prescriptive recommendations that has made the Semester's governance procedures less hierarchical and more interactive.

These developments underline the limits of centralised hierarchical governance in the EU's turbulent and polyarchic environment, where strategic uncertainty about how best to achieve common goals recommends joint exploration and recursive learning from implementation experience, while the heterogeneity of national institutions and preferences discourages one-size-fits-all solutions. At any given moment, it may be desirable to move towards greater uniformity in the rules governing tightly integrated markets (as in finance), provided that these can be rapidly updated and revised, as well as to push for increased convergence of economic, social, and employment performance across EU member states, especially within the eurozone. But under conditions of deep uncertainty, diversity – of business models, institutions, and policies – remains a vital adaptive resource, both for stability (as in finance) and for learning. Since strategic uncertainty depends on policy-makers' perceptions of their environment, there can be no guarantee that the EU will eschew centralised hierarchical solutions as its leaders pursue further integration in a variety of domains in response to the crisis. A powerful bulwark against this possibility, however, as the cases of financial regulation and the European Semester each in different ways suggest, is the abiding polyarchic structure of the EU, whereby the member states participate directly in its decision-making processes, and no single actor can impose their preferred approach without taking into account the views of others.

Notes

1. For a sceptical view of their extensiveness, see Börzel (2012).
2. This section draws on Zeitlin and Vanhercke (2014) and Vanhercke and Zeitlin (2015), which provide fuller references to EU documents and interviews with key participants in the Semester process. The analysis is based on five rounds of interviews conducted between 2010 and 2015 with more than 50 high-level policy-makers within the EU institutions and member states (Commission, Council, advisory committees, Parliament, NGOs, social partners) concerned with economic, social, and employment issues, as well as on near-complete access to the papers of the EU Social Protection and Employment Committees during this period.
3. Detailed consideration of the evolution of EU fiscal governance, which has never been characterisable as experimentalist, is beyond the scope of this paper. On the pre-crisis limitations of the rules-based approach of the Stability and Growth Pact, and its dependence on 'soft law' surveillance processes, see Schelkle (2007); for an analysis of post-crisis fiscal governance as a 'hybrid' combination of rules- and coordination-based forms, see Armstrong (2013).
4. Commission Annual Growth Surveys, proposed CSRs, and CSRs as adopted by the Council are available online at http://ec.europa.eu/europe2020/making-it-happen/index_en.htm.

Acknowledgements

Previous versions of this paper were presented at the Watson Institute for International Studies, Brown University; the Centre for the Study of Europe, Boston University; and the Nijmegen School of Management, Radboud University. For helpful comments and advice, I am grateful to the participants in these seminars and the special issue preparatory workshops at the Schuman Centre, especially Brigid Laffan, as well as to Kenneth Armstrong, Eilís Ferran, Sigrid Quack, Charles Sabel and Mark Thatcher.

Disclosure statement

No potential conflict of interest was reported by the author.

References

Anderson, S.S., and N. Sitter (2015). 'Managing Heterogeneity in the EU: Using Gas Market Liberalisation to Explore the Changing Mechanisms of Intergovernmental Governance', *Journal of European Integration*, 37:3, 319–34.

Armstrong, K. (2013). 'The New Governance of EU Fiscal Discipline', *European Law Review*, 38:5, 601–17.

Bauer, M.W., and S. Becker (2014). 'The Unexpected Winner of the Crisis: The European Commission's Strengthened Role in Economic Governance', *Journal of European Integration*, 36:3, 213–29.

Bickerton, C., D. Hodson, and U. Puetter (2015). 'The New Intergovernmentalism: European Integration in the Post-Maastricht Era', *Journal of Common Market Studies*, 53:4, 703–22.

Biedenkopf, K. (2015). 'EU Chemicals Regulation: Extending Its Experimentalist REACH', in J. Zeitlin (ed.), *Extending Experimentalist Governance? The European Union and Transnational Regulation*. Oxford: Oxford University Press, 107–36.

Black, J. (2012). 'Restructuring Global and EU Financial Regulation: Character, Capacities, and Learning', in E. Wymersch, K.J. Hopt, and G. Ferrarini (eds.), *Financial Regulation and Supervision: A Post-Crisis Analysis*. Oxford: Oxford University Press, 3–47.

Börzel, T.A. (2012). 'Experimentalist Governance in the EU: The Emperor's New Clothes?', *Regulation and Governance*, 6:3, 378–84.

de Búrca, G., R.O. Keohane, and C.F. Sabel (2013). 'New Modes of Pluralist Global Governance', *NYU Journal of International Law and Politics* 45:3, 723–86.

Chalmers, D. (2012). 'The European Redistributive State and a European Law of Struggle', *European Law Journal*, 18:5, 667–93.

Crum, B. (2013). 'Saving the Euro at the Cost of Democracy?', *Journal of Common Market Studies*, 51:4, 614–30.

Curtin, D. (2014). 'Challenging Executive Dominance in European Democracy', *Modern Law Review*, 77:1, 1–32.

Das, H.D. (2014). Banking Union: The Appropriate Degree of Centralization of European Banking Governance?, Master thesis, University of Amsterdam.

Dawson, M. (2015). 'The Legal and Political Accountability Structure of "Post-Crisis" EU Economic Governance', *Journal of Common Market Studies*, 53:5, 976–93.

ECB Banking Supervision (2015). *Annual Report on Supervisory Activities 2014*. Frankfurt: European Central Bank.

EMCO (2015). 'EMCO Review of the European Semester Process', 9 September.

European Commission (2013-15). 'EU Negotiating Texts in TTIP', available at http://trade.ec.europa.eu/doclib/press/index.cfm?id=1230.

European Commission (2015). *2015 European Semester: Country-specific recommendations*, COM (2015) 250 final, Brussels 13 May.

Ferran, E. (2012). 'Understanding the New Institutional Architecture of EU Financial Market Supervision', in E. Wymersch, K.J. Hopt, and G. Ferrarini (eds.), *Financial Regulation and Supervision: A Post-Crisis Analysis*. Oxford: Oxford University Press, 111–58.

Ferran, E. (2015). 'European Banking Union: Imperfect, but It Can Work', in D. Busch and G. Ferrarini (eds.), *European Banking Union*. Oxford: Oxford University Press, 56–90.

Ferran, E. (2016). 'The Existential Search of the European Banking Authority', *European Business Organization Law Review*, forthcoming.

Grossman, E., and P. Leblond (2012). 'Financial Regulation in Europe: From the Battle of the Systems to a Jacobinist EU', in J. Richardson (ed.), *Constructing a Policy-Making State? Policy Dynamics in the EU*. Oxford: Oxford University Press, 189–208.

Herrigel, G. (2015). 'Experimentalist Systems in Manufacturing Multinationals', unpublished paper, Department of Political Science, University of Chicago.

Ioannou, D., and L. Stracca (2011). *Have Euro Area and EU Economic Governance Worked? Just the Facts*, ECB Working Paper No. 1344.

Juncker, J.-C., D. Tusk, J. Dijsselbloem, M. Dragi, and M. Schultz (2015). *Completing Europe's Economic and Monetary Union*. Brussels: European Commission.

Koutalakis, C., A. Buzogany, and T.A. Börzel (2010). 'When Soft Regulation Is Not Enough: The Integrated Pollution Prevention and Control Directive of the European Union', *Regulation & Governance*, 4:3, 329–44.

de Larosière, J. (2009). 'Report of the High-Level Group on Financial Supervision in the EU', Brussels, 25 February.

Lithuanian Presidency of the EU (2013). *Lessons from 2013 and way forward*, Council of the EU 14618/13, 16 October.

van Middelaar, L. (2015). 'A Return of Politics – The European Union after the Crises in the Eurozone and Ukraine', *Journal of Common Market Studies*, 53:3, 495–507.

Moloney, N. (2014a). *EU Securities and Financial Markets Regulation*, 3rd ed. Oxford: Oxford University Press.

Moloney, N. (2014b). 'European Banking Union: Assessing Its Risks and Resilience', *Common Market Law Review*, 51, 1609–670.

Moloney, N. (2015). 'Banking Union and the Implications for Financial Market Governance in the EU: Convergence or Divergence?', in D. Busch and G. Ferrarini (eds.), *European Banking Union*. Oxford: Oxford University Press, 524–63.

Monar, J. (2010). 'Experimentalist Governance in Justice and Home Affairs', in C.F. Sabel and J. Zeitlin (eds.), *Experimentalist Governance in the European Union*. Oxford: Oxford University Press, 237–60.

Nouy, D. (2015a). 'Presentation of the First ECB Annual Report on Supervisory Activities at the European Parliament's Economic and Monetary Affairs Committee', 31 March, available at https://www.bankingsupervision.europa.eu/press/speeches/date/2015/html/se150331.en.html.

Nouy, D. (2015b). 'Interview with *Handelsblatt*', 1 April, available at https://www.bankingsupervision.europa.eu/press/interviews/date/2015/html/sn150401.en.html

Pochet, P., and C. Degryse (2012). 'The Programmed Dismantlement of the European Social Model', *Intereconomics*, 4, 212–17.

Posner, E. (2010). 'The Lamfalussy Process: The Polyarchic Origins of Networked Financial Rule-Making in the EU', in C.F. Sabel and J. Zeitlin (eds.), *Experimentalist Governance in the European Union: Towards a New Architecture*. Oxford: Oxford University Press, 43–60.
Posner, E. (2015). 'International Financial Regulatory Cooperation: An Experimentalist Turn?', in J. Zeitlin (ed.), *Extending Experimentalist Governance? The European Union and Transnational Regulation*. Oxford: Oxford University Press, 196–223.
Sabel, C.F., and W.H. Simon (2015). 'The Management Side of Due Process in the Service-Based Welfare State', paper prepared for 'Administrative Law from the Inside Out: A Conference on Themes in the Work of Jerry Mashaw', New Haven, October 1-2.
Sabel, C.F., and J. Zeitlin (2008). 'Learning from Difference: The New Architecture of Experimentalist Governance in the EU', *European Law Journal*, 14:3, 271–327.
Sabel, C.F., and J. Zeitlin, eds. (2010). *Experimentalist Governance in the European Union: Towards a New Architecture*. Oxford: Oxford University Press.
Sabel, C.F., and J. Zeitlin (2012a). 'Experimentalism in the EU: Common ground and persistent differences', *Regulation and Governance*, 6:3, 410–26.
Sabel, C.F., and J. Zeitlin (2012b). 'Experimentalist Governance', in D. Levi-Faur (ed.), *The Oxford Handbook of Governance*. Oxford: Oxford University Press, 169–83.
Schelkle, W. (2007). 'EU Fiscal Governance: Hard Law in the Shadow of Soft Law?', *Columbia Journal of European Law*, 13, 705–31.
SPC (2014). Ex Ante Coordination of Major Social Policy Reforms: Synthesis Report, Council of the EU 10386/14, Brussels, 3 June.
SPC (2015). 2015 European Semester – Review of Arrangements and Lessons Learnt, SPC/2015/9/1.3, 11 September.
Svetiev, Y., and A. Ottow (2014). 'Financial Supervision in the Interstices between Private and Public Law', *European Review of Contract Law*, 10:4, 496–544.
Vanhercke, B., and J. Zeitlin (2015). *Further Socializing the European Semester: Moving Forward for the Social 'Triple A'?* Brussels: European Social Observatory, 15 December.
Veron, N. (2015). *Europe's Radical Banking Union*. Brussels: Bruegel.
Zeitlin, J., ed. (2015). *Extending Experimentalist Governance? The European Union and Transnational Regulation*. Oxford: Oxford University Press.
Zeitlin, J., and B. Vanhercke (2014). *Socializing the European Semester? Economic Governance and Social Policy Coordination in Europe 2020*. SIEPS Report 2014:7. Stockholm: Swedish Institute for European Policy Studies, December.

Why the single market remains the EU's core business

Jacques Pelkmans

ABSTRACT
This paper examines the centrality of the single market to the EU. Its main conclusion is that the single market will remain central to the Union in future and that although it is not immune to crises, because it is the Union's hard core and has powerful governance, serious erosion is unlikely. The paper examines the centrality of the single market by analysing in-depth the functional logic of market integration and the progress and deficits that characterise the Union's market regime. The paper then explores the meaning of the internal market for EMU and argues that the single market is the 'E' in EMU. The issue of the euro 'ins' and 'outs' is addressed. The paper ends by asking if the single market is resilient against crises and concludes in the affirmative.

The internal market was and is the hard core of the EU. In the shadow of the Great Recession, the eurozone crisis and its multi-fold repercussions for European integration, the question is whether the single market will remain so central - indeed, the foundation of the EU also tomorrow ? We shall answer this question affirmatively and set out why. Indeed, the robustness of the single market is likely to have mitigated the overall economic impact of the Great Recession for the EU. The single market is not necessarily immune to crises but as it is the EU's hard core and its powerful governance render serious erosion unlikely.

Before addressing why the single market remains the EU's core business, even in the aftermath of a deep crisis, it is critical to first discuss what the single market is, and is not, and why it is so central. Subsequently, the rigorous logic of market integration in the EU will be explained, a permanent potential source of functionalist deepening and widening (of scope). We shall stylise how the EU has 'established' the internal market over time, how the EU attempts to ensure its 'proper functioning' and what the 'regulatory logic' of the single market is. A brief exposition of the progress of EU market integration up to today is given, again in a stylised fashion in terms of policy accomplishments, followed by a discussion of how the internal market and EMU are related, both the 'soft' Economic and Monetary Union (EMU) of all 28 member states and the 'hard' EMU in the form of the eurozone of 19 EU countries. It is crucial to focus on the single market of all 28 countries at all times. The debate here is complicated as the single market has been deepened during the crisis but there is also a lingering fear that the eurozone's deepening (e.g. with the banking union) might inflict a bias against a truly single financial market (e.g. for the 'outs'). In any case, further deepening is to be expected, if not already under way, with new single market strategies recently initiated. The penultimate section finds that the single market is resilient against crises; and the final section concludes.

Why the single market is accepted as the 'hard core' of European integration

Building up the internal market – what the treaty calls its 'establishment' - and having it 'function properly', is supposed to serve the aims of the Treaty on the Functioning of the European Union (TFEU) treaty. This was even more clearly the case for the four economic objectives of the Rome treaty.[1] Indeed, the internal market is the *principal* means serving these objectives. Although the treaty (now the TFEU) has become far more complicated, and a separate EU treaty is formulating or overarching all that the EU stands for, the internal market has remained the foundation for by far the larger part of substantive EU activities. Meanwhile, the internal market also serves as the foundation of EMU, especially the eurozone with 19 EU countries. It is therefore not comparable to 'yet another' policy domain in European integration. On the contrary, many policies 'piggyback' on the single market in its widest form. On the one hand, the EU would signify rather little economically and/or politically without maintaining a single market – in the worst case, it might dissolve into a kind of customs-union-plus of the 1970s, or allow costly forms of fragmentation. In the process, many other EU policies, which essentially constitute derivatives of the single market (see below), would be at risk of erosion as well. EMU or the eurozone would also lose its foundation, with the 'E' (economic union) melting away gradually. EU countries without exception regard the single market as the overriding reason why they have become a member of the Union, besides values and a sense of 'soft security'. A community of values without the single market risks being an elevated Council of Europe. On the other hand, EU and non-EU countries routinely signal how critical the single market is for them. A few examples will clarify this. The UK might take a BREXIT decision but its entire strategy rests on staying inside the single market - even though the UK might end up as a non-EU country, it counts on staying in the single market and PM Cameron is adamant that this ought to be possible.[2] New EU members, when still candidates, have consistently expressed a strong preference to become part of the single market, for the purpose of stimulating growth and companies' competitiveness. The three European Economic Area countries of the European Free Trade Association (EEA-EFTA) countries and (for the most part) Switzerland essentially live in the single market – indeed, the EEA Agreement and the many sectoral bilaterals with Switzerland are almost all about the single market. But the strength and depth of the single market is equally decisive for the Trans-atlantic Trade and Investment Partnership (TTIP), Comprehensive Economic and Trade Agreement (CETA) and EU trade and regulatory negotiations with Japan.

Should the single market be redesigned in the light of the recent crises in order to render it more resilient and/or to respond satisfactorily to signs of dissatisfaction among grassroots in the European electorates? 'Rethinking' market integration has been done several times in the nearly 60 years of EU history. The current 'rethink' of the single market is only very partially a response to the crisis and the Great Recession because most of the upgrading prompted by the crisis has already been accomplished in the regulation and supervision of financial markets as well as by adopting a centralised bank resolution regime. The strategic single market debates of today[3] contrast sharply with the turmoil and hectic EU decision-making about crisis measures for and urgent 'repairs' of the fault lines of the not-so-genuine EMU.

However, it would be a great mistake to conclude that there was and is no politics to the single market. The history of the single market has had its occasional turmoil and hectic political discourse or decision-making. It began in 1958 with French monetary reform (by Rueff). Had this drastic removal of export subsidies and extra import charges – a de facto devaluation, combined with a 'new' French franc – failed, the EEC would never have taken off in the first place. The empty chair in 1965 was about the politics and decision power over the agricultural policy, the (costly) underpinning of the single market for agricultural goods. The removal of vetoes led to the first ever referendum on the single market (in Denmark in 1992). More recent instances of profound political conflict on aspects of the single market include the three years of turmoil in the EP on the horizontal services directive[4] and the simultaneous deep quarrels (with open letters from some PMs to Commission President Prodi) about the new chemical regulation in Registration, Evaluation, Authorisation and Restriction of Chemicals (REACH). Finally, much of single market high politics was channelled into debates over treaty changes which comprised, for example, Qualified Majority Voting (QMV) in more and more instances and gradually stronger powers for the EP.

The functional logic of EU market integration

Defining EU market integration

EU market integration has to be 'established' (treaty language for 'realised' by law) and it has to 'function properly'. Already in the Rome treaty one can discern that establishing the internal market is the result of two policy processes: cross-border intra-EU liberalisation in several market types (like goods and services) and what is termed 'harmonisation' or approximation of national laws. The first process is essentially 'market access' inside the EU, be it in a very demanding form of non-discrimination in (numerous) national laws, an almost unconditional right of access called 'free movement' (and the right of establishment of a company or an independent) and strong disciplines for the minimisation of distortions (negative integration). However, in many markets it is dysfunctional or even impossible to solely rely on 'negative integration', because there are 'market failures'. It is pointless or (in terms of 'welfare') counterproductive to do so since these market failures are usually addressed at the member state level and will have to be addressed in some way at the EU level for the internal market to function properly. Not doing so will make it impossible for member states to agree with open access, hence justifying regulatory or technical barriers, fragmenting the internal market. Joint forms of addressing such regulatory needs and the institutions required are called 'positive integration'. Many degrees of ambition of positive integration can be envisaged, from consultation and coordination (whatever that might mean), to joint (i.e. EU) regulation in many forms, joint funds or, in the extreme, common bodies with the task of regulating themselves, within a commonly agreed EU framework. Nearly 60 years after Rome, this positive integration, with various manifestations of EU market regulation (also in common policies), is perhaps the most conspicuous aspect of the EU internal market. To put it simply, the day-to-day core business of the EU is to 'regulate'. Surely that was not what the founding fathers (see the Comité Intergouvernemental 1956 report) would have expected, or at least certainly not to this extent, in so many areas and so intrusively. The functional rigour of the internal market logic was only gradually discovered and understood.

Stylising how the EU pursues market integration

The internal market serves the (economic) treaty objectives. The left-hand side of Figure 1 is 'negative market integration', starting with the customs union (removing intra-EU tariffs; the common external tariff is part of common trade policy on the right-hand side), complemented by free movement[5] and the right of establishment. Negative integration has turned out to be ambitious, taking generations to establish, even in goods – the first market type that was tackled seriously. Without the Single Act, the internal goods market would never have enjoyed general free movement as it does today. This was mainly due to three critical reforms in or stimulated by the Single Act. First, the 'area without frontiers' encompassed regulatory and fiscal frontiers, not just customs frontiers. This had fundamental consequences for the ambition of new Commission programmes, known later as EC-1992. In one stroke it undermined many lobby and protectionist strategies in goods and services

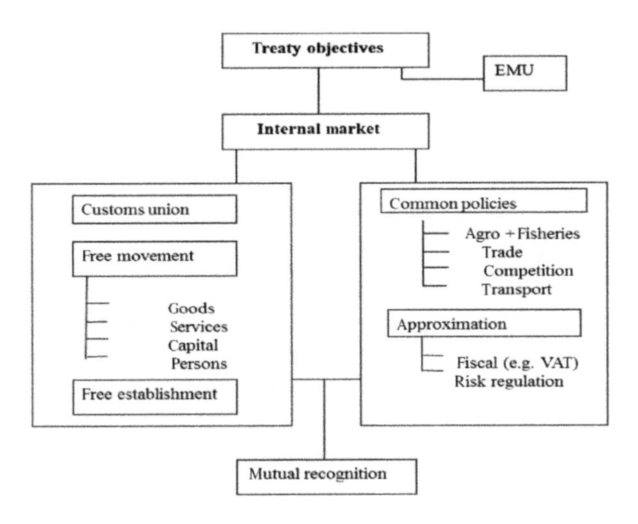

Figure 1. Internal market regime.

sectors so far still heavily fragmented. Second, many internal market questions came under QMV, which effectively meant that countries – if against – had in turn to construct blocking minorities, often leading to partial concessions of an integrationist character and/or to 'better' solutions more acceptable to some member states. In numerous other instances the Council (then still dominant) could focus on sound proposals or well-justified amendments, which increased the speed of decision-making and enabled the member states to revisit proposals or ideas that, before, proved to be impossible due to vetoes. Third, the Single Act coincided, but not by chance, with several reforms, which had the double dividend of improving the quality of EU regulation and facilitating the adoption of 'lighter' regulation, without undermining objectives (mainly of risk regulation). The example par excellence is the new approach of removing technical barriers to trade in the Union but one can also cite the new approach to (more horizontal) food regulation, the timid breakthrough in mutual recognition in professional qualifications (late 1980s), the radical reforms in EU transport policy (after the 1985 conviction of the Council by the Court of Justice of the European Union [CJEU]), the 'simple' removal of frontier controls on the roads and the partial acceptance of 'home country control' in EU financial services regulation. Another reform which suddenly became acceptable consisted in the removal of all exchange controls in the EU-12, the idea being that sound macro-economic policy was in the enlightened self-interest of every member state, so that there was simply no case to introduce or maintain restrictions in the internal market in order to protect bad national policy.

The real challenges of the next episodes were found in services, an amalgam of areas and sectors with very distinct characteristics, and in intellectual property rights (IPRs). Below we will briefly describe the progress in services.

IPRs were regarded as an issue of 'national ownership' (given the Rome treaty article 222, now article 345, TFEU). The huge vested interests in this area[6] and the technicality of the issues (in other words, the great asymmetries of information between the specialists and political decision-makers) provided endless opportunities to prevent or slow down the Europeanisation of IPRs. Also this episode is now largely over with the arrival of the European Unitary Patent, a significant breakthrough for EU-driven innovation.

The right-hand side of Figure 1 is about positive integration. In essence, this is about EU regulation in common policies (trade, competition, transport, agro-fisheries) and EU regulation as 'approximation'. The latter is overwhelmingly in risk regulation, and to a small extent in fiscal (VAT, excises, some minor issues in corporate taxation and interest taxes). Risk regulation in the single market is the dominant regulatory activity of the EU. It stands for all regulation based on the objectives of safety, health, investor/saver, environmental and consumer protection. Risk regulation is about correcting or at least reducing the impact of market failures, so that free movement is combined with the appropriate EU regulation. This allows member states to agree to lift restrictions, first kept for reason of an EU regulatory 'gap'. Risk regulation should be distinguished from 'economic' regulation where markets may not work well for economic reasons, and hence might have undesirable effects. A 'natural monopoly' (like rail track infrastructure) is likely to have undesired effects and hence has to be regulated. But of course the term 'undesirable' is not necessarily derived from economic analysis only. Thus, the common agricultural policy is a form of economic regulation where market outcomes – especially for certain types of farmers – were long regarded as undesirable and policy/regulation as well as EU money were employed to correct such outcomes. Although nowadays the EU hardly intervenes in agricultural markets, other than by general farm-based income grants, the EU tariffs in some agro-products are still very high indeed. Such economic regulation is quite different from risk regulation in agro-goods. The latter is what in the World Trade Organisation (WTO) is called SPS[7] regulation, for health and safety in food, animal feeds and plants. The EC-1992 programme included some 160-plus directives on SPS measures inside the internal market. At a later stage the full consequences were drawn by further centralising risk assessment for food[8] and introducing reforms leading to a value-chain approach called 'from farm to fork', which can only work if EU institutions, transparency and disciplines are powerful.

The proper functioning of the internal market

There are three important aspects to 'proper functioning'. The first one is about the core of the single market. Figure 2 provides a simplified picture of how the EU single market is organised to make it function properly. Also here, the EU is ambitious. No other regional economic grouping would allow this combination

Figure 2. Internal market diamond.

of far-reaching and intrusive instruments to govern the internal market, and thereby override member states.

One may see Figure 2 as a rewrite of Figure 1, but the idea behind it is different. The picture is suggestive of how the four sides of the rhombus influence the functioning of the internal market simultaneously or interactively. Thus, no free movement would be expected to come about as long as market failures (or, rarely, other reasons in the EU public interest) have not been addressed by the lower side of the rhombus. Even if that is accomplished, EU competition policy is critical to avoid market distortions caused by market power or (say) state aid distortions. In some cases, typically network industries, EU competition policy is ex ante rather than ex post, because otherwise proper market functioning would almost certainly not come about, at least not initially.[9] Moreover, EU regulation should only be employed where necessary; at times, no EU rules are needed and mutual recognition between national regulatory regimes can be sufficient; but, in turn, that requires a carefully constructed regime of procedural mutual recognition.[10]

The second aspect of proper functioning is the mutual entanglement and intense interaction between most common EU policies and the internal market. In fact, what have long been known as common policies are nothing else than sectoral single market regulatory regimes for transport, agro and fisheries, or aspect-based regulatory regimes (trade, environment, regional, industrial). What is known as EU energy policy is in fact a combination of gas and electricity internal market regulations and some climate-based regulation. With the so-called 'energy mix' still remaining sacrosanct for individual member states, no true EU 'energy policy' is feasible. Even infrastructural aspects in energy, or indeed in several other markets, are hardly EU-based. It is little recognised that labels on EU policies (for each Commissioner or Directorate-General or, for that matter, for many committees in the EP and in the Council) may be good for associating people with concrete policy activities, but conceptually they are all internal market aspects, and, more often than not, also legally based on the single market.

The third aspect of proper functioning is modern and credible enforcement. This sounds obvious but has proved to be an endless steeple chase of problems, often closely related to what is – rightly or wrongly - regarded as national policy autonomy. Enforcement has become far more disciplined and professional in the internal market than 25 years ago, but there are still problems which affect the internal market negatively (for example, foot-dragging on large packages of regulation in network industries, like the third energy package or the first rail package). Nevertheless, what is more important for the longer term is to make enforcement less legalistic as well as more effective, cheaper and faster. Pelkmans and Correia de Brito (2012) show at great length and in many different ways empirically that the EU has finally embraced such 'modern enforcement'. The critical factor here is not to regard the member state as a 'sinner', which the Commission must approach in a policing manner, as it has traditionally done, but as a partner in making the single market work better. Only when member states remain recalcitrant or are convinced that a CJEU judgment is needed can one fall back on classical (but very expensive and slow) infringement procedures. Since about 2009, after the late 2007 single market review proposals to this effect, member states have begun cooperating on a structural basis, and it works.

The proper functioning of the single market is crucial for the EU objectives to be served well. An ill-designed EU regulation, a free movement with many exceptions, a mutual recognition frustrated by member states, weak enforcement or too lax EU anti-trust nullify or at least reduce the possible economic gains from enjoying a single market.

Functional subsidiarity test indispensable for a better single market

Subsidiarity is, by its very nature, a functional principle: it implies an analytical approach to identify the level of government where a policy or a competence is most effective. It is also a two-way principle: dependent on the outcome of the subsidiarity test, powers can go to the EU or indeed remain with or go back to EU countries. The more functional subsidiarity is approached, for instance, in impact assessments of proposed EU regulation, the better it will be for the internal market because the best design in terms of levels of government can then be followed. This is welfare improving. However, in many cases one runs into political sensitivities or 'red lines' drawn in the sand by leaders of member states. This might concern the tightening of enforcement of the posted workers directive, or the (greater) autonomy of an EU agency, or proposed EU regulation on the corporate tax base (highly distortive at the moment, and a clear disadvantage compared to the uniform corporate tax base in the US), or perhaps even the language of the European patent. A most painful example of a missed opportunity of properly applying a subsidiarity test is the hopelessly fragmented bank supervision in the EU internal market for financial services up to 2008 or even later. The political neglect of functional subsidiarity led to three failings: the quest of many exceptions in the so-called common rules (some 150 in 2008), the impossibility to transcend narrow national (bank) interests in EU-wide supervisory committees that could only 'cooperate' without bite, and the complete failure of fully and credibly informing one another on bank problems as a corollary of the home country control principle. The second of these failures was always defended with the excuse that the EU had no 'fiscal capacity' to rescue a bank or bring it into 'resolution', so the national level was inevitable. This is turning subsidiarity on its head: the test would clearly show that such a capacity would have to be created at EU level, so that the regime can be optimised.

Applying a functional subsidiarity test carefully does *not* mean that a wave of centralisation would follow. But the arrangement has to be credible and effective and, in several areas, that does require an EU regime, possibly with agencies with some centralisation (operating in an EU regulatory framework, of course). Banking supervision and resolution has, in principle, nothing to do with the eurozone; it is no more than the indispensable positive integration of an internal market for banking services. The degree of centralisation is relatively high because, apart from the assurance of having sound banks, there are possibly serious implications of 'systemic risks' and contagion between big banks all over the EU, and even loading sovereigns with high debt, in other words, for financial stability. The enormous consequences of endangering EU-wide financial stability are now better appreciated.

In network industries, especially those with large sunk costs in physical infrastructure (i.e. rail freight, gas and electricity, eComms), the internal market has still not been achieved after 25 years of rather frantic work, with successive 'packages'. Here a major problem is that member states have national regulatory authorities (NRAs) under EU law but the EU internal market itself does *not* enjoy regulatory agencies which could ensure the fully fledged internal market in these network industries as well as its proper functioning. NRAs (and sometimes the Commission) use the Meroni doctrine as the formal excuse for not having such agencies.[11] Pelkmans and Simoncini (2014) make the case that the Meroni doctrine has 'mellowed' with the ESMA case[12] and, if handled properly, is no longer a barrier to setting up independent EU agencies where needed.

EU market integration: progress and deficits

For the purpose of this paper, sketching progress in EU market integration is done in three ways. First, a concise summary of the main elements of the

Table 1. Market integration deficits in services, 2014.

	Main areas	Annotations
Horizontal regimes	• Services directive, a range of follow-ups on 'fitness' for specific sectors, legal form, insurance, etc. • Public procurement in services and concessions, based on 2014 rewrite • Infrastructures, often a binding constraint	• No. of barriers for trade and FDI in services can be reduced much more • 'Concessions' new in dir. 2014/23, still many issues • Network industries can only enjoy a true single market if infrastructures can be better governed (and co-financed) at EU level; huge investments are required in rail, gas and electricity, eComms
Sectoral regimes	• 4th generation of financial services regime (2009–2014) better, but still not complete and not fully tested • Professional services exchange in the single market requires easier market access, blocked or made more difficult by lack of recognition • Electricity and gas single market does not yet exist though progress has been made • Rail freight market hopelessly fragmented; freight corridors initiative positive but long term • eComms >> no such thing as a single electronic communications market	• Today's fragmentation hinges partly on (mis)trust, new regime not complete • Professional qualifications under national powers; mutual evaluation ongoing via public interest tests • Mixed: insufficient interconnectors, national 'energy mix' and huge distortions renewables • Nine EU-wide freight rail corridors will help in the medium run; ERA and regulatory regime too soft • Essentially due to NRAs and lack of EU solutions; huge price disparities (see Maincent *et al.* 2013)
Cross-cutting regime	Retail; slow increase of competitive exposure, restrictive local rules Logistics Digital single market	• 'Economic needs' test gone, subtle barriers remain; touches various policies • Modern logistics critical for competitiveness (e.g. in value chains); links with transport and digital • Digital Agenda of June 2013 had 132 items, showing the diversity and complexity (including private law issues, copyright, etc.); now DSM

Note: ERA = European Rail Agency; NRA = national regulatory authority; DSM = digital single market.

successful EC-1992 programme will be provided. Second, the progress of the single market between 1993 and 2010 will be highlighted. Third, Table 1 summarises 'market integration deficits' in services in 2014.

The achievements of the EC-1992 programme are amazing. Starting in mid-1985, and given that the 7.5-year period comprised two commissions and also one European election, not to speak of all the national government rotations or changes, the prospects for such an ambitious undertaking would not be considered good. Yet EC-1992 was a resounding success. It would seem to defy all routine political expectations about lobbies and EU countries resisting such deep reforms (think of insurance, airlines, the car industry with its quotas vis-à-vis Japan, many SPS measures, abolishing frontiers). The success rate of the White Paper's Annex by the end of 1992 was around 95 per cent of the 284 measures (and many others were taken as well). In the process, a number of regulatory and other reforms were incorporated in the proposals.

The EU decisively moved into services, beginning with transport, financial services and, more hesitantly, professional services, followed later by network industries. These areas were less well understood and certainly full of resistance, be it out of fear of liberalisation or for other reasons. Also capital market liberalisation was accomplished fully (and enacted in the Maastricht treaty). The first taboos in IPRs were reduced as well. Free movement of goods was 'cleansed' of some protectionist exceptions (e.g. cars, clothing) and an entirely new system of animal health controls as well as other SPS provisions were rapidly enacted. The transformation of EU industrial policy, whether at national or EU level, caused it (from late 1990 onwards) to move away firmly from interventionist and sectorally specific policies (again codified in the Maastricht treaty).

Following the EC-1992 programme, the single market became subject to a 'brick-by-brick' approach until the Monti report in 2010 (Monti 2010). Despite the lack of a blueprint or a long-run programme, the functionalist pressures arising from the internal market logic remained at work, but in a highly splintered manner. The areas with the greatest potential long-run impact are the services directive 123/2006 (and the 'ownership' demonstrated by the member states in the early implementation phase) and network industries. Nevertheless, a lot more has been accomplished: the 2008 goods package, including much-improved conformity assessment, the setting up of quasi-regulatory agencies (medicines, chemicals, food) and transport safety agencies (rail, air, maritime), the Emission Trading System, addressing barriers in stock exchanges and progress in other IPRs (e.g. trademarks) illustrate the continuous activity of deepening the single market.[13]

It goes without saying that the implicit EU agenda for services in the internal market is incredibly ambitious and partly medium if not long term. The treaty is to some extent ill-designed for this agenda: for example, copyright is often still national and causes fragmentation (e.g. geo-blocking) to harden, whilst infrastructure is barely an EU competence and enjoys only minimal funds, with ad hoc supplements like the Juncker plan.

The meaning of the internal market for EMU

The single market can also be seen in a wider context than pure market integration. Ever since Balassa (1961), the first 'higher' stage than the 'common market' was to be 'economic union'. But economic union is a stage without agreed definition. Also the TFEU or Maastricht treaties do not define economic union anywhere.

One would assume that, in any event, the E of EMU must have the internal market as its centrepiece although the TFEU does not say that. In the eurozone, the 'economic union' was long de facto regarded as budgetary discipline of national governments, because loose debt and deficit disciplines might sooner or later lead to pressures on the European Central Bank (ECB) to relax monetary policy, and/or generate negative cross-border fiscal spill-overs (e.g. higher interest rates caused by less disciplined countries). In other words, although national budgets are not 'monetary' but 'economic', budgetary disciplines directly serve the proper functioning of monetary union. However, this seems to be an inappropriate notion of economic union.[14] Articles 120/121, TFEU address 'economic policy coordination' without giving much detail. It is sometimes suggested that these two articles are the 'economic union' articles. However, the term economic union is nowhere to be found. The only link with EMU is found in Article 121/4, which argues that if national economic policies are not consistent with the Broad Guidelines, they 'risk jeopardising the proper functioning of EMU'. Altogether, looking pragmatically at 'economic union', one may reasonably suggest the EU's economic union to consist of (i) the internal market, (ii) economic policy coordination, (iii) budgetary disciplines for the member states and supervised by the Economic and Finance (EcFin) Commissioner, under the treaty rules, (and for the eurozone) under the SGP, and two- and six-pack regimes. The economic rationale of having (i) and (ii) for all member states is the realisation that a very deep internal market generates such a significant economic interdependence that national 'economic policies are a matter of common concern' (Art. 121/1), whilst at the same time national policies may distort or be in the way of further developing the deep internal market. The core problem is that the relevant national economic policies at stake here are under the autonomy of the member states. One might call this the 'soft economic union'. The 'hard' economic union, in contrast, adds item (iii) fully, together with the awareness that the eurozone countries jointly own a 'collective good' called the euro. It is in their joint interest to pursue policies and disciplines at two levels of government (EU, ECB; member states) which maintain a high level of currency quality. Thus, apart from sound monetary policy, it is essential that the underlying eurozone economy is flexible and can adjust swiftly and relatively painlessly via the proper functioning of competitive goods, services, labour and capital markets and their (relative) pricing. This is the more important as other adjustment mechanisms (internal exchange rate adjustments; fiscal transfers) are not available; only relatively short-run net capital flows to finance current account imbalances are available, which are no panacea for the underlying problems. It is especially here that (a) a very deep internal market, including all types of markets, is helpful; (b) further reaching and more intrusive policy coordination as a form of joint 'management' of the eurozone economy is indispensable.

Nevertheless, the financial and sovereign debt crisis demonstrated that this modern version of linking the internal market with the E and the M of EMU is not necessarily wrong, but naively assumes away the underlying problems of a mistaken design of the internal market. The story is broadly correct if, and only if, the positive integration of the internal market of financial services is properly designed. However, that was clearly not the case. Two profound flaws caused both EMU not to function properly at all, when it was most needed, and the internal market for banking services to falter, if not to fail. First, the internal financial market was never designed on the basis of a functional subsidiarity test, for the simple reason that member states drew 'red lines' for political reasons. When large banks are Europeanising via subsidiaries and via assets (e.g. holding bonds from many EU governments), prudential supervision has to be centralised to a decisive degree, including the sensitive aspect of bank resolution, with the relevant funds ('fiscal capacity') to do so effectively and immediately when needed. This was taboo. Instead, a weak and cooperative system of intergovernmental supervisory committees, with a mutual information obligation, was set up - a system which failed utterly. At the same time, supervision should not only be based on prudential directives, but also on fully uniform application in a single rulebook: not 150 exceptions to these rules serving any wish of almost every member state. Rules should also not be 'light touch' where risks do not allow this. The recent drastic 'repairs' of the positive integration of these markets are a major improvement, although European Banking Authority (EBA) is still too intergovernmental and the toughening up had to come from the banking union initiative with full centralisation where justified. Second, the repercussions of a faltering internal financial market for systemic financial stability were totally ignored before the crisis. Again, this link calls for at least some centralisation in a eurozone context, although this should benefit non-eurozone countries as well. The so-called macro-prudential watchdog is the European Systemic Risk Board (ESRB), established in the ECB, although of significance for the entire EU. It is an information and analysis system, with advisory functions; it can give warnings and recommendations too. Its advantage is that the sole focus on budgetary disciplines is a thing of the past, thereby reducing the risks of 'bubbles' and helping to prevent the build-up of distortions (e.g. in housing markets) or longer-run deficits on current account. Once systemic risks start undermining trust in financial markets, the damage may be very great due to 'sudden stops' of finance or the drying up of daily interbank markets, not to speak of quickly rising risk premiums in interest rates of sovereign bonds from (EU) countries which are seen as vulnerable. It has also led to a sharp fragmentation of financial markets in the EU, at least for some four years or so.

The present paper does not cover banking union and its corollary, the so-called fiscal union. The essence of the banking union is merely and simply the required positive integration to make the single market for banking services function properly. This may be demanding and somewhat centralising (a problem for the 'outs' and the EEA-3 countries which are in the single banking market) but functionally this is appropriate. Given the heavy reliance on banking when demanding capital in the Union, a banking union is also more likely to pre-empt a renewed fragmentation of financial markets. The principle of 'bail-in', now enacted in the Single Resolution Mechanism, gives the right incentives not to assume excessive risks in the single market for banks and, in any event, to minimise or effectively prevent a negative fall-out for the sovereigns (i.e. taxpayers). The crisis has therefore forced the lifting of taboos, which enabled the building of a far stronger and more resilient single market for financial services. The only lingering anxiety on the part of the 'outs' is whether the further deepening of the eurozone towards a 'genuine EMU' might, in the margin, be at the expense of the single market, in particular for the 'outs'. However, there are clauses that ensure the internal market's integrity cannot be affected by the banking union and its specific application to the 'ins'. The UK is particularly sensitive about it given the very strong position of the City in financial markets. But the 'outs' have obtained a double majority in the EBA – that is, of 19 eurozone countries and of the 9 'outs'. There is an issue about limits on how much a bank can lend to its own government: the UK argues that the case for strict limits is less strong for the 'outs'. The problem in economic terms here is that financial stability is part of the regulatory regime of the single market and of the eurozone. Given that such limits are never the result of exact science, there must be compromises that remove this anxiety.

Is the single market resilient against crises?

The EU single market has emerged largely unscathed from the Great Recession. Indeed it has gained in strength and depth and a renewed impetus for further deepening and redesigning appears under way. It is also likely – but harder to prove – that the relative immunity from the crisis (except for the temporary damage to financial markets) has helped the EU to recover despite a huge debt overhang and no budgetary possibility to stimulate the economy beyond the 'automatic stabilisers'. But that was not immediately obvious. In early October 2008 President Sarkozy gave an aggressive (election) speech with a long list of interventionist, if not protectionist, policy ideas to fight the upcoming crisis (after the collapse of Lehman Brothers), and summoning French automotive investors in the Czech Republic to return to France. If Sarkozy had tested the water, he must have swiftly realised that it was ice-cold. Not only did he prompt a storm of protests from other EU government leaders, the European Commission kept a low profile, merely announcing that each and every measure announced would have to be assessed and justified according to single market rules. In a little noticed Commission Memo 09/90 of 28 February 2009, one finds confirmation that the support to the French car industry remained what had long been agreed, and the other Sarkozy measures vanished. This demonstrates that an effective bastion exists against erosion in times of crisis. The bastion consists first of all of quasi-constitutional EU rules and powerful principles underlying the single market, complemented by strict surveillance of state aids. But if the going gets rough, also peer pressure at the highest level provides clear political signalling that the single market cannot be undermined by short-run and national 'quick fixes'. Later, the European Council declared that the single market, not implying any budgetary outlays, should be seen as a robust 'protection' against too much weakening of overall demand.

During the crisis, the single market for financial services went through an overhaul, once the taboos had been swept away by the extreme circumstances. The rules for financial services and capital were decisively improved. Later, the banking union added centralised and fully neutral, technical (ECB) supervision of large banks, and a safeguard for small bank failures if and when appropriate. The 'fiscal capacity' was installed at EU level on the basis of funds, to be built up via contributions from the banks themselves. The banking union could be more robust still, for example by accepting an EU deposit insurance system as an underpinning of fiscal capacity.

In other words, the routine incremental improvement of the single market never ceased while the Great Recession was causing a loss of demand and jobs. The third gas and electricity package as well as the 2009 telecoms package and the 2010 Digital Agenda, plus an overhaul of European standardisation in 2012, illustrate the dichotomy between the macro-economic policy environment and single market policies. In 2015, plans for the Digital Single Market, the EU Energy Union and the Capital Market Union were added to this ambitious approach as well as a host of smaller propositions. Also, the external dimension of the single market – EU trade policy –was framed as a remedy for at least some growth, without any cost to budgets; hence, CETA (with Canada), TTIP (with the US), Free Trade Area (FTA) negotiations with Japan as well as FTAs with some Association of South East Asian Nations (ASEAN) countries. This does not guarantee that the single market is immune to crisis. Erosion is always a possibility, in particular if large member states would no longer treat the single market as a common asset, to be protected and managed well for the common good. However, the depth of the single market makes that prospect ever more unlikely as the stakes have grown so high for all involved. The response to BREXIT by all EU leaders is a clear case in point.

Conclusions: rethinking market integration?

The single market is the hard core of European integration but receives relatively little attention in high politics (beyond obligatory statements). Nevertheless, it has proceeded far, and is much deeper and wider in scope than could have even been dreamt of in the EC-1992 period, the only period when the single market was popular. Already for many decades, one hears soundings from scholars and others that, *so far*, the internal market has been relatively easy but the future issues will be far more intrusive for member states and more sensitive socially and politically. The EU nevertheless went on deepening and, where relevant, widening the scope. The long-run pattern is that what was sensitive or 'impossible' (a core item of 'sovereignty', whether the frontiers and their national customs, a flag-carrier in airlines, national energy strategies, bank resolution with national fiscal capacity, public procurement, exchange controls, or indeed the national currency) eventually lost its taboo status. Moreover enforcement has been tightened significantly and grown more and more into a joint responsibility. These developments have facilitated a deep internal market in 2015 and will help to pursue further improvements in the near future.

Precisely because of this intrusive single market, the EU must take great care in making the case for more and better EU regulation (via impact assessment) and ensure as much as possible its political legitimacy in formal and substantive ways. Indeed, most people might often not even realise that it is really the single market they deal with. This is largely due to the prominence, by now, of EU regulation, mostly risk regulation. These rules reflect policy concerns of many parties, including lobbies and citizens. Therefore, much of what in the present paper is presented as single market questions shows up in 'Brussels' as 'better' food regulation, climate policies, banking union, energy strategy, or product safety. The pursuit of the single market is ultimately driven by functionalist and market pressures, but, as alluded to several times, this does not mean that it is a-political. There is surely scope for policy choices up to a degree. However, it is mistaken to attribute too many of Europe's or national problems to the single market. For example, issues such as income distribution are essentially national issues subject to national political processes (one only has to verify the disparities in income distribution indicators in the EU, not to speak of the US, Brazil or China) and the speed and nature of adjustment of workers and enterprises can only be influenced at EU level in the margin (that is, most means are national, and some pressures have to do with autonomous technological progress and with global competition by developing and emerging economies seeking their place in what used to be an Organisation for Economic Co-operation and Development (OECD)-dominated world economy).

A careful application of a functional subsidiarity test is critical because there is little support for an ever more centralising EU. The single market needs selective centralisation via its rules, and sometimes via EU agencies. It also requires stronger powers and more funds for infrastructure. The banking union even disposes of a (not so large) rescue fund and a resolution fund is built up with contributions of the banks themselves. One can justifiably defend more independence for EU agencies in those network industries having large sunk costs (rail, gas and electricity, eComms) but this should not be read as if (regulatory) agencies keep on multiplying. The benefits of each case should carefully be spelled out and the costs of the alternative of inefficient and slow inter-governmentalism have to be verified.

Therefore, EU market integration does not need a wholesale 'rethinking' but, rather, a faithful and functional pursuit of the realisation of a 'genuine' single market, with appropriate degrees of selective centralisation. The single market idea needs to be modernised, as markets are changing rapidly and digitalisation is reaching all services, including the 'sharing economy' and other new business models, as well as advanced industrial production processes. This redesigning and deepening is inevitably slow and uneven. The agenda for deepening the single market for services remains a tall order. Political legitimacy has to be 'conquered' time and again. It will also have to be accepted that the single market is not the slogan that moves voters, yet it will always remain the common 'asset' of the EU that makes it a magnet for candidate countries or the EEA-3, or Switzerland or defectors from the EU. This asset ought to be well 'managed' and, if possible, increased in value and dynamic opportunities.

Notes

1. For an extensive analysis of the internal market as the principal means for the EEC to pursue the four economic objectives of the Rome treaty, see Pelkmans (2006: ch. 2) for the Rome, Single Act and Maastricht treaties.
2. Note that the detailed Single Market Review (in the UK Competences review) found almost no instances where the single market was to the detriment of the UK, or, significantly over- or mis-regulated.
3. The two strategic single market documents are: (1) the European Commission Strategy in COM(2015)550 of 28 October 2015, Upgrading the Single Market – More Opportunities for People and Business; this proposal has to be understood in a broader strategic context for the overall single market, with three other proposals, i.e. COM (2015) 192 of 6 May 2015, A Digital Single Market for Europe; COM(2015) 80 of 25 February 2015, Energy Union Package – A Framework Strategy for a Resilient Energy Union with a Forward-looking Climate Change Policy; COM (2015)468, Capital Markets Union Action Plan ; (2) the European Parliament's Report of the High Level Panel, A Strategy for Completing the Single Market: the Trillion Euro Bonus, 14 January 2016, see http://www.europarl.eu/thinktank.eu/thinktank.eu/document.html?reference+EPRS_STU(2016)558772
4. A powerful reason also for French voters to reject the draft European Constitution in 2005.
5. This should include the free movement of codified technology (e.g. IPRs etc.).
6. Case law and other literature strongly suggests that internal market fragmentation was strengthened by IPRs and provided highly profitable instances of price discrimination.
7. Sanitary and phyto-sanitary regulation.
8. In EFSA, the European Food Safety Agency.
9. A referee queried why competitiveness is not found in Figure 1. Competitiveness of firms in the EU is, insofar as the single market can influence that, a *result* of the better functioning of the single market, in turn resulting from a proper application of the regime as depicted in Figure 1.
10. Finally achieved after many problems in Reg. no. 964/2008, shifting the burden of proof largely to member states.
11. The Meroni doctrine, named after an old ECSC case (of 1956), essentially says that, since member states have delegated regulatory (hence law-making) powers

to the EU level, the Commission or the Council cannot delegate such powers to an independent agency/regulator without having an explicit legal base in the treaty.

12. ESMA is the European Securities and Markets Authority, an agency dealing with regulation and supervision of capital markets in the EU. The ESMA case C-270/12, brought by the UK, challenged the ESMA power to forbid short-selling as a violation of the Meroni doctrine. The ruling on 22 January 2014 dismissed all four aspects of the UK government's case. Pelkmans and Simoncini (2014) show that this ruling has general validity for all EU agencies, not just for ESMA.
13. It is also possible to verify progress in market integration in purely economic terms. The literature finds trends of price convergence and a lessening of 'home bias' (the propensity of buyers to purchase at home), both signs of increasing market integration. Indirectly, the increasing gains from deepening market integration also point to this: ranging from the Cecchini report (Emerson *et al.* 1989) of some 4.5 per cent increase in GDP due to the full implementation of EC-1992 to, for example, Campos *et al.* (2014) finding an increase in GDP attributable to EU membership (mainly the single market) of some 12 per cent since 1973. Note that the present contribution cannot deal with the growth and productivity effects of the single market in any detail. Up-to-date summaries of the state of the art are in the High Level Panel report of the EP (see note 3) and, for example, in Mariniello *et al.* (2015).
14. It should be remembered that neither Ireland nor Spain had a deficit or a debt ratio problem until 2008.

Disclosure statement

No potential conflict of interest was reported by the author.

References

Balassa, Bela (1961). *The Theory of Economic Integration*. Homewood: Irwin.

Campos, Nauro F., Fabrizio Coricelli, and Luigi Moretti (2014). 'Economic Growth and Political Integration: Estimating the Benefits from Membership in the European Union Using the Synthetic Counterfactuals Method', IZA Discussion Paper no. 8162.

Comité Intergouvernemental Créé par La Conférence de Messine (1956). *Rapport Des Chefs de Déléfation aux Ministres Des Affaires Entrangè*. Report of the Heads of Delegation of the Foreign Ministries. Brussels.

Emerson, Michael, Michal Aujean, Michel Catinat, Philippe Goybet, and Alexis Jacquemin (1989). *The Economics of 1992: An Assessment of the Potential Economic Effects of Completing the Internal Market of the European Community*. Oxford: Oxford University Press.

Maincent, Emmanuelle, Dimitri Lorenzani, and Attila Eordogh (2013). 'Market Functioning in Network Industries – Electronic Communications, Energy and Transport', *European Economy, Occasional Paper*, 129, 1–121.

Mariniello, Mario, Andre Sapir, and Alessio Terzi (2015). 'The Long Road towards the European Single Market', *Bruegel Working Paper*, 2015:1, 1–36.

Monti, Mario (2010). *A New Strategy for the Single Market: At the Service of Europe's Economy and Society*, Report to the President of the European Commission, 9 May.

Pelkmans, Jacques (2006). *Economic Integration, Methods and Economic Analysis*, 3rd ed. Essex: Prentice Hall Financial Times an imnprint of Pearson Education.

Pelkmans, Jacques, Anabela Correia de Brito (2012). *Enforcement in the EU Single Market'*. Brussels: Centre for European Policy Studies.

Pelkmans, Jacques, and Marta Simoncini (2014). *Mellowing Meroni: How ESMA Can Help Build the Single Market*. Brussel: Centre for European Policy Studies.

Index

Entries in *italics* denote figures; entries in **bold** denote tables.